SU**K**
COUNTY

The Roger Scruton Reader

The Roger Scruton Reader

Compiled, Edited and with an
Introduction by Mark Dooley

continuum

Published by the Continuum International Publishing Group

The Tower Building   80 Maiden Lane
11 York Road   Suite 704
London   New York
SE1 7NX   NY 10038

www.continuumbooks.com

First published 2009

British Library Cataloguing in Publication Data
A catalogue record for this book is available from the British Library.

ISBN 978-0826-42049-7

Typeset by BookEns, Royston, Herts.
Printed and bound in Great Britain by the MPG Books Group

In Memoriam

Professor John Cleary (1949–2009)

Contents

Introduction
A Philosophy of Love

Roger Scruton produced his first book in 1974. Since then he has become a publishing sensation: 40 books, hundreds of scholarly articles, and scores of magazine and newspaper columns. He has written two operas, two novels and a book of poetry. Few can rival his prodigious output, his clarity of expression and the profundity of his thoughts. And yet, even now, at the age of 65, Scruton remains one of the most misunderstood and misrepresented figures in British intellectual life. Why that is so is something which I deal with in my book *Roger Scruton: The Philosopher on Dover Beach*. In that context, I suggested that Scruton's diverse writings on philosophy, religion, culture, architecture, sex, politics, hunting and wine are united by a single theme: *the love of home*. Throughout his long career, Scruton has been vilified by the Left as a conservative reactionary, whose views are no less dangerous than those of the British National Party. It is, however, quite obvious to anyone who has taken the time to read them that his writings are far from the deranged delusions of those on the extreme Right. For what fundamentally distinguishes Scruton from such people is that they are narrow nationalists, whereas his is a gentle and dignified patriotism.

In his most recent book of political thought, *A Political Philosophy*, he contrasts nationalism and patriotism in the following terms:

Left-liberal writers, in their reluctance to adopt the nation as a
social aspiration or a political goal, sometimes distinguish
nationalism from 'patriotism' – an ancient virtue extolled by
the Romans and by those like Machiavelli who first made the
intellectual case for modern secular jurisdiction. Patriotism, they
argue, is the loyalty of citizens, and the foundation of
'republican' government; nationalism is a shared hostility to
the stranger, the intruder, the person who belongs 'outside'. I
feel some sympathy for that approach. Properly understood,
however, the republican patriotism defended by Machiavelli,
Montesquieu and Mill is a form of national loyalty: not a
pathological *form* like nationalism, but a natural love of country,
countrymen and the culture that unites them. Patriots are
attached to the people and the territory that is *theirs by right*, and
patriotism involves an attempt to transcribe that right into
impartial government and a rule of law. This underlying
territorial right is implied in the very word – the *patria* being the
'fatherland', the place where you and I belong and to which we
return, if only in thought, at the end of all our wanderings.

In defiance of those thinkers who have sought to repudiate the
patria in favour of nothingness and nowhere, Roger Scruton
strives to provide his readers with a sense of *somewhere*. If
radicals 'prefer global ideas to local loyalties', Scruton searches
instead for 'a lost experience of home' – an experience which
every left-wing movement from the social contract theory of
Jean-Jacques Rousseau to the deconstruction of Jacques
Derrida attempts to undermine. Restoring that old sense of
home, of the *patria*, of a concrete place in which we can settle
and have our identity objectively endorsed, is what primarily
motivates Scruton politically and philosophically. Hence, his
constant appeals on behalf of art, culture and beauty – those
things through which we identify a particular place as *ours*.
The culture of a territory is what renders it enchanting and
provides for those who dwell there a common source of loyalty
and membership. In the course of memorializing his beloved
England, Scruton explains:

When human beings cease their wanderings and mark out a
place as their own, their first instinct is to furnish it with things

which have no function – ornaments, pictures, knick-knacks – or with things which, while possessing a function, are valued for other reasons: for their associations, their beauty, their way of fitting in. Their instinct for the purposeless has a purpose – namely to make these objects into an expression of ourselves and our common dwelling place, to endow them with the marks of order, legitimacy and peaceful possession. In other words, objects, when they form part of the home, are endowed with a soul... The enchantment of things in the home is part of a larger spiritual project. Home has its customs, its rituals, its special times and places. Or if it does not, it is so much the less a home, so much the less a place to look back upon in adulthood, when anger and rejection have intervened. A kind of authority attaches to the way things are done at home, and to the roles of mother and father as they divide the labour between them. We take this experience of authority with us into later life, and the images of father, mother and the rituals that haloed them shape our subsequent emotions.

Culture is what binds *us* together, and it is that through which we develop our loves and our deepest longings. In deconstructing it, therefore, the high priests of postmodernism and the legionnaires of liberalism reveal their underlying political agenda, which is to unsettle the old routines and settled ways of traditional society. It is to put alienation in the place of affection and liberation in that of lasting attachments. That is why Scruton follows Edmund Burke in making the passage 'from aesthetics to conservative politics with no sense of intellectual incongruity'. Both are ways of recovering what has been wantonly wasted by those like Michel Foucault who strive to 'unmask' the prevailing political order, believing it to be a citadel of power, a prison from which we must be emancipated. Aesthetics and conservative politics contain what Scruton calls 'social knowledge', or as he explains in his classic discourse on *The Meaning of Conservatism*:

> By social knowledge I mean the kind of knowledge embodied in the common law, in parliamentary procedures, in manners, costume and social convention, and also in morality. Such knowledge arises 'by an invisible hand' from the open-ended

business of society, from problems which have been confronted and solved, from agreements which have been perpetuated by custom, from conventions which coordinate our otherwise conflicting passions, and from the unending process of negotiation and compromise whereby we quieten the dogs of war.

To do away with such knowledge is to make man blind to his social condition, for it is the practical wisdom of the ages.

Liberalism, socialism and postmodernism have each sought to evict modern man from his spiritual, cultural and political home. And they have done so by declaring war on the storehouse of social knowledge that gave a sense of meaning to all who dwelt there. In opposing this process of disenchantment, Scruton is seeking to overcome our sense of loss. Underlying that sense, he tells us,

> is the permanent belief that what has been lost can also be recaptured – not necessarily as it was when it first slipped from our grasp, but as it will be when consciously regained and remodelled, to reward us for all the toil and separation through which we are condemned by our original transgression.

That belief is, for him, 'the romantic core of conservatism', and it is one shared by all of his intellectual heroes, including Burke, Hegel, Coleridge, Ruskin, Dostoevsky and T.S. Eliot. And it is also what gives unity and coherence to his writings on everything from farming to philosophy, music to marriage, and from dwelling to dance. Restoring that love of existing things, of 'community, home and settlement' is, in other words, the central theme of Roger Scruton's social, cultural and political philosophy. In sum, his is a philosophy of consolation for people tired of repudiation and rejection, of nihilism and nay-saying.

This book is intended to give expression to that romantic core of conservatism as developed throughout Scruton's vast back-catalogue. It has three principal aims: first, to act as a companion volume to my *Roger Scruton: The Philosopher on Dover Beach*; secondly, to gather together for the first time in a single volume a selection of Scruton's writings on everything from sex and the sacred to wine and architecture; lastly, to serve as a textbook for those wishing to teach Roger Scruton's philosophy as part of a university course, or indeed for those unacquainted with his work and who simply wish to find out what it is all about. The process of selecting which pieces to include was made all the more difficult because there is such a superabundance of material to choose from. In the end, however, I opted for relatively recent writings, in as much as they serve to crystallize the main ideas of the earlier works in a mature and eloquent style which has become Scruton's standard hallmark.

The volume opens with three pieces, each of which aims to explain the central contours of Scruton's political conservatism. The first chapter on 'How I Became a Conservative', is taken from his delightful and moving memoir *Gentle Regrets*. It tells us of how, after witnessing first-hand the student riots in Paris in 1968, Scruton rejected the likes of Foucault and embraced the vision of General de Gaulle, who believed that 'a nation is defined not by institutions or borders but by language, religion and high culture'. If Foucault and his followers poured scorn on such 'spiritual things', Scruton vowed there and then to devote the rest of his life to their affirmation and preservation. He also tells of how it was Edmund Burke who first taught him that 'aesthetic judgement matters, that it is not merely a subjective opinion, unargued because unarguable', but that it 'lays a claim upon the world, that it issues from a deep social imperative, and that it matters to us in just the way that other people matter to us, when we strive to live with them in a community'.

In 'What is Right?' – originally the final chapter of arguably his most controversial book, *Thinkers of the New Left*, Scruton provides a comprehensive analysis of the conservative outlook by juxtaposing it with its socialist counterpart. The New Left, he writes

> has not generally shared that laudable respect for institutions. Its fervent denunciation of power has therefore been accompanied by no description of the institutions of the future. The goal is for a society without institutions: a society in which people spontaneously group together in life-affirming globules,

and from which the dead shell of law, procedure and established custom has fallen away.

In contrast, the New Right rejects the 'impersonal government' of the socialists in favour of personal or responsible government. Hence, it follows Hegel in recognizing a 'distinction between state and civil society, and believes that the second should arise, in general, from the unforced interaction of freely contracting individuals, moderated by custom, tradition and a respect for authority and law'.

Custom, tradition and respect for authority and law are also the prime targets of Jean-Jacques Rousseau's theory of the social contract. In Rousseau, we see the first stirrings of the liberal temperament and its attempt to recast society as the product of rational choice. But that, as Scruton argues in Chapter 3, 'Rousseau & the Origins of Liberalism', is to deny the basic fact of the human condition; it is to deny that the human being

in all his aspects, including his capacity for rational choice, is the product of a history that stretches before and after him. The search for origins is doomed to failure; at every point we encounter the historical contingency, the arbitrariness of human destiny. We are thrown together without reason or cause, and must make the best of circumstances that have been indelibly marked by a history that was not our doing. Hence, we should look for legitimacy not in origins but in procedures. Instead of asking whether the social order conforms to some abstract criterion of justice, we should ask whether, and if so how, a perceived injustice might be rectified; whether the individual can obtain redress for any injury; and whether crime is punished and loyalty rewarded. We should study the functioning of offices and roles and institutions, and ask whether they soften or heighten human conflicts. The quest for origins asks no such answerable questions. For it is a religious quest: an attempt to anchor society outside history, and to take a God's-eye view of all our brief arrangements.

In Section 2, devoted to Scruton's theory of 'The Nation', we see how his conservative ideas find concrete application in the contemporary political climate. 'The Social Contract', drawn from his highly acclaimed study *The West and the Rest*, argues that prior to any contractual arrangement there arises, as both Burke and Hegel counselled, a 'web of non-contractual obligations' which surround the individual from birth. Such is the 'bond of membership' that we all experience, and which shapes our pre-political loyalties. Not only does this bond of membership link me to absent generations; it also 'enables me to regard the interests and needs of strangers as my concern'. What distinguishes the West from the rest is that, thanks largely to the legacy of Roman law and Christianity, the western political order is held together by a rule of law, as distinct from tribal, ethnic or religious forms of membership. The citizens of the West are thus bound together by a shared loyalty to the land and the law which has shaped and settled it. 'Around this particular territorial jurisdiction', Scruton argues,

> there has arisen a remarkable and in many ways unique form of membership, in which belonging is defined neither by language nor by religion nor even by sovereignty, but by the felt recognition of a particular territory as home: the safe, law-governed and protected place that is 'ours'.

Fostering that form of membership among all those who share 'our' territory is the *sine qua non* of harmonious social relations, especially in a world where the local has been challenged to its core by the forces of globalization.

Such is the reason behind the success of America's great social and political experiment. Unlike the European Union, which has singularly sought to 'discard national loyalty and to replace it with the cosmopolitan ideals of the Enlightenment', America is first and foremost a *nation* – a 'community of strangers' bound together by the love of the home that they share. This argument, which Scruton advances to fine effect in Chapter 5, 'The Nation State and Democracy', also explains why America is likely to endure while the European future is uncertain. Americans 'unselfconsciously' rehearse their 'myths of origin' and, on a daily basis, 'repeat the narrative of their pilgrimage into the modern world'. For Europeans, on the other hand, such things are either scorned as chauvinistic or condemned as another example of that 'racism and xenophobia' which is lurking under every bed. Some of our national narratives have been scribbled over and cancelled out, like that of the Germans. Others have become stories of class-conflict and oppression, like that now told in English schools, or records of belligerent episodes that never paid off – like the national stories that no longer appeal to the French. Everywhere we find a kind of repudiation of those fortifying legends on which nations have always depended for their sense of identity.

No one foresaw the dire consequences of this politics of repudiation better than Enoch Powell. But the hysterical reaction to his infamous 'Rivers of Blood' speech in 1968 ensured that a veil of silence would fall across the issue of immigration for the following 40 years. For Roger Scruton, the case of Enoch Powell 'raises in its acutest form the question of truth: what place is there for truth in public life, and what should a politician do when comfortable falsehoods have settled down in government, and their uncomfortable negations seek forlornly for a voice?' Scruton himself has passed his career trying to combat those 'comfortable falsehoods', a position that has cost him dearly. However, as recent events have proved, Powell and Scruton were not engaging in reactionary rhetoric, but in a defence of the nation as the only political model capable of integrating newcomers into the national narrative. As Scruton reminds us in Chapter 6, 'Should he have Spoken?':

> Such predictions as Powell made in his speech, concerning the tipping of the demographic balance, the ghettoization of the industrial cities, and the growth of resentment among the indigenous working class have been fulfilled. Only the sibylline prophecy has fallen short of the mark. Even so, the Madrid and London bombings and the murder of Theo van Gogh are viewed by many Europeans as a foretaste of things to come. It is now evident to everyone that, in the debate over immigration, in those last remaining days when it could still have made a difference, Enoch Powell was far nearer the truth than those who instantly drove him from office, and who ensured that the

issue was henceforth to be discussed, if at all, only by way of condemning the 'racism' and 'xenophobia' of those who thought like Powell.

Section 3 of this reader contains three essays on 'Sex and the Sacred'. Since the publication of what many consider his magnum opus – *Sexual Desire* in 1986, Scruton has made the recovery of the traditional virtue of love a priority. For him, human beings are unlike animals by reason of the fact that for them the aim of sexual activity is not simply genital satisfaction, but the possession of *another human subject*. Or, as he puts it in the beautiful excerpt from *Death-Devoted Heart* included in Chapter 7: 'It aims to fill the surface of the other's body with a consciousness of your interest not only in the body, but in the person *as* embodied'. Perversion and obscenity, on the other hand,

> involve the eclipse of the subject, as the body and its mechanism are placed in frontal view. In obscenity flesh is represented in such a way as to become opaque to the self that inhabits it: that is why there is an obscenity of violence as well as an obscenity of sex, a torturing of the flesh which extinguishes the light of freedom and subjectivity.

They are, in other words, a 'crime against love'.

Such indeed is the crime committed by the pseudoscience of sexology as it strives to undermine traditional morality, and thus the old social order. But for Scruton, while the liberal will try to deconstruct the given political reality, on the basis that it cannot be defended from the standpoint of the first-person, there are sufficient third-person reasons for its justification as a social benefit. That is the central message of Chapter 8, 'Meaningful Marriage'. Marriage, Scruton writes, 'is something more than a contract of mutual co-operation, and something more than an agreement to live together'. It is 'divinely ordained', possessing a 'sacred aura that reinforces the undertaken duties and elicits the support of the tribe'. Moreover, it differs from a civil union in being founded upon a *vow* rather than a contract. For the conservative, as we have seen, the triumph of the contractual view of life has resulted in a loss of the social and moral capital upon which long-term human happiness depends. In the case of marriage, it represents nothing less than a 'change in the phenomenology of sexual union, a retreat from the world of "substantial ties" to a world of "negotiated deals"'. That is why the cause of marriage must be foremost in the mind of the conscientious conservative. Indeed, for Scruton it is a *sacred* obligation, in as much as 'the world of vows is a world of sacred things, in which holy and indefeasible obligations stand athwart our lives and command us along certain paths, whether we will or not'.

In Chapter 9, 'The Return of Religion', Scruton continues an ongoing debate with those he has christened 'evangelical atheists' – Richard Dawkins and Christopher Hitchens. This piece is interesting from a number of perspectives, not least the fact that it provides the reader with a compelling introduction to Scruton's philosophy of religion, his critique of scientific reductionism and his theory of the sacred, something which has consistently featured in each of his major writings. According to Scruton, religion does not, and indeed never should, deny the truths of the scientific worldview. But the world of science is one dedicated to analysing and explaining objects. What is missing from such accounts, however, is a study of the human subject as a source of meaning. Human beings are, for Scruton, both subject *and* object, person *and* animal. They are subject to nature's laws, and yet somehow not fully determined by them. We are, as he repeatedly argues, *in* the world and yet not entirely *of* it. We can stand, as it were, on the edge of our empirical world and gaze out onto that other 'transcendental' sphere which is the source of our freedom. Such is the mystery of consciousness: our ability 'to look for the reason and the meaning of things, and not just for the cause'. The astonishing thing about our universe, claims Scruton, is that 'it contains consciousness, judgement, the knowledge of right and wrong, and all the other things that make the human condition so singular'. And that fact, he adds, 'is not rendered less astonishing by the hypothesis that this state of affairs emerged over time from other conditions. If true, that merely shows us how astonishing those other conditions were. The gene and the soup cannot be less astonishing than their product'. The mystery of consciousness is what draws modern people to religion, even those who respect the findings of science. For humans have

> an innate need to conceptualise their world in terms of the transcendental, and to live out the distinction between the sacred and the profane. This need is rooted in self-consciousness and in the experiences that remind us of our shared and momentous destiny as members of Kant's 'Kingdom of Ends'. Those experiences are the root of human as opposed to merely animal society, and we need to affirm them, self-knowingly to possess them, if we are to be at ease with our kind.

For Roger Scruton, art 'has grown from the sacred view of life'. In its ideal manifestations, it draws upon and amplifies those 'experiences which are given in less conscious form by religion: experiences of the sacred and the profane, of redemption from sin and the immersion in it, of guilt, sorrow and their overcoming through forgiveness and the oneness of a community restored'. Furthermore, high culture 'ennobles the human spirit, and presents us with a justifying vision of ourselves, as something higher than nature and apart from it'. It is as such an expression of the sacred, something which sees meaning and value in things where science sees only cause and explanation. Scruton defends that position in Chapter 10, 'The Aesthetic Gaze'. Following Kant, he believes that aesthetic interest is 'disinterested', meaning that it aims not merely to consume things, but to value them as *ends in themselves*. Hence, aesthetic objects

> invite us to an 'interest of reason' – a self-conscious placing of ourselves in relation to the thing considered, and a search for meaning which looks neither for information nor practical utility, but for the insight which religion also promises: insight into the why and whither of our being here.

The complex question of how children can be taught to value something for its own sake is the focus of Chapter 11, 'Knowledge and Feeling'. Knowing what to feel on the right occasion and for the right reasons is, for Scruton, 'critical to moral education'. Following Aristotle, he argues that teaching people what to feel means instilling them with virtue. But how does one teach virtue, defined as the ability to order one's emotions and to feel rightly towards the right object in the right degree? The answer lies in a knowledge of the 'touchstones' of high culture. Scruton writes:

> we can read stories of the heroes and their adventures; we can study narratives of historical exploits, and look at pictures of the life that we share. We can listen to homilies and rehearse in ritual form the joys and sufferings of revered and exemplary people. In all kinds of ways the emotions and motives of other people 'come before us' in works of art and culture, and we spontaneously sympathize, by recreating in imagination the life that they depict. It is not that we imitate the characters depicted, but that we 'move with' them, acquiring an inner premonition of their motives, and coming to see those motives in the context that the writer or artist provides. Through imagination we reach emotional knowledge, and maybe this is the best way, in the advance of the crucial tests, of preparing ourselves for the joys and calamities that we will some day encounter.

In the previously unpublished piece 'Classicism Now' (Chapter 12), Scruton synopsizes his earlier writings on the role and function of architecture in human affairs. As in those influential works, he critically contrasts the architectural failures of modernism with the 'sacred architecture' of classicism. Building matters because it answers to the needs of rational beings who long to see in their surroundings a concrete endorsement of their values. The 'discarded wrecks of the modernist era' testify to the fact that they answer neither to man's desire for permanence or to his transcendental yearnings. Classicism, however, offers

> a vision of architecture that is universal in its aim, and comprehensive in its understanding of the relation between buildings and people. According to this vision the goal of architecture is *fittingness*: buildings must fit to each other and to the urban context; and part must fit to part in the composition of the whole. This demand for fittingness stems from a deep

human need. We seek to be at home in the world – to come in from our wandering, and to settle in the place that is ours. Hence we need to match and to harmonize, projecting thereby our common commitment to the peaceful settlement of a common place.

If classicism in architecture satisfies the human longing for lasting settlement and an enduring community, for value and transcendental meaning, then so too does classical music. The piece on music I have selected for this volume reflects on the nature of sound, tone, melody and harmony. Simply entitled 'Music' and taken from *Philosophy: Principles and Problems*, Chapter 13 describes what happens when the human subject hears sound *as* music. Like art and architecture, music answers to the needs of subjects who can see in objects more than their function. This means that music also belongs to the sphere of value, enabling the self to catch a glimpse of his 'godly home'. When we hear music, in other words, life is liberated from its 'human prison' and moves freely in a 'useless space of its own'. And while it does not 'describe the transcendental subject', it nevertheless '*shows* it, as it would be, if it *could* be shown'. That is, in music we have a clear illustration of how the sacred or the timeless enter time through human consciousness, lifting us from 'our time and space into an ideal time and space, ordered by an ideal causality, which is the causality of freedom'.

The final section of this book, entitled 'Homecomings', deals with Scruton's other great passions: the environment, wine and fox-hunting. In Chapter 14, 'Conserving Nature', he appeals to left-wing environmentalists to follow their conservative counterparts and respond to environmental degradation from a Burkean standpoint. For Burke, long-term political order cannot be sustained by a contract between the living members of society without regard to the unborn and the dead. Rather it requires 'a relation of trusteeship, in which inherited benefits are conserved and passed on'. In defending that claim, Burke wished to safeguard the social and moral ecology from those 'converts of Rousseau' and 'disciples of Voltaire' as he described them, people who sought and ultimately succeeded in plundering those timeless resources for the satisfaction of their own short-term aims. In so doing, he was endeavouring to remind us of a motive that, according to Scruton,

> arises naturally in human beings, and which can be exploited for the wider purpose of environmental and institutional conservation: namely, love. This motive leads people both to create good things and to destroy them. But it turns of its own accord in a direction that favours conservation, since human love extends to the dead and the unborn: we mourn the one and plan for the other out of a natural superfluity of good will.

Love puts restraint and sacrifice in the place of selfishness and impulse. Hence there is no motive

> more likely to serve the environmentalist cause than this one, of the shared love for our home. It is a motive in ordinary people. It can provide a foundation both for a conservative approach to institutions and a conservationist approach to the land. It is a motive that might permit us to reconcile the demand for democratic participation with the respect for absent generations and the duty of trusteeship.

It is, Scruton concludes, 'the only serious recourse that we have, in our fight to maintain local order in the face of globally stimulated decay'.

It is that love of home and soil, of 'all the customs, ceremonies and practices whereby the sacred is renewed, so as to be a real presence among us, and a living endorsement of the human community', that gives wine its moral and religious significance for Roger Scruton. In Chapter 15, 'The Philosophy of Wine', he seamlessly synthesizes his thoughts on conservatism, conservation, culture and the sacred when he remarks that

> the experience of wine is a recuperation of that original cult whereby the land was settled and the city built. And what we taste in the wine is not just the fruit and its ferment, but also the peculiar flavour of a landscape to which the gods have been invited and where they have found a home. Nothing else that we eat or drink comes to us with such a halo of significance, and cursed be the villains who refuse to drink it.

As someone who gave up nowhere to settle somewhere, Scruton is acutely aware that 'the act of settling, which is the origin of civilisation, involves both a radical transition in our relation to the earth – the transition known in other terms as that from hunter-gatherer to farmer – and also a new sense of belonging'. That is something he learned when, in 1995, he gave up full-time academia for a life on the farm. Hence it is fitting that this volume should conclude with some thoughts on hunting, that activity which has, more than any other, taught Scruton how to love the settled space that he now calls 'home'. Chapter 16, 'Thoughts on Hunting', is a beautifully crafted reflection on the deeper meaning of hunting for all those who identify with, and find consolation in, its ancient traditions. For Scruton, hunting gives modern people an experience of 'homecoming to our natural state'. And it does so by reviving

in transfigured form, some of the long-buried emotions of our forebears. The reverence for a species, expressed through the pursuit of its 'incarnate' instance; the side-by-sideness of the tribal huntsman; the claim to territory and the animals who live in it; and the therapy for guilt involved in guiltless killing.

But it is more than that. Through the rituals of the hunt, we also experience 'ceremonial hospitality', defined as 'an attempt to raise the relations among neighbours to a higher level: to confer legitimacy and permanence on the current patterns of ownership'. When looked at in that way, it then becomes easier to understand why, according to Scruton, 'it is not just permissible to hunt, but morally right'.

* * *

In the end, my earnest hope is that this collection will serve to remind those already acquainted with his writings, as well as those curious to learn more, that Roger Scruton is an enormously cultivated philosopher, whose range and scope far exceeds that of most public intellectuals. I once asked him how he might describe his work, to which he replied: 'Consoling thoughts for a happy and fulfilling life'. I doubt that anyone who reads the chapters of this book, even those who disagree with their content, will doubt the sincerity of his message or the graciousness with which it is expressed. For it is, as I have already said, a message of love, of affirmation and of hope in a world dedicated to their ruin.

That is why Roger Scruton matters: he shines a light on our failures not in order to condemn them, but in order to lead us from despair, loneliness and desecration back home to beauty and its sacred source. As he says,

> we can, at any moment, turn away from desecration and ask ourselves instead what inspires us and what we should revere... We can turn our attention to things we love – the woods and streams of our native country, friends and family, the 'starry heavens above' – and ask ourselves what they tell us about our lives on earth, and how that life should be lived. And then we can look on the world of art, poetry and music and know that there is a real difference between the sacrilegious, with which we are alone and troubled, and the beautiful, with which we are in company and at home.

I would like to thank Roger Scruton for his kind and helpful suggestions with regard to the content of this volume, as well as for his inspiration and friendship. I am also grateful to my editor, Robin Baird-Smith, for his continued encouragement and support. A great debt is owed to my Editorial Assistant, Elizabeth Meade, and to my wife Laura for their generous help in preparing the manuscript. Lastly, I wish to express my gratitude to the editors of *The American Spectator*, *Axess Magazine*, Encounter Books, Oxford University Press, *The New Criterion*, *The World of Fine Wine* and Continuum International for permission to reproduce the pieces contained in this book.

Dublin, St Patrick's Day, 2009

SECTION 1

Conservatism

1

How I Became a Conservative
(From *Gentle Regrets*, 2005)

I was brought up at a time when half the English people voted Conservative at national elections and almost all English intellectuals regarded the term 'conservative' as a term of abuse. To be a conservative, I was told, was to be on the side of age against youth, the past against the future, authority against innovation, the 'structures' against spontaneity and life. It was enough to understand this to recognize that one had no choice, as a free-thinking intellectual, save to reject conservatism. The choice remaining was between reform and revolution. Do we improve society bit by bit, or do we rub it out and start again? On the whole my contemporaries favoured the second option, and it was when witnessing what this meant, in May 1968 in Paris, that I discovered my vocation.

In the narrow street below my window the students were shouting and smashing. The plate-glass windows of the shops appeared to step back, shudder for a second, and then give up the ghost, as the reflections suddenly left them and they slid in jagged fragments to the ground. Cars rose into the air and landed on their sides, their juices flowing from unseen wounds. The air was filled with triumphant shouts, as one by one lamp-posts and bollards were uprooted and piled on the tarmac, to form a barricade against the next van-load of policemen.

The van – known as a *panier à salade* on account of the wire mesh that covered its windows – came cautiously round the corner from the Rue Descartes, jerked to a halt, and disgorged a score of frightened policemen. They were greeted by flying cobble-stones and several of them fell. One rolled over on the ground clutching his face, from which the blood streamed through tightly clenched fingers. There was an exultant shout, the injured policeman was helped into the van, and the students ran off down a side-street, sneering at the *cochons* and throwing Parthian cobbles as they went.

That evening a friend came round: she had been all day on the barricades with a troupe of theatre people, under the captainship of Armand Gatti. She was very excited by the events, which Gatti, a follower of Antonin Artaud and the 'theatre of cruelty', had taught her to regard as the high point of situationist theatre – the artistic transfiguration of an absurdity which is the day-to-day meaning of bourgeois life. Great victories had been scored: policemen injured, cars set alight, slogans chanted, graffiti daubed. The bourgeoisie were on the run and soon the Old Fascist and his régime would be begging for mercy.

The Old Fascist was de Gaulle, whose *Mémoires de Guerre* I had been reading that day. The memoirs begin with a striking sentence – '*Toute ma vie, je me suis fait une certaine idée de la France*' – a sentence so alike in its rhythm and so contrary in its direction to that equally striking sentence which begins *À la recherche du temps perdu*: 'Longtemps, je me suis couché de bonne heure'. How amazing it had been, to discover a politician who begins his self-vindication by *suggesting* something – and something so deeply hidden behind the bold mask of his words! I had been equally struck by the description of the state funeral for Valéry – de Gaulle's first public gesture on liberating Paris – since it too suggested priorities unimaginable in an English politician. The image of the cortège, as it took its way to the cathedral of Notre Dame, the proud general first among the mourners, and here and there a German sniper still looking down from the rooftops, had made a vivid impression on me. I irresistibly compared the two bird's-eye views of Paris, that of the sniper, and my own on to the riots in the *Quartier latin*. They were related as yes and no, the affirmation and denial of a national idea. According to the Gaullist vision, a nation is defined not by institutions or borders but by language, religion and high culture; in times of turmoil and conquest it is those spiritual things that must be protected and reaffirmed. The funeral for Valéry followed naturally from this way of seeing things. And I associated the France of de Gaulle with Valéry's *Cimetière marin* – that haunting invocation of the dead which conveyed to me, much more profoundly than any politician's words or gestures, the true meaning of a national idea.

Of course I was naïve – as naïve as my friend. But the ensuing argument is one to which I have often returned in my thoughts. What, I asked, do you propose to put in the place of this 'bourgeoisie' whom you so despise, and to whom you owe the freedom and prosperity that enable you to play on your toy barricades? What vision of France and its culture compels you? And are you prepared to die for your beliefs, or merely to put others at risk in order to display them? I was obnoxiously pompous: but for the first time in my life I had felt a surge of political anger, finding myself on the other side of the barricades from all the people I knew.

She replied with a book: Foucault's *Les mots et les choses*, the bible of the *soixante-huitards*, the text which seemed to justify every form of transgression, by showing that obedience is merely defeat. It is an artful book, composed with a satanic mendacity, selectively appropriating facts in order to show that culture and knowledge are nothing but the 'discourses' of power. The book is not a work of philosophy but an exercise in rhetoric. Its goal is subversion, not truth, and it is careful to argue – by the old nominalist sleight of hand that was surely invented by the Father of Lies – that 'truth' requires inverted commas, that it changes from epoch to epoch, and is tied to the form of consciousness, the *episteme*, imposed by the class which profits from its propagation. The revolutionary spirit, which searches the world for things to hate, has found in Foucault a new literary formula. Look everywhere for power, he tells his readers, and you will find it. Where there is power there is oppression. And where there is oppression there is the right to destroy. In the street below my window was the translation of that message into deeds.

My friend is now a good bourgeoise like the rest of them. Armand Gatti is forgotten; and the works of Antonin Artaud have a quaint and *dépassé* air. The French intellectuals have turned their back on '68, and the late Louis Pauwels, the greatest of their post-war novelists, has, in *Les Orphelins*, written the damning obituary of their adolescent rage. Foucault is dead from AIDS, contracted during well-funded tours as an intellectual celebrity. However his books are on university reading lists all over Europe and America. His vision of European culture as the institutionalized form of oppressive power is taught everywhere as gospel, to students who have neither the culture nor the religion to resist it. Only in France is he widely regarded as a charlatan.

By 1971, when I moved from Cambridge to a permanent lectureship at Birkbeck College, London, I had become a conservative. So far as I could discover there was only one other conservative at Birkbeck, and that was Nunzia – Maria Annunziata – the Neapolitan lady who served meals in the Senior Common Room and who cocked a snook at the lecturers by plastering her counter with kitschy photos of the Pope.

One of those lecturers, towards whom Nunzia conceived a particular antipathy, was Eric Hobsbawm, the lionized historian of the Industrial Revolution, whose Marxist vision of our country is now the orthodoxy taught in British schools. Hobsbawm came as a refugee to Britain, bringing with him the Marxist commitment and Communist Party membership that he retained until he could retain it no longer – the Party, to his chagrin, having dissolved itself in embarrassment at the revelation of its crimes. No doubt in recognition of this heroic career, Hobsbawm was rewarded, at Mr Blair's behest, with the second highest award that the Queen can bestow – that of 'Companion of Honour'. This little story is of enormous significance to a British conservative. For it is a symptom and a symbol of what has happened to our intellectual life since the sixties. We should ponder the extraordinary fact that Oxford University, which granted an honorary degree to Bill Clinton on the grounds that he had once hung around its precincts, refused the same honour to Margaret Thatcher, its most distinguished post-war graduate, and Britain's first woman Prime Minister. We should ponder some of the other recipients of honorary degrees from British academic institutions – Robert Mugabe, for example, or the late Mrs Ceausescu – or count (on the fingers of one hand) the number of conservatives who are elected to the British Academy.

Suffice it to say that I found myself, on arrival in Birkbeck College, at the heart of the left establishment that governed British scholarship. Birkbeck College had grown from the Mechanics Institute founded by George Birkbeck in 1823, and was devoted to the education of people in full-time employment. It was connected to the socialist idealists of the Workers' Education Association, and had links of a tenacious but undiscoverable kind to the Labour Party. My failure to conceal my conservative beliefs was both noticed and disapproved, and I began to think that I should look for another career.

Because of Birkbeck's mission, as a centre of adult education, lectures began at 6 p.m. and the days were nominally free. I used my mornings to read for the Bar: my intention was to embark on a career in which realities enjoyed an advantage over utopias in the general struggle for human sympathy. In fact I never practised at the Bar, since I had a mortgage by then, and could not afford the unpaid year of pupillage without which no barrister can take a case of his own. I therefore received from my studies only an intellectual benefit – though a benefit for which I have always been profoundly grateful. The common law of England is proof that there is a real distinction between legitimate and illegitimate power, that power can exist without oppression, and that authority is a living force in human conduct. English law, I discovered, is the answer to Foucault.

Inspired by my new studies I began to search for a conservative philosophy. In America this search could be conducted in a university. American departments of Political Science encourage their students to read Montesquieu, Burke, Tocqueville and the Founding Fathers. Leo Strauss, Eric Voegelin and others have grafted the metaphysical conservatism of Central Europe on to native American roots, forming effective and durable schools of political thought. American intellectual life benefits from American patriotism, which has made it possible to defend American customs and institutions without fear of being laughed to scorn. It has benefited too from the Cold War, which sharpened native wits against the Marxist enemy, in a way that they were never sharpened in Europe: the wholesale conversion of the social democratic Jewish intelligentsia of New York to the cause of neo-conservatism is a case in point. In 1970's Britain, conservative philosophy was the preoccupation of a few half-mad recluses. Searching the library of my college I found Marx, Lenin and Mao, but no Strauss, Voegelin, Hayek or Friedman. I found every variety of socialist monthly, weekly or quarterly, but not a single journal that confessed to being conservative...

To my rescue came Burke. Although not widely read at the time in our universities, he had not been dismissed as stupid, reactionary or absurd. He was simply irrelevant, of interest largely because he got everything wrong about the French Revolution and therefore could be studied as illustrating an episode in intellectual pathology. Students were still permitted to read him, usually in conjunction with the immeasurably less interesting Tom Paine, and from time to time you heard tell of a 'Burkean' philosophy, which was one strand within nineteenth-century British conservatism.

Burke was of additional interest to me on account of the intellectual path that he had trodden. His first work, like mine, was in aesthetics. And although I didn't find much of philosophical significance in his *Essay on the Sublime and the Beautiful*, I could see that, in the right cultural climate, it would convey a powerful sense of the meaning of aesthetic judgement and of its indispensable place in our lives. I suppose that, in so far as I had received any intimations of my future destiny as an intellectual pariah, it was through my early reactions to modern architecture, and to the desecration of my childhood landscape by the 'horizontal vernacular'. I learned as a teenager that aesthetic judgement matters, that it is not merely a subjective opinion, unargued because unarguable, and of no significance to anyone besides oneself. I saw – though I did not have the philosophy to justify this – that aesthetic judgement lays a claim upon the world, that it issues from a deep social imperative, and that it matters to us in just the way that other people matter to us, when we strive to live with them in a community. And, so it seemed to me, the aesthetics of modernism, with its denial of the past, its vandalization of the landscape and townscape, and its attempt to purge the world of history, was also a denial of community, home and settlement. Modernism in architecture was an attempt to remake the world as though it contained nothing save atomic individuals, disinfected of the past, and living like ants within their metallic and functional shells.

Like Burke, therefore, I made the passage from aesthetics to conservative politics with no sense of intellectual incongruity, believing that, in each case, I was in search of a lost experience of home. And I suppose that, underlying that sense of loss is the permanent belief that what has been lost can also be recaptured – not necessarily as it was when it first slipped from our grasp, but as it will be when consciously regained and remodelled, to reward us for all the toil of separation through which we are condemned by our original transgression. That belief is the romantic core of conservatism, as you find it – very differently expressed – in Burke and Hegel, in Coleridge, Ruskin, Dostoevsky and T.S. Eliot.

When I first read Burke's account of the French Revolution I was inclined to accept, since I knew no other, the liberal humanist view of the Revolution as a triumph of freedom over oppression, a liberation of a people from the yoke of absolute power. Although there were excesses – and no honest historian had ever denied this – the official humanist view was that they should be seen in retrospect as the birth-pangs of a new order, which would offer a model of popular sovereignty to the world. I therefore assumed that Burke's early doubts – expressed, remember, when the Revolution was in its very first infancy, and the King had not yet been executed nor the Terror begun – were simply alarmist reactions to an ill-understood event. What interested me in the *Reflections* was the positive political philosophy, distinguished from all the literature that was currently à la mode, by its absolute concretion, and its close reading of the human psyche in its ordinary and unexalted forms.

Burke was not writing about socialism, but about revolution. Nevertheless he persuaded me that the utopian promises of socialism go hand in hand with a wholly abstract vision of the human mind – a geometrical version of our mental processes that has only the vaguest relation to the thought and feelings by which real human lives are conducted. He persuaded me that societies are not and cannot be organized according to a plan or a goal, that there is no direction to history, and no such thing as moral or spiritual progress. Most of all he emphasized that the new forms of politics, which hope to organize society around the rational pursuit of liberty, equality, fraternity or their modernist equivalents, are actually forms of militant irrationality. There is no way in which people can collectively pursue liberty, equality and fraternity, not only because those things are lamentably underdescribed and merely abstractly defined, but also because collective reason doesn't work that way.

People reason collectively towards a common goal only in times of emergency – when there is a threat to be vanquished, or a conquest to be achieved. Even then, they need organization, hierarchy and a structure of command if they are to pursue their goal effectively. Nevertheless, a form of collective rationality does emerge in these cases, and its popular name is war. Moreover – and here is the corollary that came home to me with a shock of recognition – any attempt to organize society according to this kind of rationality would involve exactly the same conditions: the declaration of war against some real or imagined enemy. Hence the strident and militant language of the socialist literature – the hate-filled, purpose-filled, bourgeois-baiting prose, one example of which had been offered to me in 1968, as the final vindication of the violence beneath my attic window, but other examples of which, starting with the *Communist Manifesto*, were the basic diet of political studies in my university. The literature of left-wing political science is a literature of conflict, in which the main variables are those identified by Lenin: 'Who? Whom?' The opening sentence of De Gaulle's memoirs is framed in the language of love, about an object of love – and I had spontaneously resonated to this in the years of the student 'struggle'. De Gaulle's allusion to Proust is to a masterly evocation of maternal love, and to a dim premonition of its loss.

Three other arguments of Burke's made a comparable impression. The first was the defence of authority and obedience. Far from being the evil and obnoxious thing that my contemporaries held it to be, authority was, for Burke, the root of political order. Society, he argued, is not held together by the abstract rights of the citizen, as the French Revolutionaries supposed. It is held together by authority – by which is meant the right to obedience, rather than the mere power to compel it. And obedience, in its turn, is the prime virtue of political beings, the disposition which makes it possible to govern them, and without which societies crumble into 'the dust and powder of individuality'. Those thoughts seemed as obvious to me as they were shocking to my contemporaries. In effect Burke was upholding the old view of man in society, as subject of a sovereign, against the new view of him, as citizen of a state. And what struck me vividly was that, in defending this old view, Burke demonstrated that it was a far more effective guarantee of the liberties of the individual than the new idea, which was founded in the promise of those very liberties, only abstractly, universally and therefore unreally defined. Real freedom, concrete freedom, the freedom that can actually be defined, claimed and granted, was not the opposite of obedience but its other side. The abstract, unreal freedom of the liberal intellect was really nothing more than childish disobedience, amplified into anarchy. Those ideas exhilarated me, since they made sense of what I had seen in 1968. But when I expressed them, in a book published in 1979 as *The Meaning of Conservatism*, I blighted what remained of my academic career.

The second argument of Burke's that impressed me was the subtle defence of tradition, prejudice and custom, against the enlightened plans of the reformers. This defence engaged, once again, with my study of aesthetics. Already as a schoolboy I had had been struck by Eliot's essay entitled 'Tradition and the Individual Talent', in which tradition is represented as a constantly evolving, yet continuous thing, which is remade with every addition to it, and which adapts the past to the present and the present to the past. This conception, which seemed to make sense of Eliot's kind of modernism (a modernism that is the polar opposite of that which has prevailed in architecture), also rescued the study of the past, and made my own love of the classics in art, literature and music into a valid part of my psyche as a modern human being. Burke's defence of tradition seemed to translate this very concept into the world of politics, and to make respect for custom, establishment, and settled communal ways, into a political virtue, rather than a sign, as my contemporaries mostly believed, of complacency.

Burke's provocative defence, in this connection, of 'prejudice' – by which he meant the set of beliefs and ideas that arise instinctively in social beings, and which reflect the root experiences of social life – was a revelation of something that until then I had entirely overlooked. Burke brought home to me that our most necessary beliefs may be both unjustified and unjustifiable from our own perspective, and that the attempt to justify them will lead merely to their loss. Replacing them with the abstract rational systems of the philosophers, we may think ourselves more rational and better equipped for life in the modern world. But in fact we are less well equipped, and our new beliefs are far less justified, for the very reason that they are justified by ourselves. The real justification for a prejudice is the one which justifies it *as* a prejudice, rather than as a rational conclusion of an argument. In other words it is a justification that cannot be conducted from our own perspective, but only from outside, as it were, as an anthropologist might justify the customs and rituals of an alien tribe.

An example will illustrate the point: the prejudices surrounding sexual relations. These vary from society to society; but until recently they have had a common feature, which is that people distinguish seemly from unseemly conduct, abhor explicit sexual display, and require modesty in women and chivalry in men, in the negotiations that precede sexual union. There are very good anthropological reasons for this, in terms of the long term stability of sexual relations, and the commitment that is necessary if children are to be inducted into society. But these are not the reasons that motivate the traditional conduct of men and women. This conduct is guided by deep and immovable prejudice, in which outrage, shame and honour are the ultimate grounds. Sexual liberators have no difficulty in showing that those motives are irrational, in the sense of being founded on no reasoned justification available to the person whose motives they are. And they may propose sexual liberation as a rational alternative, a code of conduct that is rational from the first-person viewpoint, since it derives a complete code of practice from a transparently reasonable aim, which is sexual pleasure.

This substitution of reason for prejudice has indeed occurred. And the result is exactly as Burke would have anticipated. Not merely a breakdown in trust between the sexes, but a faltering in the reproductive process – a failing and enfeebled commitment of parents, not merely to each other, but also to their offspring. At the same time, individual feelings, which were shored up and fulfilled by the traditional prejudices, are left exposed and unprotected by the skeletal structures of rationality. Hence the extraordinary situation in America, where lawsuits have replaced common courtesy, where post-coital accusations of 'date-rape' take the place of pre-coital modesty, and where advances made by the unattractive are routinely penalized as 'sexual harassment'. This is an example of what happens, when prejudice is wiped away in the name of reason, without regard for the real social function that prejudice alone can fulfil. And indeed, it was partly by reflecting on the disaster of sexual liberation, and the joyless world that it seems to have produced around us, that I came to see the truth of Burke's otherwise somewhat paradoxical idea.

The final argument that impressed me was Burke's response to the theory of the social contract. Although society can be seen as a contract, he argued, we must recognize that most parties to the contract are either dead or not yet born. The effect of the contemporary Rousseauist ideas of social contract was to place the present members of society in a position of dictatorial dominance over those who went before, and those who came after them. Hence these ideas led directly to the massive squandering of inherited resources at the Revolution, and to the cultural and ecological vandalism that Burke was perhaps the first to recognize as the principal danger of modern politics. In Burke's eyes the self-righteous contempt for ancestors that characterized the Revolutionaries was also a disinheriting of the unborn. Rightly understood, he argued, society is a partnership between the dead, the living and the unborn, and without what he called the 'hereditary principle', according to which rights could be inherited as well as acquired, both the dead and the unborn would be disenfranchized. Indeed, respect for the dead was, in Burke's view, the only real safeguard that the unborn could obtain, in a world that gave all its privileges to the living. His preferred vision of society was not as a contract, in fact, but as a trust, with the living members as trustees of an inheritance that they must strive to enhance and pass on.

In those deft, cool thoughts, Burke summarized all my instinctive doubts about the cry for liberation, all my hesitations about progress and about the unscrupulous belief in the future that has dominated and (in my view) perverted modern politics. In effect, Burke was joining in the old Platonic cry, for a form of politics that would also be a form of nurture – 'care of the soul', as Plato put it, which would also be a care for absent generations. The graffiti paradoxes of the *soixante-huitards* were the very opposite of this: a kind of adolescent insouciance, a throwing away of all customs, institutions and achievements, for the sake of a momentary exultation which could have no lasting sense save anarchy. All that was implied in the 'C'est interdit d'interdire' that had been sprayed on the wall below my garret...

Vociferous conservatives are accepted in politics, but not in the intellectual world. I suppose it was naïve of me not to see this. I should have learned from Spinoza, who refused to publish his *Ethics*, and who chose for his device the single word *caute* – 'be cautious' – inscribed beneath a rose, the symbol of secrecy. Instead I decided to go public, with *The Meaning of Conservatism*, a somewhat Hegelian defence of Tory values in the face of their betrayal by the free marketeers. My credentials as an anachronism were thereby established, and when the Salisbury Group, a loose collection of reactionaries founded in memory of the great third Marquess of Salisbury, the Prime Minister who kept everything so well in place that nothing now is known about him, decided to found a journal and looked round for someone sufficiently anachronistic to serve as its editor, they alighted on me with something like the expressions attributed by Ronald Searle in the Molesworth books to Gabbitas and Thring, those ruthless hunters of recruits to the teaching profession.

The first difficulty was that of finding people to write in an explicitly conservative journal. I had friends in the academic world who were prepared in private to confess to conservative sympathies, but they were all acutely aware of the risks attached to 'coming out'. They had seen what a caning I had received for *The Meaning of Conservatism*, and few of them were far enough advanced in their academic careers to risk a similar treatment.

The second difficulty was that of establishing a readership. The money we had raised would cover the printing costs of three issues: after that the *Review* would have to pay for itself, which would require 600 subscribers or more. I was confident that there were at least 600 intellectual conservatives in Britain, most of whom would welcome a journal dedicated to expressing, examining and exploring their endangered world-view. The problem was finding them.

The third difficulty was that of conservatism itself. I was often told by Maurice Cowling (a member – though in a spirit of irony – of the Salisbury Group) that I was deceiving myself if I thought that conservative politics could be given a philosophical backing sufficient to put it on a par with socialism, liberalism, nationalism and all the other isms that conservatism isn't. Conservatism, Maurice told me, is a political practice, the legacy of a long tradition of pragmatic decision-making and high-toned contempt for human folly. To try to encapsulate it in a philosophy was the kind of naïve project that Americans might undertake. And that was one of the overwhelming reasons for not teaching, still less living, in America.

One of our earliest contributors was Ray Honeyford, the Bradford headmaster who argued for a policy of integration in our schools, as the only way of averting ethnic conflict. Ray Honeyford was branded as a racist, horribly pilloried (by some of my academic colleagues in the University of Bradford, among others) and eventually sacked, for saying what every-one now admits to be true. My attempts to defend him led to extensive libels of me and the *Review*. Other contributors were persecuted (and also sometimes sacked) for coming to Ray's defence. This episode was our first great success, and led to the 600 subscriptions that we needed.

Our next success came in 1985, when, at the annual congress of the British Association for the Advancement of Science, the *Review* was subjected to a show-trial by the sociologists, and found guilty on the dual charge of 'scientific racism' and intellectual incompetence. Neither I nor any contributor to the *Review* was invited to attend this show-trial, and besides there was no way in which the charge could be disproved. Our contributors included Jews, Asians, Africans, Arabs and Turks. But the advantage of the charge of *scientific* racism is that it can be proved without showing racial discrimination, and merely by examining words. It is a 'thought-crime' in the sense made famous by Orwell. Thereafter the *Review* and its writers were ostracized in the academic world. The consequences of this for my career soon became apparent. Invited to give a paper to the Philosophy Society in the University of Glasgow I discovered, on arrival, that the Philosophy Department was mounting an official boycott of my talk, and had announced this fact to the world. I wandered around the campus for a while, watched a desultory procession of apparatchiks who were conferring an honorary degree on Robert Mugabe, and was eventually rescued by a fellow dissident, Flint Schier, who had arranged for the talk to go ahead as an 'unofficial seminar'.

I was used to such things from Eastern Europe, and in time got used to them in England too. On the whole, however, the communist secret police treated one rather better than the reception parties organized by the Socialist Workers Party: a slight roughing up and maybe a night in jail, but relieved by intellectual discussion at a much higher level than could be obtained in our provincial universities. After a particularly frightening experience giving a lecture on 'toleration' at the University of York, and following a serious libel in *The Observer*, I began to wonder whether my position as a university professor was really tenable.

Eastern Europe was the occasion of another success. To my astonishment, a *samizdat* edition of *The Salisbury Review* began to appear in Prague in 1986. By then I had been expelled from Czechoslovakia, and was regularly followed in Poland. Things were not much better in Britain, where the *Review* might just as well have been a *samizdat* publication, so great was the venom directed towards those who wrote for it. So the news that the *Review* had achieved, under 'real socialism', an honour accorded, to my knowledge, to no other Western periodical, was especially gratifying. Examples were smuggled to us and their wafer-thin pages – the final carbon copies from sheaves of ten – had the spiritual quality of illuminated manuscripts. They were testimony to a belief in the written word that had been tried and proved through real suffering.

In 1987 the Police Museum in Prague – a propaganda institute to which teachers would take their quiet crocodiles of 'young pioneers' – composed a new exhibit devoted to the 'unofficial secret agent'. The central item was a maquette of a youngish man in Western clothes, with spy camera and binoculars. From his open briefcase there spilled – along with Plato and Aristotle – copies of *The Salisbury Review*. Some time later one of our regular contributors, Ján Čarnogursky, was arrested in Slovakia and charged with subversion of the state in collaboration with foreign powers. The indictment mentioned *The Salisbury Review* as clinching evidence. This was, I suppose, our greatest triumph: the first time that anybody with influence had conferred on us the status of an equal. Unfortunately, however, the trial never took place, with the communists out of power and Ján on his way to becoming Prime Minister of Slovakia.

It was not only the issues of ethnic relations and national identity that had provoked the British intellectual establishment. *The Salisbury Review* was belligerently anti-communist, with a regular series of articles smuggled to us from underground writers in the Soviet bloc; it took a stand against CND and the Peace Movement; it drew attention to the plight of Christians in North Africa and the Middle East; it carried articles denouncing foreign aid; it was explicitly critical of feminism, modernism, postmodernism and deconstruction. Above all, it was anti-egalitarian, defending achievement against mediocrity and virtue against vice. Although all those positions are now widely accepted, we had the good fortune to express them at a time when each was actively censored by some group of sanctimonious half-wits. Hence we survived. One by one the conservatives came out and joined us, recognizing that it was worth sacrificing your chances of becoming a Fellow of the British Academy, a vice chancellor or an emeritus professor for the sheer relief of uttering the truth. With contributors ranging from Peter Bauer and A.L. Rowse to Václav Havel and P.D. James, we were able to deflect the charge of intellectual incompetence. Without claiming too much credit for this, I remain convinced that *The Salisbury Review* helped a new generation of conservative intellectuals to emerge. At last it was possible to be a conservative and also to the *left* of something, to say 'Of course *The Salisbury Review* is beyond the pale; but...'.

Still, there was a price to pay. It became a matter of honour among English-speaking intellectuals to dissociate themselves from me, to write, if possible, damning and contemptuous reviews of my books, and to block my chances of promotion. Some of the criticisms were justified; once stigmatized as a conservative, however, there was nothing I could do to avoid them. However hard I tried, however much scholarship, thought and open-minded argument I put into what I wrote, it was routinely condemned as ignorant, sloppy, pernicious or just plain 'silly' – A.J. Ayer's verdict on *Sexual Desire*, a book which I honestly believe to offer a cogent philosophical account of its subject-matter, and an answer to the mendacious three-volume 'history' by Foucault.

One academic philosopher wrote to Longmans, who had published one of my books, saying that 'I may tell you with dismay that many colleagues here [i.e. in Oxford] feel that the Longman imprint – a respected one – has been tarnished by association with Scruton's work.' He went on to express the hope that 'the negative reactions generated by this particular publishing venture may make Longman think more carefully about its policy in the future.' Even more curious was the letter sent to my head of department by another colleague, who acted as external assessor for academic promotions. He would have had no difficulty in recommending me, he wrote, before my articles began to appear in *The Times*, and on the strength of my academic work. But those articles, with their unremitting conservative message, were the real proof of my intellectual powers, and the conclusive demonstration that I was unfit to hold a university chair.

In time I came to see that he was right. Someone who believes in real distinctions between people has no place in a humanities department, the main purpose of which is to deliver the ideology required by life in the postmodern world.

What the *soixante-huitards* hoped to achieve by violence has been accomplished far more effectively by the peaceful self-censorship natural to the academic mind. The attacks that I suffered showed the health of the university organism, which surrounds each invading germ with antibodies, and expels it from the system. Perceiving the rightness and necessity of this I left the university and took up farming – or rather 'metafarming', a practice that I describe in *News from Somewhere*.

Nevertheless I remain what I have been since May 1968 – a conservative intellectual, who not only loves the high culture of Europe, but believes it to be a source of consolation and the repository of what we Europeans should know. It is, to put it bluntly, our best hope for the past. Such a hope animated de Gaulle; it enabled him to save his country not once but twice from destruction. And, by deflecting us from our self-centred projects, it offers a guarantee of national survival. That, to me, is the lesson of conservative politics, and it is one that will never be understood by those who place their hopes solely in the future, and without faith in the past.

The years of conflict have taught me that few will share my convictions, and that all attempts to conserve things come too late. But the philosopher who most clearly perceived this truth brought a message of peace: 'when philosophy paints its grey-in-grey, then is a form of life grown old. The Owl of Minerva spreads its wings only with the gathering of the dusk.' Hegel's words describe not the view from that attic window in the *Quartier latin*, but the soul that absorbed it. It was not to change things, or to be part of things, or to be swept along by things, that I made my pilgrimage to Paris. It was to observe, to know, to understand. And so I acquired the consciousness of death and dying, without which the world cannot be *loved for what it is*. That, in essence, is what it means to be a conservative.

2

What is Right?

(From *Thinkers of the New Left*, 1986)

Writing in the *The Communist Journal* of September 1847, Marx dissociated himself from 'those communists who are out to destroy liberty and who want to turn the world into one large barracks or gigantic workhouse'. He promised to return to the question of freedom in a future issue, but never did. For us, looking back over the history of Marx's influence, there is a sombre lesson in this dishonoured promise. The gigantic system of control – at once barracks and workhouse – which now dominates the world in Marx's name, has yet to be understood by those who defend its aims and ideology. In the writings of the left the concept of freedom looms large: emancipation is both the individual purpose and the great social cause. And yet the nature of this freedom is rarely analysed, and the institutions needed to secure it still more rarely discussed. 'Socialist relations of production' are by definition free. And if a state exists in which freedom is not a reality, then by definition it cannot – *yet* – be socialist, even when founded on the theories, aims and methods which socialists defend.

POWER AND DOMINATION

This identification of socialism and freedom results, in part, from an obsession with power, and a confusion between questions of freedom and questions of power. Everywhere about him the radical sees domination: of man over man, of group over group, and of class over class. He envisages a future without domination, in which there is no power to secure obedience from the powerless. And he imagines that this condition is not only possible, but also a state of universal *freedom*. In other words, he sees equality and freedom as deeply compatible, and achievable together by the destruction of power.

This yearning for a 'powerless' world – which finds its most eloquent expression in the writings of Foucault – is incoherent. The condition of society is essentially a condition of domination, in which people are bound to each other by emotions and loyalties, and distinguished by rivalries and powers. There is no society that dispenses with these human realities, nor should we wish for one, since it is from these basic components that our worldly satisfactions are composed. But where there is loyalty there is power; and where there is rivalry there is the need for government. As Kenneth Minogue has put it:

> ... the worm of domination lies at the heart of what it is to be human, and the conclusion faces us that the attempt to overthrow domination, as that idea is metaphysically understood in ideology, is the attempt to destroy humanity.[1]

Our concern as political beings should be, not to abolish these powers that bind society together, but to ensure that they are not also used to sunder it. We should aim, not for a world without power, but for a world where power is peacefully exercised and where conflicts are resolved according to a conception of justice acceptable to those engaged in them.

The radical is impatient with this 'natural justice', which lies dormant within human social intercourse. Either he discards it, like the Marxist, as a figment of 'bourgeois ideology', or else he diverts it from its natural course, insisting that priority be given to the underdog and the fruits of adjudication removed from the hands of his 'oppressor'. This second stance – illustrated at its most subtle in the work of Dworkin – is anti-revolutionary in its methods but revolutionary in its aims. The American liberal is as convinced of the evil of domination as is the Parisian *gauchiste*. He is distinguished by his recognition that institutions are, in the end, necessary to his purpose, and that ideology is no substitute for the patient work of law.

COMMUNITY AND INSTITUTIONS

The New Left has not generally shared that laudable respect for institutions. Its fervent denunciation of power has therefore been accompanied by no description of the institutions of the future. The goal is for a society *without* institutions: a society in which people spontaneously group together in life-affirming globules, and from which the dead shell of law, procedure and established custom has fallen away. This *'groupe en fusion'* as Sartre calls it, is another version of the *fascio* of the early Italian socialists: a collective entity in which individual energies are pooled in a common purpose and whose actions are governed by a 'general will'.[2] When others proclaim this ideal the leftist denounces them (quite rightly) as fascists. Yet it is precisely his own ideal that angers him, when it stands before him armed in a doctrine that is not his own.

Institutions are the necessary inheritance of civilized society. But they are vulnerable to the 'armed doctrine' (as Burke described it) of the revolutionary, who looks to society not for the natural and imperfect solaces of human contact but for a personal *salvation*. He seeks a society that will be totally fraternal, and also totally free. He can therefore be content with no merely negotiated relation with his neighbours. For the institutions of negotiation are also the instruments of power.

In pursuit of a world without power the leftist finds himself plagued not only by real institutions but also by hidden devils. Power is everywhere about him, and also within him, implanted by the alien ideas of a dominating order. As Foucault writes:

> A stupid despot may constrain his slaves with iron chains; but a true politician binds them even more strongly by the chains of their own ideas ... the link is all the stronger in that we do not know what it is made of.[3]

Such a vision fuels the paranoid fantasies of R. D. Laing and Aaron Esterson, and also the more sober methodical suspicions of Sartre and J. K. Galbraith. Everywhere, without and within, are the marks of power, and only a leap of faith – a leap into the 'totality' – brings freedom.

At the heart of the New Left thinking lies a paradox. The desire for total community accompanies a fear of 'others', who are the true source of social power. At the same time, no society can have the powerless character which the New Left requires. The attempt to achieve a social order without domination inevitably leads to a new kind of domination, more sinister by far than the one deposed. The seeds of the new structure of power are present in the organization necessary for the violent overthrow of the old. A study of the logic of 'revolutionary *praxis*' must, I believe, confirm the celebrated observation of Roberto Michels, that an 'iron law of oligarchy' constrains all revolutionary parties towards the opposite of their emancipatory goal.[4] It is three-quarters of a century since Michels – himself a radical socialist – expressed those thoughts, and no socialist has really bothered to answer him. He is but one among the staggeringly many pertinent writers whom the left in general – and the New Left in particular – have decided to ignore.

POWER AND COERCION

The obsession with power has an important consequence. The radical is unable to see that the 'system' which he seeks to overthrow is consensual, while that towards which his thinking tends is not. Real human freedom is constrained by human circumstance, and therefore cannot be free from 'the worm of domination'. Freedom consists, not in the absence of domination, but in the presence of a domination congenial to those contained by it. Thinkers of the New Left invariably confuse power with coercion: power is so inherently hateful to them (and especially the 'secret' power that controls our inner thoughts) that they cannot understand how human beings can really accept it – unless it be by some monstrous fraud, some 'false consciousness', perpetrated by power itself. Nor are they alone in this confusion. Indeed, it is one of the most influential of Marx's legacies, and a natural offshoot of the 'sociological' method, which leads us to look always below the human surface to the 'structures' upon which it depends.

Consider Max Weber. We may not go so far as the *Great Soviet Encyclopedia,* whose 1951 edition describes him as 'a

German reactionary sociologist ... and the worst enemy of Marxism'. But we should certainly be reluctant to identify Weber as a 'thinker of the left', not the least because he recognized that socialism would require more organization, more bureaucracy and more impersonal power than the capitalism which it offered to replace. Nevertheless, like Marx, Weber wished to look below the surface of human society, to its real 'laws of motion'. And, by a faulty but persuasive logic, this led him to see 'coercion' wherever there is power, and power wherever there is authority.

Thus for Weber, the state is defined as a monopoly of violence ('physical coercion'), while 'a norm is a law depending on the probability that the state will violently enforce it'.[5] He concludes, therefore, that the law, like the state which acts through it, is a system of coercion. Moreover, he defines the idea of 'voluntary compliance' so widely as to imply that all coercive orders are also voluntarily accepted: 'domination implies a minimum of voluntary compliance, that is, an *interest* ... in obedience'.[6] From which it follows that any order, however tyrannical, is voluntarily obeyed. For what does the tyrant do with his threats and tortures, except endow his subjects with an *interest* in obedience?

The net result of the Weberian method is to abolish the distinction between consent and coercion. Most of us are *not* coerced by the law, provided the law enacts the procedures and principles of natural justice. We do not *wish* to rape, steal, murder or defraud, and are therefore in no way coerced by the laws which forbid us to do so. Only the criminal is coerced, and for him law comes as a retribution rather than a prior act of violence. But this feature of 'capitalist' society and the legal system which inheres in it is for Weber imperceptible, as is the real distinction in human freedom between socialism and capitalism. He writes:

> In a socialist community, direct mandatory and prohibitory decrees of a central economic control authority, in whichever way it may be conceived, would play a greater role than such ordinations are playing today. In the event of disobedience observance will be produced by means of some sort of 'coercion' but not through struggle in the market. Which

system would possess the more real coercion and which one more real personal freedom cannot be decided, however, by the mere analysis of the actually existing or conceivable formal legal system.[7]

Democratic socialism, he goes on to say, rejects coercion, both of a personal kind and of the kind 'exercised in the market through the possession of private property'. Thus the market – a paradigm of consensual relations – is reduced to a system of coercion, not different in kind from the control exerted, through forced labour, compulsory purchase and rationing, by the socialist state. The argument given for this conclusion by Weber is the argument given by Marx, and the one which has proved irresistible to a thousand subsequent thinkers: the owner of the means of production, it is said, coerces the man who owns nothing but his labour power.

There is an evident difference between slavery, in which one man is forced to work for another, and the wage contract. Suppose a travelling salesman comes to town, offering goods which will make life far more agreeable to the residents. Does he coerce those who purchase from him, just because they can obtain what he offers only by accepting his terms? It would be a gross misuse of language to say so. What makes the decisive difference, therefore, for the socialist, is the element of *need*, which supposedly poisons the wage contract and removes its consensual character. But why does that change the case? Suppose the salesman comes to a town where everyone is dying from a disease which only his brand of chocolate can cure. Does that suddenly transform him into a tyrant? And why should the man who brings labour to a community that is dying for the lack of it be branded as coercing those whose suffering he relieves? Should he have stayed away, just because he is in a position to profit from their need?[8]

To ask such questions is neither to exonerate capitalism nor to condemn the socialist 'alternative': it is simply to define the terms of debate, by refusing the socialist mis-description. No doubt the circumstances of the wage contract are frequently cruel and undignified; and no doubt traditional 'capitalism' offered little hope to those at the bottom of the pile. But to say that is not to prove that capitalism is 'wage slavery'. We should never overlook the salient moral feature of our political order: that its fundamental economic transaction is consensual. Nor should we ignore the fact that, under the impact of socialist doctrine, this consensual order has in many countries been replaced by a new kind of slavery.

The socialist will perhaps argue that he blames, not the individual employer, but the system of which he is a part and which is the true source of human suffering. But what does it mean to blame a 'system'? The system may be the product of human intention: but it is surely the expression of no human design. It arises by an 'invisible hand', according to processes which we do not really control, even when we believe that we do so.

The radical goes even further. For him the 'system' is not the product but the producer of the contracting individual whose 'freedom' it bestows. The invisible hand is untouched by the visible handshake. But this reversal of Adam Smith's hypothesis does not alter the case. Whichever view the socialist takes, he must recognize that to condemn one system he must suggest a better, and also show us how to obtain it: and it is precisely that which he is so reluctant to do. It is not sufficient to dwell on the fact of human need, which spurs us to sell even that which is nearest to us – our labour – for the precious benefit of survival. Without need there would be no motive for production, and without a fundamental inequality between the parties – each of whom wants what the other offers him – no contract can be freely engaged in. But to speak of coercion wherever there is need is to render freedom unobtainable. And in a sense that is precisely the achievement of 'actual socialism'.

CLASS AND AGENCY

The Marxist believes, however, that he can demonstrate that the wage contract is coercive in the fullest sense of the term. He arrives at this result by substituting for the individual human agent the social *class* of which he is a member. The person who offers employment to the worker is not, it is true, the one who first reduced his ancestors to misery. Nevertheless the one who employs and the one who 'originally' expropriated, are of the same social *class*. (This is, I believe, a tautological consequence of the classical Marxian theory.) Seeing the situation in 'class terms', we are tempted to the conclusion that the class which expropriates is also the class which employs. In which case the class which owns nothing but its labour power is *coerced* by the class which owns the means of production.

To steal from a man what he needs, and then to offer it on terms, is certainly to coerce him. But suppose we accept the schematic, and indeed mythopoeic, theory of the original 'separation of the producers from the means of production'.[9] It surely does not follow that capitalism is a system of coercion. For in the normal case the individual who offers a livelihood is not the one who first removed it. No *individual* exercises coercion in this arrangement, which proceeds at every point through contracts which are freely undertaken by those who are bound by them. Such contracts may indeed be *unfair:* but that is not to say that they can be described as having been forced.

It is at this point that there arises the most important and persistent of theoretical obfuscations: the misperception of agency. Despite Marx's warnings to the contrary the radical is tempted to identify classes as agents, to whom actions and responsibilities can be ascribed, and reward and punishment allotted. If classes are agents, then it is possible to say that the bourgeoisie as a class coerces the proletariat: in other words, the proletariat's lack of power is also a lack of freedom. Moreover, it is now possible to blame the bourgeoisie as a class, and each member of it individually, for the sufferings of the powerless. Acts of retribution, expropriation and violence, committed in the cause of revolution, become not merely expedient but also deserved. The collective agency of the upper class is also a collective liability, and if this or that bourgeois is stripped of his rights for the sake of the new society, this is no more than a just return for the sufferings which his class engendered.

That pattern of thought leads as logically to the Gulag as the Nazi ideology of race led to Auschwitz. And, like the Nazi ideology, it is riddled with intellectual confusion and moral exorbitance. Every advanced society contains points of control – places in the activities of production, trade and government which give to those who occupy them effective control over decisions. Whether we agree with Marx that the crucial factor is the control over the means of production is not in point. What matters is that, for the Marxist, the ruling class is *defined* as the class of those who occupy the main points of control. If such 'points of control' are ineliminable, then it follows logically that the ruling class will always rule: for while this or that man may be displaced from his position of dominance, he suffers only as an individual. He ceases, in his fall, to be a member of the class which dominates, just as the one who replaces him loses his status as a serf. This – which might be called the 'iron law of domination' – is no more than a tautological consequence of two indisputable premises: that society requires organization, and that organization breeds control. Of course societies vary enormously in the 'chances' possessed by individuals. But the New Left asks not for increased mobility but for a society from which the 'worm of domination' has been finally removed. Even the complete 'liquidation' of the present ruling class will not achieve this result, since its dominion is the result not of collective agency but of something else. The ruling class can do nothing, either to sustain or to relinquish its power, which is as inseparable from that class as life itself.

COERCION AND CONSENT

The iron law of domination implies that nothing can disseminate power so effectively as social mobility: the gift which capitalism offers in abundance. The left pours scorn on social mobility, in terms anticipated by Marx:

> ... the more a ruling class is able to assimilate the foremost minds of a ruled class, the more stable and dangerous becomes its rule.[10]

But unless we regard 'danger' and 'stability' as synonymous (and in this Marx gives roughly the opposite of the truth), the accusation is entirely fraudulent. Social mobility is not a conspiracy of the elite, whereby it perpetuates its power, but a structural weakness of the elite, whereby it is always changing.

And what better way to alleviate the concentration of power than to ensure that power is offered to those who – through personal experience and personal loyalty – retain their sympathy for those who do not possess it? Observe the worlds of 'real capitalism' and 'real socialism' and ask yourself which is most responsive to the needs and aspirations of the powerless. You will see then what a monstrous fraud has been perpetrated on the workers by the Marxist theory of class. Not only has the vanguard party, in its vigilant effort to exclude all but the faithful and the craven from its ranks, closed the avenues of social improvement: the powerless have become increasingly helpless, increasingly separated from any reward save that which is offered to them from above. In such a situation the powerless really are the victims of coercion, and dominion really is a threat.

In saying that the order by which we are surrounded is consensual I do not mean that it is consented to. I mean, rather, that this society, while not the *object* of consent, is nevertheless the *product* of consent, arising by an invisible hand from the countless negotiations, agreements, votes and compromises that compose the body politic. Philosophers of the 'social contract' attempt to translate this consensual order into an order consented to: to make the result of our contracts into the first object of them. In that attempt, however, lies a deep and enduring error: the error of supposing that we could understand the outcome of social interaction before we had engaged in it, and that we could agree *now* on a social order which arises from choices that we cannot *now* envisage.

Likewise, in saying that the society of 'actual socialism' is coercive, I do not mean that it is imposed. The ruling party did not envisage the result and then seek by all means to establish it. On the contrary, the result is so disheartening that the party forbids its subjects to describe it, or even to think about it, except in carefully measured euphemisms that parody the ancestral voices of the Marxist church. The coercive order is no more chosen by the party than the consensual order is chosen by the citizen. It too arises by an 'invisible hand', from transactions which are, in themselves, devoted to no such end. If the order is coercive, it is because these transactions are coerced.

CIVIL SOCIETY AND STATE

Underlying the New Left vision of society, therefore, are two deep and contestable assumptions: first, that wherever there is power there is coercion; second, that classes are not the products of social interaction but the agents which control it. Those two assumptions arise from a kind of moral impatience, a need, faced with the ocean of human misery, to discover the culprit who turned on the tap. From the same impatience arises the political science of the New Left, which dismisses or ignores the concepts necessary to the defence of 'capitalist' society and which, by aiming always for the 'deep' explanation, misses the surface (and the truth) of social action.

Consider the distinction between civil society and state. It was Hegel who first gave this distinction currency, and it was Marx's attack on Hegel that first threatened to overthrow it. In Antonio Gramsci's theory of hegemony (and Louis Althusser's derived idea of the 'ideological state apparatus') the Marxian enterprise obtains canonical utterance. All powers within civil society – even though exercised by free association, autonomous institutions and corporations limited by law – are ascribed to the state (and to the 'ruling class' which controls it). They are as much part of the state, for the follower of Gramsci, as are the army, the judiciary, the police and parliament.

Someone who accepts that theory can no longer perceive the destruction of autonomous institutions by the state as a radical and innovatory departure. For the New Left, there is no significant difference between the control exercised by a triumphant communist party and that exercised through the 'hegemony' of a 'ruling class'. Once again, therefore, a true achievement of 'capitalist' politics – the effective separation of society and state – is rendered imperceivable, and the reality of totalitarian dictatorship clouded in euphemism and apology. For someone nurtured on the Gramscian theory, the effort of Poland's Solidarity – described by its principal protagonists precisely as the effort to establish society (*spoteczenstwo*) outside the control of the state (*wtada*) – is either a restoration of the old communist 'struggle', or else a gross self-delusion. In other words, those who most fiercely oppose communism and are prepared even to pay the supreme price for its destruction, are seen as fighting to install it, in a 'true' and 'realized' form.

This is not to say that the distinction between state and society is either easy to characterize or easy to defend. It is, indeed, one of the lasting problems of political philosophy how the two might best be related. We should understand their ideal relation in terms of a human analogy. The human person is neither identical with his body nor distinct from it, but joined to it in a metaphysical knot that philosophers labour fruitlessly to untie. When treating someone as a person, we address ourselves to his rational and decision-making part: when treating him as a body (when he is ill or incapacitated) we study the anatomical functions which lie outside his will. Civil society is like the human body: it is the substance which composes the state, but whose movement and functions arise by an 'invisible hand'. And the state is like the human person: it is the supreme forum of decision-making, in which reason and responsibility are the only authoritative guides. State and society are inseparable but nevertheless distinct, and the attempt to absorb the one into the other is the sure path to a stunted, crippled and pain-wracked body politic.

It is hardly a distinguishing fault of the New Left that it has relied so heavily on shoddy rhetoric in its discussion of this issue. The same goes for thinkers of every persuasion, and no theory yet provided – from the 'dialectical' analysis of Hegel to Hayek's conception of 'spontaneous order' – does justice to the extreme complexity of political realities. Nevertheless, it is characteristic of the New Left to be easily contented with theories that fuel its angry sentiment. When so much is at stake, this 'willing suspension of disbelief' is far from innocent.

It is difficult to assess the practical consequences of political theories. Nevertheless, it is not unreasonable to suggest that the New Left, in attributing agency to that which does not possess it (to class and society) – has connived at the removal of responsibility from that which does – from the state and the party. The world of communism is a world of impersonal dominion, where all power lies with a party that can never answer for its actions. This state of affairs is no accidental correlate of a ruling philosophy which encourages the myth of class agency, and which sees every moderating institution, including law itself, as an elaborate crime. It is precisely in locating agency in entities which are answerable for nothing that communism has created such an agency, and placed it at the summit of power. By identifying itself with a 'class' the party has appropriated both the agency that its theory wrongly attributes to the proletariat and the unanswerability that truly characterizes every social class. This, I believe, is the source of its criminal momentum. By its own self-confessed nature, the Communist Party is an agency – indeed a vast conspiracy – whose collective decisions are subject to no law and answerable to no human purpose but its own.

LEFT AND RIGHT

Were we to define the right as the force which leans from the left in an opposite direction, then we should have succumbed to the most dangerous feature of leftist rhetoric. We too should be seeing politics as a 'struggle' between opposing forces, an 'either/or', poised between two equally absolute and equally final goals. Nevertheless, the labels 'left' and 'right' are inevitably forced on us, and we must venture a description – however partial and however brief – of the 'right-wing' attitude that is now most readily available. It is by reference to communism, I believe, that this outlook is best defined. The New Right (if I may appropriate the label) believes in responsible rather than impersonal government; in the autonomy and personality of institutions; and in the rule of law. It recognizes a distinction between state and civil society, and believes that the second should arise, in general, from the unforced interaction of freely contracting individuals, moderated by custom, tradition and a respect for authority and law. Power, for the New Right, is an evil only when abused. For power arises naturally from human intercourse, and is merely the unobjectionable consequence of an arrangement whose virtue lies elsewhere.

CORPORATE PERSONALITY

Perhaps the simplest way to indicate the theoretical base and practical effect of this 'right-wing' politics is through an idea which Otto von Gierke and F. W. Maitland have argued to be essential to the understanding of European politics: the idea of corporate personality.[11]

Roman Law, the *Genossensrecht* of medieval Germany, the English law of trusts and corporations – all such legal systems recognize that the features of individual human beings, whereby we are moved to praise or blame them, to accord to them rights and liabilities, to oppose them and to ally ourselves with them, can be displayed by collective entities. Such systems also recognize that collective agency is a danger, until brought before the law as a composite person, equal to the individual whom it threatens to oppress. A university, a trading company, a club, an institution, even the state itself: all may be endowed with 'legal personality', and so made answerable before the law. (Hence the existence of 'unincorporated associations' is regarded as a legal *problem*.) A trading company can perform actions which are the actions of no individual. It has reasons for what it does. It may behave rationally and irrationally in pursuit of its goals. It has rights in law: rights of ownership, trade and action; rights of way, light and air; rights of usufruct and interest. It also has duties and liabilities: duties according to the law of contract, tort and crime. The factory which pollutes a river can therefore be compelled to compensate those who suffer. It can also be charged with a crime, and fined to the point of bankruptcy. (We should not be surprised, therefore, that problems of environmental pollution are far worse in the under-productive world of Communist government than in the over-productive world of private enterprise.)

By this device of corporate liability, the 'capitalist' world has ensured that, wherever there is agency, there is also liability. No such maxim holds in the world of communism. The Communist Party is the supreme agent. But it cannot be held liable for its crimes, for its spoliation or for its massive encroachments upon the rights and privileges of everyone who stands in its way. Indeed it provides one of the major justifications for the 'capitalist' society which Marxists so intemperately condemn.

THE RULE OF LAW

The abolition of true corporate liability means the abolition of effective law. Although there are laws of a kind in communist countries, and although they nominally apply to the 'collectives' and the official institutions, they cannot be enforced against the Communist Party. Nevertheless, the Communist Party is the major source of collective action, and acts *through* all subordinate institutions without partaking of their liabilities. This circumstance is a direct result of the 'classist' ideology of communism, an ideology that is shared by the left as a whole. Convinced of the absolute evil of domination, the leftist sees his task as the abolition of power. He is therefore impatient with those institutions which have the *limitation*, rather than the abolition, of power as their primary object. Because these institutions stand in the way of power, and because the violent overthrow of the old order requires a greater power than that upon which it rested, the leftist inevitably sanctions the destruction of limiting institutions. And once destroyed, they are never resurrected, except as instruments of oppression. They are never again turned against the power that the leftist himself installed, but only against the power of his ancestral enemy, the 'bourgeois', who for some reason continues to survive in the hidden crevices of the new social order.

The case of Foucault shows clearly how the radical's hostility to power leads to a hostility to law, and to a thoroughgoing mis-perception of judicial institutions. This hostility is also fuelled by the Marxian theory of history, with its distinction between political superstructure and economic base. The distinction is untenable, but of immense theological importance: hence the interest of the New Left in Gramsci and Althusser, who provide the language by which the refutation of Marx's theory can be presented as though it were really a proof of it. The theory leads to a devaluing of politics and law, a refusal to judge them by their own carefully elaborated criteria, and a spurious invocation of the 'class struggle' as the major political fact. Judicial independence is no longer seen for what it is – a means of standing back from human conflict and endeavouring to take an impartial view of it – but as another instrument of domination, another functional device, whereby the power of the old ruling class is embellished with excuses and meticulously preserved.

The net result of the two ideas – the idea of 'class agency' and the (strictly incompatible) idea of a distinction between political superstructure and economic base – is a fundamental political ignorance. Communist government – in which the judiciary really does act as part of the ruling power, and where the ruling power really is an agent – is no longer seen as the perversion of politics, but as politics of a new and promising kind. Our European systems of law, patiently constructed upon the established results of Roman Law, Canon Law and the common laws of the European nations, embody centuries of minute reflection upon the realities of human conflict. Such legal systems have tried to define and to limit the activities of every important social power, and to install in the heart of the 'capitalist' order a principle of answerability which no agent can escape. The rule of law is no simple achievement, to be weighed against the competing benefits of some rival social scheme and renounced in their favour. On the contrary, it is definitive of our social condition and represents the high point of European political achievement. There is a rule of law, however, only where every power, however large, is subject to the law and limited by it. It is precisely this limitation of itself by the law that the Communist Party cannot tolerate. In supporting the ideology through which law may be despised and set aside, the New Left ceases to be an innocent observer of the crimes committed in that ideology's name.

IDEOLOGY AND OPPOSITION

Nor should we dissociate the New Left from the attitude that communism has taken towards its opponents. For such thinkers, the opponent is never better than an 'opportunist'. What he speaks is not reason but 'ideology' (in the peculiar Marxian sense of that term). His claim to truth is automatically discounted by the class interest which speaks through him. And because he is opposed to the 'socialist' ideas of the 'proletariat' – as represented in its intellectual vanguard – he speaks only for the 'bourgeoisie'. Gramsci's idea of 'class hegemony' again proves its utility, in explaining how the voices of reaction may occur throughout society, impeding the movement of historical progress and placing in the heart of the proletariat the canker of 'false consciousness'. Whenever you encounter opposition, you encounter the class enemy, even if he is wearing some cunning disguise. This enemy is not to be argued with, for he cannot utter truth; still less is he to be the object of a compromise. Only after his final elimination from the social order will the truth be generally perceived.

It is precisely this philosophy, offering to bring intellectuals to power, that constitutes the greatest threat to intellectual freedom. Once in power the intellectual 'expropriates the means of communication' (until then in 'bourgeois' hands), and dissolves the institutions of 'bourgeois' democracy in the proletarian cause. The universal result is the elimination of effective opposition.

This lack of opposition is the decisive feature of communist government. Of course, there are people who disagree with the party line, and people who oppose it. But the political process in a communist state makes no room for them. And in order to drown the still, small voice of opposition, the ruling party has recourse to ideology – a set of doctrines, for the most part doctrines of a staggering imbecility, designed to close the avenues of intellectual enquiry. The purpose of this ideology is not that people should believe it. On the contrary, the purpose is to make belief irrelevant, to rid the world of rational discussion in all areas where the party has staked a claim. The idea of a 'dictatorship of the proletariat' is not supposed to describe a reality: it is supposed to bring enquiry to an end, so that reality cannot be perceived ...

Nor is this ideology a harmless eccentricity – a convenient substitute for religion in minds too proud to recognize the virtue of atonement. It is a dangerous weapon, which threatens the very structure of rational thought and action. The first effect of ideology in power is to mark out areas where discussion is closed and where it is rash for the ordinary man to venture. Because these are the areas in which opposition might take root – the areas of fundamental political choice – ideology is an important instrument in the war against opposition. It abolishes the element of rational choice from political decisions, for it abolishes the language in which opposing principles might be uttered. Fundamentals can no longer be questioned, not because they are accepted but because they are taboo.

The failure to discuss with opponents, to open the mind to doubt and hesitation, is a rooted characteristic of the New Left. All discussions are conducted with those who share the fundamental illusions, and they remain arguments within Marxism, not without it. Exactly the same failure is exhibited by communist government, which makes fundamental choices without the benefit of criticism and without corrective measures. Such a government cannot be bound by obligations, since it cannot listen to the voice that strives to make it answerable to something other than itself. Hence it constantly seeks to increase its power, in order that opposition will never rise up to accuse it. It stands above all laws and sees no person as anything but a means to the supreme revolutionary goal of 'social justice'. Its leaders (unless canonized as Revolutionary Heroes) are forgotten as soon as they have left office, and no procedure exists either for electing or for removing them. Power is the sole commodity, and it is power that is beyond rational appraisal. The impersonal advance of power is no-one's responsibility, since no individual can either criticize the workings of power or feel personally liable for them when he serves as the channel through which they flow.

Nor should we ignore the consequences for *us*, who have so far escaped the yoke of communism, of this power which the New Left encourages us to see as evil only in the way that all power is evil, our own power most of all. The effect of Marxist ideology is precisely to set the communist state on the road to domination. Nobody believes that it *should* dominate, least of all those who apologize for its 'errors' and 'deviations'. Nor does any citizen of a communist state wish it to increase its power so alarmingly. But no one knows how to stop it, since no reason for stopping it can be uttered without instant penalty. The ideology of communism holds that the work of commun-ism will be ended only when communism is everywhere triumphant. Although this is not believed, it is acted upon: the purpose of ideology is precisely to make belief irrelevant to action, to close up the places at which reasoned discussion might enter, and to bend all action to a single-minded goal. The machine-state of communism is not only out of control and beyond reproach: it is also bound by an impersonal aim of monumental proportions, from which it can be deflected only by force. The force necessary to oppose it is ever greater, and the will to apply it ever less. People are therefore tempted to see the communist states as they see our own: they look for excuses that will make us seem equally to blame for the present tensions, not realizing that it is our very capacity to accept and respond to blame which provides our exoneration.

POLITICS OF THE RIGHT

The totalitarian structure of communist government is not an *inevitable* consequence of Marxist conceptions. Nevertheless, under their justifying surveillance compromise, constitution and the institutions of civil society have been steadily perverted or abolished. The resulting form of government, lacking the corrective devices of free opinion, judicial independence and parliamentary opposition, is locked on a course which, however irrational, cannot be peacefully altered. It is against the reality of communist government, I believe, that our own laws and institutions should be judged, and the 'right' point of view defended. The matter could be put simply: our inherited forms of government, founded upon representation, law and autonomous institutions which mediate between the individual and the state, are also forms of *personal* government. The state as we know it is not a thing but a person. This is true not only in the legal sense but in a deeper sense, once captured in the institution of monarchy but displayed more widely and more discreetly through the rule of law. Like every person, the state is answerable to other persons: to the individual subject, to the corporations and to other states. It is also answerable to the law. It has rights against the individual and duties towards him; it is tutor and companion of society, the butt of our jokes and the recipient of our anger. It stands to us in a human relation, and this relation is upheld and vindicated by the law, before which it comes as one person among others, on equal footing with its own subjects.

Such a state can compromise and bargain. It is disposed to recognize that it must respect persons, not as means only but as ends in themselves. It tries not to liquidate opposition but to accommodate it. The socialist too may influence this state, and provided that he recognizes that no change, not even change in his favoured direction, is or can be 'irreversible', he presents no threat to its durability. The immense human achievement represented by such a state is neither respected nor even noticed by the New Left radical. Bent on a labour of destruction, he sees behind the mask of every institution the hideous machinery of power. For him there is, in the end, no real difference between the impersonal, abstract power of communism, and the personal, mediated and concrete power of the 'bourgeois democracies'. By demoting law and politics to epiphenomena, and by seeing all states as 'systems' based on structures of economic organization and control, the New Left radical effectively removes from his perception all the real distinctions between the world of representative government and the world of communism, and in doing so connives at the communist destruction of compromise and law. He sees, not the personal face of Western government, but the skull beneath the skin. He compares societies as an anatomist compares bodies: recognizing the similarity in function and structure and failing to see the person, whose rights, duties, reasons and motives are the true objects of our concern. The body of the communist state may be like the body of the Western democracy: after all, in each case, the main ingredient – people – is the same. But one body is animated by a person, while the other is no more than a corpse, marching ever onwards, its limbs moved lifelessly by the fearful puppet-master of the Communist Party.

CONCLUSION

The inhuman politics of communism is the objective realiza-tion of the Marxist vision of society, which sees true politics as no more than a mendacious covering placed over the realities of power. For such a vision, political systems can no longer be judged as persons – by their virtues and vices and by the movement of their intrinsic life – but only by their goals. The excuses made for the Soviet Union originate, not in a love of tyranny, but in the failure to *perceive* tyranny when its goal is also one's own. Whatever 'errors' have been committed in the name of communism, it is supposed, they have been the work of individuals, such as Stalin, who perverted the system from its true and humanizing purpose.

Despite this devotion to goals – a devotion which is in itself at variance with the spirit of European law and government – the radical is extremely loath to tell us what he is aiming at. As soon as the question of the 'New Society' arises, he diverts our attention back to the actual world, so as to renew the energy of hatred. In a moment of doubt about the socialist record, E. J. Hobsbawm writes:

> If the left may have to think more seriously about the new society, that does not make it any the less desirable or necessary or the case against the present one any less compelling.[12]

There, in a nutshell, is the sum of the New Left's commitment. We know nothing of the socialist future, save only that it is both necessary and desirable. Our concern is with the 'compelling' case against the present, that leads us to destroy what we lack the knowledge to replace. A blind faith drags the radical from 'struggle' to 'struggle', reassuring him that everything done in the name of 'social justice' is well done and that all destruction of existing power will lead him towards his goal. He desires to leap from the tainted world that surrounds him into the pure but unknowable realm of human emancipation. This leap into the Kingdom of Ends is a leap of thought, which can never be mirrored in reality. 'Revolutionary praxis' therefore confines itself to the work of destruction, having neither the power nor the desire to perceive, in concrete terms, the end towards which it labours. By an inevitable transition, therefore, the 'armed doctrine' of the revolutionary, released in pursuit of an ideal freedom, produces a world of real enslavement, whose brutal arrangements are incongruously described in the language of emancipation: 'liberation', 'democracy', 'equality', 'progress' and 'peace' – words which no prisoner of 'actual socialism' can now hear uttered without a pained, sardonic smile.

So much is perhaps obvious to those who have not succumbed to the ideological temptation of the left. But the consequence is not always accepted. The 'right' (which in this context means those who defend personal government, autonomous institutions and the rule of law) does not, after all, bear the onus of justification. It is not for us to defend a reality which, for all its faults, has the undeniable merit of existence. Nor is it for us to show that the consensual politics of Western government is somehow closer to human nature and more conducive to man's fulfilment than the ideal world of socialist emancipation. Nevertheless, nothing is more striking to a reader of the New Left than the constant assumption that it is the 'right' which bears the burden and that it is sufficient to adopt the *aims* of socialism in order to have virtue on one's side.

This assumption of *a priori* correctness, added to the turgid prose and the sheer intellectual incompetence of much New Left writing, presents a formidable challenge to the reader's patience. No doubt I have frequently been driven, in my exasperation, to lapse from accepted standards of literary politeness. But what of that? Politeness is no more than a 'bourgeois' virtue, a pale reflection of the 'rule of law' which is the guarantee of bourgeois domination. In engaging with the left one engages not with a disputant but with a self-declared enemy. Nobody has perceived more clearly than the reformed totalitarian Plato that argument changes its character when the onus is transferred from the man who would change things to the man who would keep them secure:

> How is one to argue on behalf of the existence of the gods without passion? For we needs must be vexed and indignant with the men who have been, and still are, responsible for laying on us this burden of argument.[13]

Like Plato's wise Athenian, I have tried to pass the burden back to the one who created it.

NOTES

1. Kenneth Minogue, *Alien Powers: The Pure Theory of Ideology* (London: 1985), p. 226.
2. See the criticisms of the later work of Sartre in Raymond Aron, *D'une Sainte Famille a une autre* (Paris: 1975).
3. Michel Foucault, *Surveiller et Punir* (Paris: 1975).
4. Roberto Michels, *Political Parties,* Trans. C. and E. Paul (London: 1915).
5. Max Weber, *Economy and Society,* Trans. E. Fischoff et al., Vol. 1 (New York: 1968). Part II, Ch. 1, §1.
6. Ibid., Part I, Ch. 3 §1.
7. Ibid., Part II, Ch. 8.
8. On this point see the now well-known arguments of Robert Nozick in *Anarchy, State and Utopia* (New York and Oxford: 1974).
9. See Jean Baechler's devastating critique of the theory of 'primitive accumulation', in both its *Grundrisse* and *Capital* versions, in *The Origins of Capitalism,* Trans. Barry Cooper (Oxford: 1975).
10. Karl Marx, *Capital,* Standard Edition (Moscow: 1971), Vol. III, p. 601.
11. F. W. Maitland, *Trust and Corporation* (Cambridge: 1904). Otto von Gierke, *Das deutsche Genossenschaftsrecht,* 4 Vols (Berlin: 1868).
12. E. J. Hobsbawm, 'Should Poor People Organise?' in *Worlds of Labour* (London: 1984).
13. Plato, *Laws,* X, 887.

3

Rousseau and the Origins of Liberalism

(From *The New Criterion*, 1998)

The modern world gives proof at every point that it is far easier to destroy institutions than to create them. Nevertheless, few people seem to understand this truth. Britain's Labour Party has embarked upon a series of 'constitutional reforms' that can be relied upon to undermine the old authority of Parliament, but that will put no new authority in its place. The churches have initiated massive liturgical changes, so losing their old consolations, their old beliefs, and their old congregations without making converts among the young. From the curriculum reformers in schools to the gay activists in the military, people are engaged in revising inherited institutions in the interests of their present members, each of whom is supposed to have an equal stake in whatever church, school, brigade, or work force he belongs to. Yet no one has the faintest conception of what the long-term costs and benefits will be.

This process of revision seems eminently rational and just to those who have embarked on it. Who can stand in the way of reform, when the liberal idea requires it? Yet the fact remains that reform will easily destroy an institution, but will not reliably replace it with another one. We have seen this in the churches, in the schools, in the universities, and in government. And we shall go on seeing it for as long as the liberal consensus prevails. It is for this reason that it is always worthwhile to return to the first and greatest of the liberal reformers, Jean-Jacques Rousseau, whose impact on modern culture and modern politics has been equalled by no other thinker of the Enlightenment. In the work of Rousseau, we discover what is really at stake in the contest between conservative and liberal in all the areas of social life where this contest can be witnessed. What is at stake is not freedom, equality, or power, but the inherited store of social knowledge.

Rousseau's discussions of the social contract, the general will, the nature of sovereignty and citizenship, the origins of inequality, and the possibility of democratic choice are of great philosophical interest. But they should be seen in the context of his work as a whole. Rousseau was not only a great philosopher; he was also a philosopher who thought through feeling and felt through ideas. All that emerges from his pen bears the stamp of an inimitable life; and if any writer were to make liberalism plausible, it would be Rousseau, who felt his way to the moral and emotional heart of it. His view of life was also a form of life, and he expressed it not only in his philosophical works, but also in an immensely influential novel – *Julie, ou la Nouvelle Heloise* – which can be favourably compared with the only other indisputable work of art from the hand of a philosopher: Plato's *Symposium*.

In his compositions and his writings on music, Rousseau gave voice in another way and through another – though, for him, connected – medium to his fundamental outlook. And of course he gave to posterity, in his *Confessions*, the first and perhaps the finest example of the romantic autobiography – the noble lie in its quintessentially modern form. Add to those achievements his brilliant anticipation of the distinction between hunter-gatherer and agricultural societies; his insight into language and the depth of the scientific problem that it poses; and his profoundly original, profoundly influential, and profoundly dangerous views on education, and you quickly come to see that there is no way in which Rousseau can be adequately discussed, still less dismissed, in a single article. Nevertheless, there is a lesson to be drawn from him, which can without distortion be given in fewer words than the philosopher would ever have bestowed on a subject so important as himself.

I have already used the term 'liberalism' in its modern sense – or one of its modern senses. It is not a term that Rousseau would have used; nor would he have recognized his ideas in those thinkers whom we now describe as 'classical liberals'. Liberalism is an intellectual tradition formed from the interplay of two political ideals: liberty and equality. Liberals differ according to whether liberty or equality is more important to them. Libertarians believe that liberty should be traded for nothing else save liberty, whereas the present-day American 'liberal' tends to sacrifice liberty for equality when the two conflict. Both libertarians and egalitarians are hostile to vested authority, and this hostility often unites the two in practice, even if it is hard to reconcile them in theory. Rousseau cared passionately for both liberty and equality. But he also brought to the fore some of the deep tensions between them. He observed with disgust what people did with their freedom, and his disgust was proof of the deep inequality that set him apart from so many of his contemporaries.

True liberty, for Rousseau, is 'moral liberty'. It does not consist merely in a lack of obstacles. Liberty involves autonomous choice. People are free only when they can bind themselves. From this thought stems another, inherent in Rousseau, and made explicit by Kant, namely that freedom is also a submission to law: 'obedience to a law which we prescribe to ourselves is liberty', as Rousseau wrote in *Du contrat social*. For Rousseau, a society can be free only if freely consented to, and obligations can be binding only if self-imposed. Hence, society must be founded in a contract: each person promises obedience in exchange for a like promise from everyone else. But there is a contradiction here, and Rousseau several times returns to it. The ability to promise, to commit oneself, to act autonomously – all these involve language, which in turn requires society. The autonomous agent does not exist in a state of nature: he is a social artefact. As Rousseau himself makes clear, our natural liberty is destroyed by the social contract, which puts 'civil liberty' in the place of it. From civil liberty springs moral liberty, but it is only with the coming of moral liberty that we can bind ourselves by a contract. So, how can society be founded on a contract, when no contract can exist until society has been founded? Here is a potent paradox, and one which awakens in Rousseau the will to believe. We must live as if bound by a contract, while knowing this to be impossible.

Inequality is of two kinds – natural and artificial. Inequalities that arise in society, Rousseau believes, are limitations on freedom, both for those at the top and those at the bottom. The rich man becomes slave to luxury and dependent on others to serve and obey him; the poor man becomes slave to need and dependent on others to command and reward him. But again there is a paradox. In a free society, where each may pursue his projects, natural power translates into social power, and natural inequality into inequality of another kind. All social advantages stem from the interest that people have in each other. Looks, intelligence, strength, prowess, energy, liveliness, the very attachment to life – all these are unequally distributed. Yet, it is these qualities that we find most interesting, and that determine our chances in the world. To prevent social inequalities, therefore, we must ensure that people are not free to exploit their natural powers. Only a massive programme of social engineering could succeed in bringing this about.

Rousseau was aware of the paradoxical nature of egalitarianism. His whole life was proof to him that natural talent leads to social distinction unless impeded by force. The human relations that most elicited his sympathy were fraught with inequality, both natural and social. The relations between Emile and his tutor, between Julie (*La Nouvelle Heloise*) and her lover St Preux (who is also her tutor), and between himself and the mother-figures who one by one take charge of him in the *Confessions* – all these offer living proof of the way in which social and natural inequalities feed each other. He observed how inequality is accepted and endorsed by love; and he observed the compassion that people feel, when permitted to look down on – and up at – their neighbours. Hence, the only equality that is ever dwelt upon in Rousseau's writings is that which arises when power and authority go on holiday. Such equality is, as the Swiss philosopher Jean Starobinski has written in *Jean-Jacques Rousseau, Transparency and Obstruction* (1988), a 'holiday affair', typified by the idyll of the grape harvest in *La Nouvelle Heloise*, when all classes, released from toil by sudden abundance, gather round for a common feast.

Why was Rousseau so eager to embrace the paradoxes to which I have alluded? What in his intellectual and emotional project entailed such a *credo quia absurdum?* The question takes us to the heart of Rousseau's thinking. 'J'aime mieux etre homme paradoxes qu'homme a prejuges', he wrote in *Emile*. Prejudices come from the desire to protect existing things; paradoxes from the attempt to question them. Paradox is the mark of *a priori* thinking – thinking from first principles in a situation where human nature has been encrusted by custom and habit. Man, in Rousseau's account, has been corrupted by society. To rediscover our freedom, we must measure every activity against its 'natural' counterpart. Not that we can return to our 'natural' state; the very idea of a state of nature is a philosophical abstraction. Nevertheless, in everything there is another way, an as yet undiscovered route to authenticity, which will allow us to do freely what we now do only by constraint. No existing institution should be accepted, therefore, just because it is *existing*. All practices and customs should be questioned, measured against an *a priori* standard, and amended if they fail to come up to the mark ...

Rousseau's attack on society in the name of 'nature' exemplifies what to me is the root error of liberalism in all its forms, namely, the inability to accept, or even to perceive, the inherited forms of social knowledge. By social knowledge, I mean the kind of knowledge embodied in the common law, in parliamentary procedures, in manners, costume, social convention, and, also, in morality. Such knowledge arises 'by an invisible hand' from the open-ended business of society, from problems that have been confronted and solved, from agreements that have been perpetuated by custom, from conventions that coordinate our otherwise conflicting passions, and from the unending process of negotiation and compromise whereby we quieten the dogs of war.

It was such knowledge that Edmund Burke had in mind when he attacked the *a priori* thinking of the French revolutionaries in *Reflections on the Revolution in France* (1790). 'We are afraid to put men to live and trade on their own private stock of reason', he wrote, 'because we suspect that this stock in each man is small, and that individuals would do better to avail themselves of the general bank and capital of nations, and of ages'. Burke's imagery is in one respect misleading. Social knowledge does not accumulate as money does, nor does it grow in the manner of scientific knowledge, which can be stored in books. It exists only in and through its repeated exercise: it is social, tacit, practical, and can never be captured in a formula or plan. The best way to understand it, indeed, is through the failures of the planned economy.

The Austrian economists – for example, Ludwig von Mises in *Socialism: An Economic and Sociological Analysis* (1951) – argued, plausibly enough, that prices in a market contain information that is indispensable to economic life. This information exists only in the free exchange of goods and services; it is information about the real pressure of human needs. Hence the attempt to encompass economic life in a rational plan, with prices controlled from the centre, will destroy the information on which the plan must draw. Rationalism in economics is irrational. Indeed, it is a living instance of the self-contradictions discovered by Rousseau whenever he searched for the first principles of human society.

The Austrian theory parallels Michael Oakeshott's attack on rationalism in politics in *Rationalism in Politics and Other Essays* (1963). It can also be applied in other spheres where social knowledge is the foundation of rational conduct, as F. A. von Hayek has shown in *Law, Legislation, and Liberty* (1982). The common law, for example, contains information that could not be contained in a legislative programme – information about conflicts and their resolution, about the sense of justice in action, and about human expectations, which is dispersed through the record of the law and is never available when legislation is the sole legal authority. Hence, the attempt to remake the legal order, through a legislative code that embodies all permissible solutions, is profoundly irrational. Such a code will destroy the source of legal knowledge, which is the judgement of the impartial judge as he confronts the unforeseeable course of human conflict. Rousseau's social contract leads to an abstract and *a priori* code, established not by the attempt to rectify injustices as they one by one arise, but by the supreme act of a Legislator who, being not God but Jean-Jacques, is destined to fail. The Legislator is the unhappy Atlas on whom the unsustainable burden of humanity falls ...

Social knowledge arises from the search over time for

agreement. Even the common law, which leans on coercion, involves the attempt to find socially agreed solutions. Hence, the outcome of a case in common law is always clear: rights and liabilities are determined. But the principle – the *ratio decidendi* – may not be clear at all, and may emerge only later in the tradition of judicial reasoning. Law, custom, convention, ceremony, moral norms, and the market are the varying ways in which human beings attempt to live by agreement. The resulting social order will be marked by inequalities and constraints. How could it be otherwise? But it will arise, in the normal case, from transactions freely engaged in. If transactions are coerced, then the resulting conventions and norms will not contain the knowledge that is so important to us: the knowledge of what to do in order to live in harmony with our fellows.

Rousseau's rejection of society in favour of free choice and uncorrupted nature should be seen in this context. It is not enough for Rousseau that institutions should arise from consent in the manner of the common law or the market; they must be the *object* of consent. We must stand outside our institutions and ask ourselves whether we would freely choose them from among alternatives. If the answer is yes, then this forms the basis of a social contract. In entering such a contract, we establish a legitimate order – but only then. For only then do our institutions reflect our own autonomous submission to government. Only then is authority bestowed upon government by the governed. Only then, in other words, does the self win against the others.

In Rousseau, of course, the contract does not amount to much. No sooner are we released from social burdens than we submit to a 'general will' that brooks no opposition, and that adds to its commands the insolent assertion that, in obeying it, we are doing our own will. Freedom is no sooner obtained than thrown away. All who have studied Robespierre's 'despotism of liberty' will know how dangerous Rousseau's paradoxes can be when their inner (that is to say, religious) meaning is brought to the surface.

Just as dangerous, however, is the assumption that we can jettison all institutions, traditions, and conventions and decide how to make them anew. This is the root assumption of liberalism, and it recurs in all versions of the social contract – even the hypothetical contract of the philosopher John Rawls. It implies that we can make rational choices, knowing what to do and how to do it, without the benefit of social knowledge – in other words, without the hard-earned legacy of consensual solutions.

It is not just that there is no reason to think that this is so. It is rather that there is every reason to think the opposite. We know what to do only when we have a sense of right and wrong, an implicit awareness of the unseen multitudes whom our actions affect, and the instinctive knowledge of what is admirable or despicable, that are percolated through the channels of tradition. Without traditions we have no 'conception of the good', as the philosopher John Rawls describes it. And, for all that Rawls says to the contrary, a social contract between creatures with no conception of the good is a parody of rational choice – the kind of parody that Rawls places before us, imagining that he has given a final proof, and not a refutation, of the liberal view of society.

Jean Starobinski attributes to Rousseau an emotional need to reject all mediation – every institution, custom, and practice that comes between the self and its desire. Whether in love, in religion, or in education, Rousseau's goal is to remove the veil of 'society' so that the individual can take immediate possession of the good that belongs to him by nature, and that has been withheld by the 'others' who stand in his way. This perception of society, as a realm of 'otherness' or alienation, has a religious meaning. For Rousseau, the self is naturally good and naturally free, living in a state of unmediated unity that is also a state of love: the *amour de soi* from which our life begins. Evil is to be explained by the sundering of this primal unity, the setting of the self against itself, which occurs when we live as others require. Society induces a fall from innocent *amour de soi* to guilt-ridden *amour-propre*. Only through the social contract, which remakes society as the expression of individual free choice, can we overcome our alienation. The contract therefore has a redemptive meaning and leads to a 'civil religion' imposing on every citizen the unmediated relation with the godhead that his nature requires ...

There is another way of seeing Rousseau's social contract, not as the redemption of society through the sacrament of choice, but as the rejection of society as an obstacle to choice. This other way of seeing the matter underlies Burke's criticism of the official doctrines of revolutionary France. Society, Burke pointed out, is an open-ended partnership (he even said 'contract') between generations. The dead and the unborn are as much members of society as the living. To dishonour the dead is to reject the relation on which society is built – the relation of obligation between generations. Those who have lost respect for their dead have ceased to be trustees of their inheritance. Inevitably, therefore, they lose the sense of obligation to future generations. The web of obligations shrinks to the present tense. Such, for Burke, was the lesson of the French Revolution.

It is undeniably true that the contractual view of society grants enormous privileges to the living, and disenfranchizes the rest. If taken seriously, as the sole ground of legitimacy, the social contract licenses the continuous pillaging of all resources in obedience to the whims of their temporary trustees. That is exactly what we have witnessed since the Enlightenment. All customs and all institutions have been measured and remade against the standard of choice. The question of their authority has been replaced by another – do we the living want them? If we don't, then they must go. The social knowledge that comes into existence not from my free choice, but as the by-product of other people's – dead people's – choices, has been little by little depleted ...

Rousseau is often singled out as the originator of the cult of 'sensibility', the one who wished to place the emotions in the centre of human life and at the same time to deprive reason of its former sovereignty. I don't think this captures the real temper of his thought. Emotion and reason, for Rousseau, were inextricable, and our greatest emotions, he believed, derive from our predicament as rational beings – our predicament as freely choosing, self-committing agents, with a consciousness of self that sets us apart from nature. It is this apartness from nature that defines our condition and the bad effects that we must overcome. We overcome it not by giving free rein to passion – on the contrary, for Rousseau our emotions should be intensely focused, rather than promiscuously dispersed. Julie, in *La Nouvelle Heloise*, owes her tragic fate not to chastity and fidelity, but to the fact that she allows a socially engendered sense of duty to take precedence over a self-engendered, but chaste and faithful, passion.

We overcome our alienation, Rousseau believed, not through passion but through rational choice. We must remake the world in the image of freedom; we must rescue human life from custom and recast it as a thing intended, a shrine for the liberated self. That is why, in the last analysis, a social contract is necessary: so that society should cease to be an external force, and become instead an expression of our inner freedom. By beginning everything anew, from procedures that conserve the sovereignty of the self, we find redemption – so Rousseau and many others have thought. But what if the self and its freedom, conceived in this a-historical way, are myths? Where then do we look for legitimate government and the foundations of political order?

There is at the heart of Rousseau's vision a culpable *a priorism* – a failure to take seriously the fact that the human being, in all his aspects, including his capacity for rational choice, is the product of a history that stretches before and after him. The search for origins is doomed to failure; at every point we encounter the historical contingency, the arbitrariness of human destiny. We are thrown together without reason or cause, and must make the best of circumstances that have been indelibly marked by a history that was not our doing. Hence, we should look for legitimacy not in origins but in procedures. Instead of asking whether the social order conforms to some abstract criterion of justice, we should ask whether, and if so how, a perceived injustice might be rectified; whether the individual can obtain redress for any injury; and whether crime is punished and loyalty rewarded. We should study the functioning of offices and roles and institutions, and ask whether they soften or heighten human conflicts. The quest for origins asks no such answerable questions. For it is a religious quest: an attempt to anchor society outside history, and to take a God's-eye view of all our brief arrangements.

Rather than aiming at that unattainable perspective, we should follow Hume and give the benefit of the doubt – and the subsequent benefit of doubting – to those activities for which 'custom' is the comprehensive name. Customs are shared and gain their significance from the fact of being shared, but are not, in the normal case, compulsory. Customs are social constraints that you are free to defy. They include all the normal ways in which we confirm and celebrate our social membership, all the normal ways in which the finite store of knowledge is enhanced and passed on, and all the normal ways in which conflicts are discovered and resolved.

How customs arise is immaterial; that they arise is the sign that human beings are able, against the odds, to form the large and complex societies that are necessary for their survival, and that could never be the subject matter of a contract. It is in the nature of customs that they cannot be chosen: they arise by an invisible hand from our consensual dealings. Hence, no custom could feature among the terms of a social contract. If we look on customs as the objects of self-conscious choice, then they cease to be customs and become 'lifestyles' – as inheritance becomes 'heritage' when put on sale. But customs are an irreplaceable source of social and moral knowledge; we should therefore neither hastily uproot them nor deceive ourselves into thinking that we know how they might be replaced. We don't know and we cannot know, since the relevant kind of knowledge is socially created and historically dispersed.

This is not to say that customs should be unquestioningly accepted. But the 'benefit of doubting' comes only after the benefit of the doubt – only when we have conceded that the survival of a custom is one powerful proof of its authority. Even if we should question customs, enough of them must be held constant if our questions are to have a purpose. When everything is questioned, then nothing makes sense – including the question.

Of course, if we believe in the natural innocence of the human being, our imperfect social arrangements will seem to us to be the sign of some terrible mistake. We might then try to think our way back into the state of primeval innocence, in order to see what would have been chosen by people who had yet to succumb to 'society'. But there never was such a state of innocence. The possibility of error is inherent in our condition. Custom, too, is the product of error, for it is the way in which error is overcome.

The virtue that the Romans described as *pietas* consisted not in a rejection of customs, institutions, and laws, but, on the contrary, in an underlying acceptance – a humble recognition that we are not the producers but the products of our world. We must strive to be worthy of an inheritance that we did not create, and to amend it only when we have first understood it. Piety is not confined to the temple and the altar. It is an attitude to life, based in a recognition of our frailty and a respect for the dead.

In place of this, Rousseau erected a God who is not in the world but impassibly removed from it, whose traces on earth lie in a past so distant that they are now indiscernible. All honour is owed to this 'real absence' – and to the self as His vicar on earth. No custom or ceremony is worthy of devotion, since all human institutions are polluted until freely chosen. Henceforth, our religious energies are to be diverted from the labour of repairing and upholding traditions, and devoted instead to the task of destroying them. Only in this way will we regain the Paradise from which we were sundered by our human fault. This explains the extraordinary zeal with which the followers of Rousseau embarked upon their revolution. Theirs was a holy war, a war against superstition in the name of God. But God was no more than a name. The 'Supreme Being' of Robespierre, the 'Being that exists by himself' of Rousseau, the abstract deity of Voltaire – all these terms denote not God himself, but the God-shaped hole in the heart of things, which is henceforth to be filled by human sacrifice.

In the sixth part of *La Nouvelle Heloise*, Julie, by then living on sublimated terms with her former lover, writes to him that 'the country of chimaeras is the only one in this world that is worthy of habitation, and such is the nothingness (*neant*) of human things that, apart from the Being who exists by Himself, nothing is beautiful except that which is not'. This sentence captures some of the religious origin of Rousseau's social philosophy, and also the immense negative energy behind his account of our condition. The nothingness that he perceived in human things he also brought to them. His description of God is really a description of himself – the self existing by itself in solitude, among chimaeras of its own creation. There are only two sources of authority, two legitimate powers, in this world of usurpation: God and self. And in a mysterious way these are not two things, but one, joined in an imagined Paradise that, paradoxically, is more real, because more free, than anything actual. As for the world of ordinary human things, it contains nothing beautiful. It was created not by God or Rousseau, but by society, which is the real presence of the Devil.

And perhaps, looking back at his great achievement across two centuries of ruin, this is how we should see Jean-Jacques Rousseau – as a religious thinker bent on destroying the old gods, but with only a void to put in place of them. That which he attacked as 'society', and as the instrument of our Fall, was really the fertile topsoil of culture, in which all that we value is rooted. Sacred and profane, virtue and vice, good and evil – all these compete in the undergrowth of custom. Clear custom away, and you take away much evil. But you also take away the knowledge of evil. Hence, you make way for evil of another kind, in which people – inoculated against remorse and assuming an absolute right to demolish whatever impedes their rational plan for human happiness – embark on vast social experiments. This happened at the French Revolution. It has happened many times in modern Europe. It has even happened in America in the revolution that has destroyed American schools. And it will happen wherever people try to reconcile equality and liberty, and to destroy custom as the enemy of both.

There is a lesson to be drawn from Rousseau that is of great importance today. Social contests and tensions have been conceptualized in a way that favours the liberal cause. Every conflict is seen in terms of power: who enjoys it and who suffers it, 'who? whom?', in Lenin's summary. But the deep conflicts concern not power but knowledge. Which institutions, which procedures, and which customs preserve and enhance the store of social knowledge? Liberals attack the traditional curriculum, for example, on the grounds that it confers power on white males, and 'disempowers' the remainder. Hence women's studies, black studies, gay studies, and all the other mock subjects that will in time destroy our universities. But the question of the curriculum has been wrongly posed. The traditional curriculum existed not because it empowered people, but because it contained an accumulation of social knowledge – knowledge of the human mind, the human character, and the human heart – whose utility is obvious to those who have studied it, but inconceivable to those who have not. The modern Rousseau, obsessed with inequality and social power, will therefore never understand the institutions that most offend him, and his relentless efforts to undermine them will deprive both him and everyone else of the knowledge required to put the damage right.

SECTION 2

The Nation

4

The Social Contract

(From *The West and the Rest*, 2003)

The word 'religion' derives from Latin *religio*, the root of which, according to a disputed ancient tradition, is *ligere*, to bind. Looked at from the outside, religions are defined by the communities who adopt them, and their function is to bind those communities together, to secure them against external shock, and to guarantee the course of reproduction. A religion is founded in piety, which is the habit of submitting to divine commands. This habit, once installed, underpins all oaths and promises, gives sanctity to marriage, and upholds the sacrifices that are needed both in peace and in war. Hence communities with a shared religion have an advantage in the fight for land, and all the settled territories of our planet are places where some dominant religion has once staked out and defended its claims.

But religion is not the only form of social binding. There is also politics, by which I mean the government of a community by man-made laws and human decisions, without reference to divine commands. Religion is a static condition; politics a dynamic process. Where religions demand unquestioning submission, the political process offers participation, discussion and law-making founded in consent. So it has been in the Western tradition, and at least one thinker has seen the contest between the religious and the political forms of social order as the process which formed the modern world.

However, the contest between religion and politics is not in itself a modern one. This we know not only from the Bible, but also from Greek tragedy. The action of Sophocles' *Antigone* hinges on the conflict between political order, represented and upheld by Creon, and religious duty, in the person of Antigone. The first is public, involving the whole community; the second is private, involving Antigone alone. Hence the conflict cannot be resolved. Public interest has no bearing on Antigone's decision to bury her dead brother, while the duty laid by divine command on Antigone cannot possibly be a reason for Creon to jeopardize the State.

A similar conflict informs the *Oresteia* of Aeschylus, in which a succession of religious murders, beginning with Agamemnon's ritual sacrifice of his daughter, lead at last to the terrifying persecution of Orestes by the furies. The gods demand the murders; the gods also punish them. Religion binds the house of Atreus, but in dilemmas that it does not resolve. Resolution comes at last only when judgement is handed over to the city, personified in Athena. In the political order, we are led to understand, justice replaces vengeance, and negotiated solutions abolish absolute commands. The message of the *Oresteia* resounds down the centuries of Western civilization: it is through politics, not religion, that peace is secured. Vengeance is mine, saith the Lord; but justice, says the City, is mine.

The Greek tragedians wrote at the beginning of Western civilization. But their world is continuous with our world. Their law is the law of the city, in which political decisions are arrived at by discussion, participation and dissent. It was in the context of the Greek city-state that political philosophy began, and the great questions of justice, authority and the constitution are discussed by Plato and Aristotle in terms that are current today.

However, two great institutions intervene between the modern world and its premonition in ancient Greece: Roman Law, conceived as a universal jurisdiction, and Christianity, conceived as a universal church. St Paul, who transformed the ascetic and self-denying religion of Christ into an organized form of worship, was a Roman citizen, versed in the law, who shaped the early Church through the legal idea of the *universitas* or corporation. The Pauline Church was designed, not as a sovereign body, but as a universal citizen, entitled to the protection of the secular and imperial powers but with no claim to displace those powers as the source of legal order. This corresponds to Christ's own vision, in the parable of the tribute money, in which Caesar's public jurisdiction is tacitly contrasted with the inner authority of religion, governing the person-to-person relationship between the individual and God: 'Render therefore unto Caesar the things which are Caesar's; and unto God the things that are God's' (Matthew 22, 30). And it contrasts radically with the vision set before us in the Koran, according to which sovereignty rests with God and his Prophet, and legal order is founded in divine command.

The Christian separation of religious and secular authority recalls Aeschylus' solution to the dilemmas thrust upon mortals by the gods. This Christian approach was developed by St Augustine in *The City of God* and endorsed by the 5th-century *Pastoral Rule* of St Gregory, which imposed the duty of civil obedience on the clergy. The 5th-century Pope Gelasius I made the separation of Church and State into doctrinal orthodoxy, arguing that God granted 'two swords' for earthly government, that of the Church for the government of men's souls and that of the imperial power for the regulation of temporal affairs. This idea persists in the medieval distinction between *regnum* and *sacerdotium*, and was enshrined in the uneasy coexistence of Emperor and Pope on the two 'universal' thrones of medieval Europe. Much wise and subtle argument was expended by medieval thinkers on the distinction between the two sources of authority in human affairs, with the early 14th-century thinker Marsilius of Padua expressing what was to become the accepted Western view of the matter in his *Defensor Pacis*. According to Marsilius it is the State and not the Church that guarantees the civil peace, and reason, not revelation, to which appeal must be made in all matters of temporal jurisdiction.

With the breakdown of Papal jurisdiction and the rise of the Reformed churches ecclesiastical law had less and less influence on the business of government. This result did not come about without conflict, and in several cases (England being the most striking instance) there resulted an explicitly 'national' church, under the authority of a secular monarch. Nevertheless throughout the course of Christian civilization we find a recognition that conflicts must be resolved and social order maintained by political rather than religious jurisdiction. The separation of Church and State was from the beginning an accepted doctrine of the Church. Indeed, this separation *created* the Church, which emerged from the Dark Ages as a legal subject, with rights, privileges and a domestic jurisdiction of its own. And it was through his theory of conciliar government that Nicholas of Cusa, in 1433, introduced the modern understanding of corporate personality, and made it fundamental to our understanding of the Church.

No similar institution exists in Islamic countries. There is no legal entity called 'The Mosque' to set beside the various Western Churches. Nor is there any human institution whose role it is to confer 'holy orders' on its members. Those Muslims who have religious authority – the *'ulama'* ('those with knowledge') – possess it directly from God. And those who take on the function of the *imam* ('the one who stands in front'), so leading the congregation in prayer, are often self-appointed to this role. Islam has never incorporated itself as a legal person or a subject institution, a fact which has had enormous political repercussions. Like the Communist Party in its Leninist construction, Islam aims to control the state without being a subject of the state.

Freedom of conscience requires secular government. But what makes secular law legitimate? That question is the starting point of Western political philosophy, and is now mired in academic controversy. But, to cut an interminable story indecently short, the consensus among modern thinkers is that the law is made legitimate by the consent of those who must obey it. This consent is shown in two ways: by a real or implied 'social contract', whereby each person agrees with every other to the principles of government; and by a political process through which each person participates in the making and enacting of the law. The right and duty of participation is what we mean, or ought to mean, by 'citizenship', and the distinction between political and religious communities can be summed up in the view that the first are composed of citizens, the second of subjects.

That account of legitimacy may not be endorsed by every Western philosopher. But it is endorsed by almost every Western politician, at least when out of office. There seems to be no better justification for imposing a decision on a group of people, than to show that the decision is theirs. The social contract and the participatory process are envisaged as mechanisms for transforming the choices of members into the choice of the group. And what better guarantee can I have that a choice made in my name is legitimate, than that I myself have made it?

It is for this reason that politicians, asked to define what they mean by the 'West', and what the 'war against terrorism' is supposed to be defending, will invariably mention freedom as the fundamental idea. Without freedom there cannot be government by consent; and it is the freedom to participate in the process of government, and to protest against, dissent from and oppose the decisions that are made in my name, that confer on me the dignity of citizenship. Put very briefly, the difference between the West and the Rest is that Western societies are governed by politics; the Rest are ruled by power.

The idea of the social contract helps us to see both the strength of the Western systems of government, and their weaknesses. Although the social contract exists in many forms, its ruling principle was announced by Hobbes, with the assertion that there can be 'no obligation on any man, which ariseth not from some act of his own'. My obligations are my own creation, binding because freely chosen. When you and I exchange promises, the resulting contract is freely undertaken, and any breach does violence not merely to the other but also to the self, since it is a repudiation of a well-grounded rational choice. If we could construe our obligation to the state on the model of a contract, therefore, we would have justified it in terms that all rational beings must accept. Contracts are the paradigms of self-chosen obligations – obligations which are not imposed, commanded or coerced but freely undertaken. When law is founded in a social contract, therefore, obedience to the law is simply the other side of free choice. Freedom and obedience are one and the same. This was the thought that so excited Rousseau, and which Kant was to develop into a comprehensive theory of secular morality ...

However, human societies are not composed of all people everywhere, and are indeed, in their nature, exclusive, establishing privileges and benefits which are offered only to the insider, and which cannot be freely bestowed on all-comers without sacrificing the trust on which social harmony depends. The social contract begins from a thought-experiment, in which a group of people gather together to decide on their common future. But if they are in a position to decide on their common future, it is because they already have one: because they recognize their mutual togetherness and reciprocal dependence, which makes it incumbent upon them to settle how they might be governed under a common jurisdiction in a common territory. In short, the social contract requires a relation of membership, and one, moreover, which makes it plausible for the individual members to conceive the relation between them in contractual terms. Theorists of the social contract write as though it presupposes only the first-person singular of free rational choice. In fact it presupposes a first-person plural, in which the burdens of belonging have already been assumed.

Even in the American case, in which a decision was made to adopt a constitution and make a jurisdiction *ab initio*, it is nevertheless true that a first-person plural was involved in the very making. This is confessed to in the document itself. 'We, the people. . .' Which people? Why, *us*; we who *already belong*, whose historic tie is now to be transcribed into law. We can make sense of the social contract only on the assumption of some such precontractual 'we'. For who is to be included in the contract? And why? And what do we do with the one who opts out? The obvious answer is that the founders of the new social order already belong together: they have already imagined themselves as a community, through the long process of social interaction that enables people to determine who should participate in their future and who should not.

Furthermore the social contract makes sense only if future generations are included in it. The purpose is to establish an enduring society. At once, therefore, there arises that web of non-contractual obligations that links parents to children and children to parents and that ensures, willy-nilly, that within a generation the society will be encumbered by non-voting members, dead and unborn, who will rely on something other than a mere contract between the living if their rights are to be respected and their love deserved. Even when there arises, as in

America, an idea of 'elective nationality', so that newcomers may choose to belong, *what* is chosen is precisely not a contract but a bond of membership, whose obligations and privileges transcend anything that could be contained in a defeasible agreement.

There cannot be a society without this experience of membership. For it is this that enables me to regard the interests and needs of strangers as my concern; that enables me to recognize the authority of decisions and laws that I must obey, even though they are not directly in my interest; that gives me a criterion to distinguish those who are entitled to the benefit of the sacrifices that my membership calls from me, from those who are interloping. Take away the experience of membership and the ground of the social contract disappears: social obligations become temporary, troubled and defeasible, and the idea that one might be called upon to lay down one's life for a collection of strangers begins to border on the absurd. Moreover, without the experience of membership, the dead will be disenfranchised, and the unborn, of whom the dead are the metaphysical guardians, will be deprived of their inheritance. The mere 'contract between the living' is a contract to squander the earth's resources for the benefit of its temporary residents. And critics of Western societies do not hesitate to point out that that is exactly what is happening, as the contractual vision of society gains ground over the experience of membership that made it possible...

MEMBERSHIP

People become conscious of their identity, and of the distinction between those who share it and those who do not, in many ways. Language, kinship, religion and territory are all important, and all have fed in to the various national and trans-national ideologies that have animated modern politics. Political organization presupposes membership; but it also affects it, and many of the artificial states of the modern world have attempted to shape a 'body politic' which will correspond to their borders and their laws, through the invention of a 'nation' of which they are the legal and political guardians. This process can be witnessed in the new states of Africa and

Asia, formed from disintegrating empires. It can also be witnessed in the Middle East. But, beneath the artificial divisions drawn on the map lie other and more visceral differences: differences of tribe, sect, language, loyalty and lifestyle, which constantly threaten the web of laws and powers and boundaries that have been laid across them. When these visceral differences subvert or extinguish the secular law, cancel the rights of citizenship and set group against group within the community, a country ceases to be part of the West and joins the rest – as is happening now in Zimbabwe.

To put the point in another way: Western civilization is composed of communities held together by a political process, and by the rights and duties of the citizen as defined by that process. Paradoxically, it is the existence of this political process that enables us to live without politics. Having consigned the business of government to defined offices, occupied successively by people who are the servants and not the masters of those who elected them, we can devote ourselves to what really matters – to the private interests, personal loves and social customs in which we find our satisfaction. Politics, in other words, makes it possible to separate Society from the State, so removing politics from our private lives. Where there is no political process, this separation does not occur. In the totalitarian state or the military dictatorship everything is political precisely because nothing is. Where there is no political process everything that happens is of interest to those in power, since it poses a potential threat to them. In Saddam's Iraq, as in Soviet Russia, social life is carried on furtively, under the vigilant eyes of a secret police force that can never be certain that it has discovered the real conspiracy that may one day destroy it.

Totalitarian states and military dictatorships are abnormalities. But so too, judged from the historical perspective, are states founded on the Western model. The political process is an *achievement* – one that might not have occurred, and which has not occurred in those parts of the world where Roman Law and Christian doctrine have left no mark. Even today most communities are held together in other ways – by tribal sentiment, by religion, or by force.

The tribe is often described as 'natural', meaning that it arises spontaneously, and is never the result of a decision –

certainly not of a political decision. Members of a tribe are joined by marriage and kinship, and the first-person plural is coextensive with the sense of kin (which may be amplified by the imagination to include all neighbours and familiars). Tribes can grow and take on a quasi-political structure, as their members move to foreign parts or lose touch with their ancestral community. Moreover, the majority of members of the tribe are either dead or unborn, and yet just as much members as those who are temporarily alive. This is what relations of kinship mean: you and I are descended from a common source, and owe our membership to the fact that our common ancestor is also still a member. All tribal ceremonies in which membership is at stake – marriages, funerals, births, initiations – are also attended by the dead, who in turn are the guardians of those unborn. And the consolation of tribal membership resides partly in this union with absent generations, through which the fear of death is allayed and the individual granted the supreme endorsement of existing as a limb of the eternal organism.

Communities bound by religion – or 'creed-communities', to use Spengler's term – grow naturally from the tribe, just as religion grows naturally from kinship. Through ceremonies of membership, in which the dead bear witness to our need of them, the gods enter the world. Every invocation of the dead is a transition to the supernatural; and whatever it is that people worship is located in the supernatural sphere: which is not to say that it is wholly outside nature or in any way inaccessible. On the contrary, the gods of the tribesman are as real and near to him as the spirits of his ancestors, and may be carried around in tangible form, like the household gods of the Romans. But that too is a sign of their supernatural character. For only what is supernatural can be *identical* with its own representation, as the god is identical with the idol, which exists nevertheless in a hundred replicas, each endowed with the same supernatural power.

The creed community is, however, distinct from the tribe. For here the criterion of membership has ceased to be kinship, and become worship and obedience. Those who worship my gods, and accept the same divine prescriptions, are joined to me by this, even though we are strangers. Moreover, creed communities, like tribes, extend their claims beyond the living. The dead acquire the privileges of the worshipper through the latter's prayers. But the dead are present in these new ceremonies on very different terms. They no longer have the authority of tribal ancestors; rather they are subjects of the same divine overlord, undergoing their reward or punishment in conditions of greater proximity to the ruling power. They throng together in the great unknown, just as we will, released from every earthly tie and united by faith.

Creed communities can expand beyond the kinship relation most easily when they enjoy a sacred text, in which the truths about the divine order are set down for all time. The existence of such a text sanctifies the language in which it is written: the language is lifted out of time and change to become immemorial, like the voice of God. Hence true creed communities resist not only changes to the ceremonies (which define the experience of membership), but also changes to the sacred text and to the language used in recording it. By this means Hebrew, Arabic, Latin and the English of King James I have been lifted out of history and immortalized. Membership of the creed community may often require an apprenticeship in the sacred language: certainly no priest or mullah can be allowed to ignore it. But the creed community inevitably grants privileges to the native speakers of that language, and endows them with a weapon that permits them to rule the world (or at least the only bit of the world that matters – the world of the faithful). The neighbouring occurrence of two of the sacred languages – Arabic and Hebrew – as spoken languages in today's Middle East is of enormous socio-political importance. Although Hebrew has been strenuously revived in order to become a modern vernacular, and although spoken Arabic everywhere differs from the classical archetype, both languages resound with a message of religious membership. The fact that the languages are close cousins serves to fuel the conflict between those who speak them. For it is the one who is near to me, not the one who is far away and unrelated, who poses the greatest threat to my spiritual territory.

The initial harmony between tribal and credal criteria of membership may give way to conflict, as the rival forces of family love and religious obedience exert themselves over small communities. This conflict has been one of the motors of Islamic history, and can be witnessed all over the Middle East, where local creed communities have grown out of the monotheistic religions and shaped themselves according to a tribal experience of membership. There is at least one such community – the Druze – in which a credal idea of membership has come to depend on a tribal criterion. Each child of a Druze is held to be a member of the sect solely by virtue of his or her birth, and each new member of the sect is believed to inherit the soul of a Druze that died. The community can neither grow nor dwindle, but is an eternal communion of the unborn and the dead, each member of which is simultaneously in both conditions, while also being alive!

For a long time Europe existed as a kind of creed community – but one in which sovereignty had crystallized in the hands of individual families, whose claims were either endorsed by the Pope or asserted against him. But Christianity was a creed community with a difference. From its beginning in the Roman Empire it internalized some of the ideas of imperial government; in particular, it adopted and immortalized the greatest of all Roman achievements, which was the universal system of law as a means for the resolution of conflicts and the administration of distant provinces. Although Islam has its law, it is explicitly a holy law, laying down the path to salvation, and dealing with all the minute particulars, from the times of prayer to the rituals of personal hygiene, through which a person makes and unmakes his relationship with God...

The Roman Law by contrast was secular, and unconcerned with the individual's religious well-being. It was an instrument for governing people regardless of their credal differences; and its decisions were not validated by tracing them to some sacred source, but by autonomous principles of judicial reasoning and an explicit statement of the law. The law itself could change in response to changing circumstances; and its validity derived purely from the fact that it was commanded by the sovereign power, and enforced against every subject.

That conception of law is perhaps the most important force in the emergence of the European forms of sovereignty. It ensured the development of law as an entity independent of the sovereign's command, and the maintenance of a kind of universal jurisdiction through the courts of canon law. At the same time, each sovereign, through his own courts, was able to qualify and narrow the universal law, so that it adapted itself to his territorial claims. Thus there arose the idea of kingdoms, not as local power centres, but as territorial jurisdictions, whose monarchs were constrained by the law and also appointed by it. Often the law was, as in England, the creation of judges: and the common law principles (including those of equity) have ensured that, wherever the English law has prevailed, it is law and not the executive power that has the last word in any conflict between them.

Under the European experience of the sovereign state, therefore, territorial jurisdiction has had at least as much importance as language and religion in shaping people's attachments. Following the Reformation in Europe, three distinct conceptions of membership exerted their forces over the popular imagination. First religion, and in particular those fine differences of doctrine and practice that distinguished Catholic from Protestant and sect from sect. (Fine differences are always more important in determining membership than large differences, precisely because they permit comparisons. The person whose religion differs from mine by a tiny article, or a barely perceivable gesture, is not a believer in other gods, but a blasphemer against my gods. Unlike the person with other deities, he is automatically an object of hostility, since he threatens the faith from a point within its spiritual territory.) Secondly language, and in particular the languages that had attained sanctity, through some authoritative translation of the sacred texts (for instance English and German), and that had been dispersed by the art of printing. Thirdly, the gravitational force of territorial jurisdictions, under which contracts could be enforced, disputes settled, marriages and institutions legalized, with uniform effect over a continuous territory. In the course of time it was this last conception of membership that was to shape the modern world, by laying the foundations for secular government, in which neither religion nor tribe nor dynasty would be the arbiter of collective choice, but in which all such factors would be subservient to the political process.

When law is defined over territory, so as to apply to everyone residing there, and when the source of its authority is the sovereign power, the reality of law, as a human artefact, rather than a divine command, becomes apparent. The law is detached from the demands of religion and reconstrued as an abstract system of rights and duties. It begins to show a preference for contract over status, and for definable interests over inarticulate allegiances. In short, it becomes a great reformer of membership, coaxing it in a contractual direction. It makes our ties judiciable and therefore articulate; and in doing so it loosens them.

At the same time we must not think of territorial jurisdiction as a merely conventional arrangement: a kind of ongoing and severable agreement, of the kind distilled in the social contract theory. It involves, in the normal case, a genuine 'we' of membership: not as visceral as that of kinship; not as uplifting as that of worship; and not as inescapable as those of language and kin: but a 'we' all the same. For a jurisdiction gains its validity either from an immemorial past, or from a fictitious contract between people who already *belong together*. In the English case, law comes with the authority of long usage; ancestors speak as clearly through it as they speak through the King James Bible; and the fact that English law is common law, arising from the particular decisions made in concrete cases and not through the impositions of a sovereign, gives to it an added authority as the 'law of the land'. Around this particular territorial jurisdiction, therefore, there has arisen a remarkable and in many ways unique form of membership, in which belonging is defined neither by language nor by religion nor even by sovereignty, but by the felt recognition of a particular territory as home: the safe, law-governed and protected place that is 'ours'. . .

THE CHRISTIAN LEGACY

The social contract, I have suggested, is a kind of theological abstraction from the experience of territorial jurisdiction. It is a representation in ideal form of a committee, a coming together of people in a single place, in order to agree the terms of their common protection. But the contract makes sense of Western politics only because of the long history that endowed Western communities with a territorial, rather than a religious loyalty. I have referred to the role of Roman Law in preparing the way for this. And I have emphasized the Christian distinction between *regnum* and *sacerdotium*, as installing the ideal of secular government among people who are nevertheless bound by a common creed. But the history of the Middle East reminds us of a far more important legacy of Christianity, which is the extolling of forgiveness as a moral virtue.

The Muslim faith, like the Christian, is defined through a prayer. But this prayer takes the form of a declaration: There is one God, and Muhammad is his prophet. To which might be added: and you had better believe it. The Christian prayer is also a declaration of faith; but it includes the crucial words: 'forgive us our trespasses, as we forgive them that trespass against us'. In other words, the appeal to divine mercy, which prefaces every Sura of the Koran with the beautiful words *bism illah il-rahman il-rahim*, 'in the name of Allah, the Compassionate, the Merciful', is made conditional, in the daily prayer of Christians, upon the habit of forgiving our enemies. The 'imitation of Christ' is conceived in the same terms: not as a vanquishing of God's enemies, but as a self-sacrifice, a willing oblation, an acceptance of the worst that human beings can do in a spirit of forgiveness. Needless to say Christians have not always followed this ideal, the Crusades being but one example. But it is also characteristic of Christianity that its adherents should apologize for the Crusades, taking on themselves the burden of a guilt incurred by their fellow believers, and seeking forgiveness from those whom their faith has wronged. Christianity contains within itself that idea of a political solution which Aeschylus presents in the *Oresteia*: a solution which steps out of the cycle of vengeance, in order to seek peace through conciliation.

The philosopher and critic René Girard sees this transition as critical to the Christian revelation. In the absence of a judicial process, Girard argues, societies are invaded by 'mimetic desire', as rivals struggle to match each other's social and material acquisitions, so heightening antagonism and precipitating the cycle of vengeance. The traditional solution is to identify a victim, one marked by fate as 'outside' the community and therefore not entitled to vengeance against it, who can be the target of the accumulated blood-lust, and who can bring the cycle of retribution to an end. Scapegoating is society's way of recreating 'difference' and so restoring itself. By uniting against the scapegoat people are released from their rivalries and reconciled.

Most religions incorporate this cycle of violence into themselves, and so legitimize it as the will of God. The triumph of Christianity, in Girard's eyes, is to have broken free from the cycle entirely. In the Gospels the scapegoat achieves transcendence and divinity through an acceptance of his fate, through an attitude of serene detachment from the aggressors, and through a manifest awareness that, while the aggressors do not know what they are doing, he does. For the first time the aggression that is at the root of the sacrificial rite is understood and forgiven by the victim, who is able both to accept his sacrifice, and also to believe in his own innocence. By freely offering himself as scapegoat, therefore, Christ lifted humanity from the cycle of 'mimetic desire' and 'mimetic violence', into the realm of conciliation.

That theory is of course highly controversial. Nevertheless, even without going so far as Girard, one must recognize that the idea of forgiveness, symbolized in the Cross, distinguishes the Christian from the Muslim inheritance. There is no coherent reading of the Christian message which does not make forgiveness of enemies into a central item of the creed. Christ even commanded us, when assaulted, to turn the other cheek. Pacifists take this remark to mean that we should not defend ourselves, but overcome violence as Christ did, by example. But it is possible to accept the Christian doctrine and yet to stop short of pacifism. Christ suffered the most violent death, not in order to recommend defencelessness, but in order to redeem mankind. At the same time he bore witness to the fact that it was not through *him* that evil had entered the world. In enjoining us to turn the other cheek he was setting before us, as always, a personal ideal, not a political project. If I am attacked and turn the other cheek, then I exemplify the Christian virtue of meekness. If entrusted with a child who is attacked, and I then turn the *child's* other cheek, I make myself party to the violence.

That, surely, is how a Christian should understand the right of defence, and how it is understood by the medieval theories of the Just War. The right of defence stems from your obligations to others. You are obliged to protect those whom destiny has placed under your care. A political leader who turns not his own cheek but ours makes himself party to the next attack. Too often this has happened. But by pursuing the terrorist and bringing him, however violently, to justice, the politician serves the cause of peace, and also that of forgiveness, of which justice is the instrument.

The Christian injunction to forgive is therefore compatible with defensive warfare. But it is incompatible with terrorism, and inimical to those visceral antagonisms which lead one group into a war of extermination against another. To remove the violent core from human societies is no easy task, for the urge to violence is planted in us by evolution, and war is a fact of sociobiology. Nevertheless, the Christian experience gives grounds for hope. Added to the tradition of secular law and territorial sovereignty, Christianity leads to the idea of a political order established without reference to tribe or faith, in which even the most fundamental differences can be accommodated, provided only that the territorial jurisdiction is given absolute sovereignty over those that reside within its borders.

The social contract provides the theology of such a territorial jurisdiction. But it does not, of itself, make such a jurisdiction possible. The political order as we in the West know it requires not only territory, but the sharing of it, and the sense of belonging that makes sharing possible. This sense of belonging does not come all at once, or without conflict. A group of incoming refugees, bound by family ties and religious duties to an amorphous 'elsewhere', does not have the sense of belonging that is shared by the native population. It can acquire that sense, but only by renouncing an identity that binds it to another time and another place. Meanwhile it must rely on that habit of forgiveness and conciliation which tells the Christian to see the Other not as a threat but as an invitation to sympathy.

The triumph of America is that it has been able to persuade wave after wave of immigrants to relinquish all competing attachments, and to identify with this *country*, this *land*, this great *experiment in settlement*, and to join in its common defence. Many factors have contributed to this triumph: but the hitherto prevailing Christian culture must surely be counted as the most important.

5

The Nation State and Democracy

(From *The American Spectator*, 2007)

American foreign policy was set on its modern path by Woodrow Wilson. Attributing the First World War to imperial competition, Wilson concluded that Europe should be divided into autonomous nation states, their rivalries brokered by a 'League of Nations'. Although those nation states were soon involved in another catastrophic war, American foreign policy remained fixed on the Wilsonian path. The post-World War II settlement was again a settlement among nation states, with a 'United Nations', guided by a well-meaning charter and a declaration of rights, taking the place of the League. Even though one member of the Security Council – the Soviet Union – was not a nation state but an empire, and even though most of those who turned up at the meetings of the UN were sent there by gangsters who bore only a nominal relation to the 'nations' that they purported to represent, American foreign policy remained fixed in the Wilsonian groove, and has remained so to this day. Hence the assumption that, because there is a seat at the UN for a place called Iraq, and because that seat has been filled by a petty thug with the title of Iraqi President, Iraq is a nation like any other, whose people are bound by a single national loyalty, and whose problems will be solved by a change of regime.

Meanwhile, however, the nation state was undergoing a strange transformation, in the very continent where it had been born. In 1951, under pressure from a coterie of civil servants and politicians who met in secret and whose names are only now becoming known, the 'European Coal and Steel Community' was formed. It seemed innocent enough, though the acute observer might have suspected, in the word 'community', an agenda that went beyond the topic of raw materials. The Coal and Steel Community was joined in 1957 by the European Economic Community and the European Atomic Energy Commission. Between them these formed the 'common market' which, despite the odd language, was generally assumed to be a well-meaning attempt to secure free trade and economic stability on a continent that had been ravaged by war.

Half a century later, following a process whose forward movement had been somehow embryonic in those initial 'communities', we find a Europe in which the nation states have lost control of law-making, of immigration, of commercial regulations, and of effective sovereignty, in which their parliaments are obliged to adopt a code of law (the *acquis communautaire*) which now extends to 100,000 pages, not one item of which they can reverse and not one error in which they can correct – and all for purposes that have never been confessed to and which indeed were hidden within the original treaties as part of a secret plan. The process whereby this plan was advanced, regardless of the perceived national interests of the Member States, and regardless of public opinion, has been carefully exposed by Christopher Booker and Richard North in *The Great Deception*. The claims made in that book have not been refuted by the Eurocrats, who are in any case now invulnerable to criticism, and therefore in the habit of ignoring it.

Booker and North identify Jean Monnet, architect and first president of the European Coal and Steel Community, as the prime conspirator. Following the horrors of the First World War, Monnet conceived the life-long ambition to create a united states of Europe, as the condition of a permanent European peace. Unlike Woodrow Wilson, who wished to divide the continent into nations and achieve peace through a balance of power, Monnet wished to unite the continent in a new and more self-sustaining empire, though one from which the ghost of nationalism had been finally exorcized. He left public office in 1955 to form the Action Committee for the United States of Europe, dedicated to lobbying on behalf of transnational institutions that would be capable of overriding national sovereignty. This idea was opposed by President de Gaulle, who favoured a Europe of sovereign nation states, and with whom Monnet was at loggerheads during the 1960s. As a result Monnet developed the 'Monnet method' of 'integration by stealth', in which unification would be advanced step by step without the goal ever being clearly perceived or clearly perceivable.

There seems little doubt, now, that Monnet played a major part in shaping the European Union as an instrument with which to destroy the nation state. But other figures, equally powerful and equally devious, had significant roles. Among them was Alexandre Kojève, that wily, mesmerizing nihilist, ostensibly a French refugee from Russian communism, though recently exposed as an NKVD agent, who advanced to the top of the French Civil Service, there to use his influence in promoting transnational government against the nation state. Kojève helped to set up both the embryonic European Union and the GATT. But he is better known today for his freelance seminar on Hegel, through which he formed the minds and souls of a whole generation of French intellectuals, including André Breton, Georges Bataille, Jacques Lacan and many others who achieved pre-eminence in the post-war period. In his seminars Kojève argued that the need of human beings for equal recognition will lead of its own accord to the 'end of history'. National boundaries and exclusive communities will wither away, and a bland democratic capitalism will spread like a fungus over the face of all mankind. This thesis, shaped for American consumption by Francis Fukuyama (*The End of History and the Last Man*), can be read in another way, as a codified admission of the secret plan for Europe's future, which will also be the future of the world.

Unlike Woodrow Wilson, who blamed the First World War on the Empires, the founders of the European experiment blamed that war and its successor on the spirit of the nation state. A united states of Europe seemed to them to be the only recipe for lasting peace. This view is for two reasons entirely unpersuasive. First, it is purely negative: it rejects nation states for their belligerence, without giving any positive reason to believe that transnational states will be any better. Indeed it resolutely ignores the history of the most belligerent state in recent times, the Soviet Union, which inherited all the ambitions of imperial Russia and added to them imperial ambitions of its own. Secondly, it identifies the normality of the nation state through its pathological examples. As Chesterton has argued about patriotism generally, to condemn patriotism because people go to war for patriotic reasons, is like condemning love because some loves lead to murder. The nation state should not be understood in terms of the French nation at the Revolution or the German nation in its twentieth-century frenzy. For those were nations gone mad, in which the sources of civil peace had been poisoned and the social organism colonized by anger and resentment.

The European Union has tried to destroy the nation states of Europe, in the belief that there is no peace while there are serious national rivalries; the United States has attempted to deal with the world as though each part of it with a name and a border can be treated as a national unity, in the belief that there is no democracy without the nation state. The American project for world peace is therefore the polar opposite of that embarked on by the European Union. The question which policy is the right one goes to the heart of our situation today – a situation in which, under pressure from transnational forces for which our political systems are not prepared, the Western alliance is being torn apart by the conflict between the American and the European vision of its goal.

It seems to me that, whatever the weaknesses in American foreign policy, it is right to take the nation state as its premise. A nation state is a form of customary order, the by-product of human neighbourliness, shaped by an 'invisible hand' from the countless agreements between people who speak the same language and live side by side. It results from compromises established after many conflicts, and expresses the slowly forming agreement among neighbours both to grant each other space and to protect that space as common territory. It depends on localized customs and a shared routine of tolerance. Its law is territorial rather than religious and invokes no source of authority higher than the intangible assets that its people share. All those features are strengths, since they feed into an adaptable form of pre-political loyalty. However, they also ensure that nation states are vulnerable at every point to subversion from those with a grand design. What Monnet set out to achieve in Europe was in one sense identical to what Lenin and Hitler had set out to achieve – to capture the unguarded instruments of social power, and to turn them against the people who had provided them.

The result of Jean Monnet's plan is there for all to see: an unaccountable bureaucracy presiding over a continent that has been cast adrift from its traditional aspirations and historical ties. Europeans have been disenfranchized by the European machine, which has at the same time resolutely refused to address the real problems of Europe's future. Of course these problems (demographic decline, adverse immigration, the imminent collapse of the welfare state) might have arisen without the project of Union: but one thing is certain, which is that the project has weakened the authority of European governments and put no rival authority in their place. The unaccountable nature of the European institutions, their ability to spend money on themselves and to clutter the continent with their fantasy projects, their endless production of absurd and malicious regulations – all these things have deprived the EU of legitimacy in the eyes of the European people. But the Union remains, immune to any action that its 'citizens' can take, cushioned from all popular resentment by the national governments that shield it from the people. If proof were needed for the proposition that the nation state is the friend of democracy, and transnational government the foe, then the European Union is it.

But why did things not work that way in America? Why did the experiment in federal government, which has led to an unaccountable empire in Europe, lead to a viable democracy in America? The answer is simple: because American federalism created not an empire but a nation state. This happened despite the dispute over states' rights, despite the civil war, despite the legacy of slavery and ethnic conflict. It happened because the American settlement established a secular rule of law, a territorial jurisdiction and a common language in a place that the people were busily claiming as their *home*. Under the American settlement people were to treat each other, first and foremost, as *neighbours*: not as fellow members of a race, a class, an ethnic group or a religion, but as fellow settlers in the land that they shared. Their loyalty to the political order grew from the obligations of neighbourliness; and disputes between them were to be settled not by priests or tribal elders but by the *law of the land*.

The nation state emerged in Europe as a perceived solution to the religious wars that had blighted the continent in the wake of the Reformation; it offered a political order in which religion would be discounted in favour of a shared attachment to the soil. But its foundation lies deeper than the needs of seventeenth-century government. All the ways in which people come to define their identity in terms of the *place where they belong* have a part to play in cementing the sense of nationhood. For example, the common law of the Anglo-Saxons, in which laws emerge from the resolution of local conflicts, rather than being imposed by the sovereign, has had a large part to play in fostering the English (and subsequently American) sense that the law is the common property of all who reside within its jurisdiction rather than the creation of priests, bureaucrats or kings. A shared language and shared curriculum have a similar effect in making familiarity, proximity and day-to-day custom into sources of common loyalty. The essential thing about nations is that they grow from below, through habits of free association among neighbours, and result in loyalties that are firmly attached to a place and its history, rather than to a religion, a dynasty, a family or a tribe.

We do not need reminding that there are many parts of the world which do not benefit from a developed sense of nationhood. This is particularly true in the Islamic world where, with the notable exception of Turkey, most people live in a deeply conflicted situation, being exhorted every Friday to rehearse their membership of an Islamic *ummah* that recognizes no national boundaries and the authority of no secular powers. A country like Iraq is not, never has been and never will be a nation state. This is not merely because it contains communities that identify themselves in terms of their religious and ethnic allegiance; it is also because for these communities their place of settlement has never been a *country*, a place defined as *ours*, where *our* way of doing things prevails, and which must be defended at all costs if *our* way of life and web of affections is to survive. Country has always taken second place to religion, family or tribe. Iraq was carved out of the Ottoman Empire by Western diplomats who imagined, like Woodrow Wilson, that nation states lie concealed beneath every Empire, that national boundaries are already inscribed in the affections of the people, held in place by lines of force that have the same historical fixity as those which created the nation states of Europe. This piece of wishful thinking is very far from the truth. Even if Iraq were to divide today into three regions, Sunni Arab, Shi'ite and Kurd, these would not succeed in becoming nation states. Authority would still be attributed to family, tribe and creed above that of country, and in emergencies the people of the resulting territories would still unite behind those old ideas of identity, and not behind the 'law of the land'.

This matters for many reasons, not the least being that democracy is a form of government that depends upon a national, rather than a credal or tribal idea of loyalty. In a nation state the things that divide neighbours from each other – family, tribe and religion – are deliberately privatized, made inessential to the shared identity, and placed well below the country and its well-being on the list of public duties. It is this, rather than any Enlightenment idea of citizenship, that enables nation states so easily to adopt democracy. In a place where tribal or religious loyalties take precedence, democratic elections, if they occur at all, occur only once.

Of course, even in a nation state, democracy is not achieved overnight. Democratic government depends upon a pre-existing rule of law and established customs upholding the freedom of individuals and the rights of minorities. Those benefits were historical achievements of the European legal and judicial systems. They preceded democracy and have not been replicated everywhere. Until they are in place, the introduction of elections may merely let the majority loose upon whatever minority provokes its indignation. We see this problem clearly in the Islamic states of the Middle East, where majorities either are kept in place by tyranny, like the Iraqi Shi'ites under Saddam Hussein, or (when freed from tyranny) look around to assert themselves against their sectarian rivals, like the Shi'ites in Iraq today. Democracy involves the ability to grant a share in government to people with whom you profoundly disagree, including people of another faith. This is possible only where government is secular, and where nevertheless people revere the process of government as the expression of a shared national identity.

The secular law of Western states has been made possible by territorial jurisdiction, and the territory in question has been defined by permeable but historically vindicated national boundaries. Our political culture has been a culture of the home and the homeland, rather than the faith and the faithful. The British people were until recently brought up on a conception of national history and national identity that promoted mutual trust and solidarity between neighbours. Although religion had a part to play in their political education, it was that of the 'Church of England', in which expression it was 'England', not 'Church', that was the operative term. The American people likewise have been brought up on the narratives of nationhood. God is invoked, but largely as the transcendental guarantee of a *nation*, a source of blessing that rains down on the land and its people, regardless of their local disagreements over who exactly He is.

That kind of territorial patriotism has suffered erosion in Europe, not only from globalization, but also from the mass immigration of minorities that do not share it, who define their communities in terms of religion rather than territory, and who do not in their heart accept the authority of a merely secular law. It has suffered too from a culture among European intellectuals who, for a variety of reasons, not all of them bad, have tried to discard national loyalty and to replace it with the cosmopolitan ideals of the Enlightenment. The problem, as I see it, is that cosmopolitan ideals are the property of an élite and will never be shared by the mass of human kind. Moreover, when embodied in transnational institutions, they have an innate tendency to degenerate into the kind of corrupt and profoundly anti-democratic bureaucracies exemplified by the UN and the EU. The nation, suitably tempered and purged of its endogenous excesses, may be the best we can hope for, by way of a pre-political community that can accept the jurisdiction of a purely secular law.

Nevertheless people often attempt to express what is distinctive about Western democracies in terms of the Enlightenment idea of citizenship. Americans, they say are citizens, whereas Syrians (for example) are subjects. There is truth in this: but it is important to see that the concept of the citizen, whose relation to the state is not one of passive obedience but one of mutual right and duty, is itself a product of the nation state. A society of citizens is a society in which strangers can trust one another, since everyone is bound by a common set of rules. This does not mean that there are no thieves or swindlers; it means that trust can grow between strangers, and does not depend upon family connections, tribal loyalties or favours granted and earned. This strikingly distinguishes a country like Australia, for example, from a country like Kazakhstan, where the economy depends entirely on the mutual exchange of favours, among people who trust each other only because they also know each other and know the networks that will be used to enforce any deal. It is also why Australia has an immigration problem, and Kazakhstan a brain drain.

As a result of this, trust among citizens can spread over a wide area, and local baronies and fiefdoms can be broken down and over-ruled. In such circumstances markets do not merely flourish: they spread and grow, to become co-extensive with the jurisdiction. Every citizen becomes linked to every other, by relations that are financial, legal and fiduciary, but which presuppose no personal tie. A society of citizens can be a society of strangers, all enjoying sovereignty over their own lives, and pursuing their individual goals and satisfactions. Such have Western societies been, when organized as nation states. They have been societies in which you form common cause with strangers, and which all of you, in those matters on which your common destiny depends, can with conviction say 'we'. . .

All that is important today, as we see the old nation states of Europe being steadily deprived of their territorial sovereignty. There are nation states of a kind in South America; India and Japan have each an established claim to nationhood, as do one or two fragments of the British Diaspora, such as Australia, Canada and New Zealand. But it is more and more apparent that the United States of America is nearly unique among the states that have a seat at the United Nations in being both united and a nation. It is the last integrated nation state in a world of imperial, tribal and religious powers. And the growing anti-Americanism in Europe is partly the result of this. Collective antipathies do not, as a rule, arise in response to injury. They arise out of envy, resentment, and a sense that the other has succeeded where you yourself have failed. Europeans see in America an image of their own past, in the days before cynicism and nihilism wiped away their sense of home. They observe a country able to shape its own destiny and laws, and to take an active and eager interest in the affairs of the world. They observe a country trusting its own people, as they once trusted theirs, to rise in the common defence. They see a country that can still confess to its faults and repent of its mistakes, because it is confident in its good intentions.

Of course, not everything about America is good. Europeans are right to question American foreign policy, and right to distance themselves from its frequently naïve assumptions – not least the assumption that the world divides into nation states. They are right to resist the globalization – which to many Europeans means the Americanization – of their economies, even though it is a process in which the business élites of Europe are as eager to join as their American competitors. They are right to see American popular culture as a temptation to be resisted rather than a gift to be received. But these things do not explain the vehemence of their antagonism. This antagonism stems not from what they have and the Americans haven't, but from what the Americans have kept and they have lost. Witnessing the mysterious *togetherness* of the Americans, even in times like the present when the country is deeply divided over issues of domestic and foreign policy, they recall their own recent experiences and acknowledge that 'we too were like that'. We too used to make our own laws, elect our own governments, decide who should and who should not reside among us; we too used to join together in our national festivals, adopt our national customs and salute the national flag; we too used to look on our country, its landscape and its cities with a sense of ownership, and stand ready to defend them in the face of threat. Above all, we too were a 'we' – a community of strangers, bound together by our love of the home that we shared. And what has happened to that 'we'? Ask the question and Europeans veer away into silence. For this is forbidden territory. National feelings come under that ever expanding category of forbidden passions, which in European Law go by the name of 'racism and xenophobia', and which are soon to be extraditable crimes throughout the Union.

The American example reminds us of one of the essential requirements of nationhood, which is a 'myth of origins'. We in England had such a myth, in the form of the Arthurian legends, which established a claim to the land that could never be defeated, since it was founded in stories that could never be disproved. It worked, partly because those stories located the origin of England in a misty past beyond the reach of rational enquiry, to be understood in terms of the long history that stemmed from it, and not in terms of exact historical events. In America the myth of origins focuses on a precise moment, the moment of the Founding Fathers, heroes who stand higher in the narrative of history than ever they stood in reality, and who bequeathed to their countrymen a text every bit as sacred as the Hebrew Bible or the Holy Koran. And this text is all the more efficacious in the turbulent world that is now emerging, in being both sacred in its origins and secular in its effect. It is a revelation, but a revelation from man, not God. And its principles do not merely enshrine the Enlightenment conception of citizenship, purged of all belligerence and defiance. They unfold a clear idea of nationhood – of a people committed to each other despite all the differences of doctrine, opinion and life-style that might otherwise force them apart.

One of the most remarkable features of America in the eyes of a European visitor is the unselfconscious manner in which Americans still rehearse the myth of their origins, and repeat the narrative of their pilgrimage into the modern world. In Europe such things are either scorned as chauvinistic or condemned as another example of that 'racism and xenophobia' which is lurking under every bed. Some of our national narratives have been scribbled over and cancelled out, like that of the Germans. Others have become stories of class-conflict and oppression, like that now told in English schools, or records of belligerent episodes that never paid off – like the national stories that no longer appeal to the French. Everywhere we find a kind of repudiation of those fortifying legends on which nations have always depended for their sense of identity. Whether this is the cause of our loss of sovereignty or an effect of it is hard to tell. Maybe it is a bit of both. But it is certain that the European Union does its best to encourage the debunking of national narratives. The EU-sponsored history textbook, which is now proposed as a basic text for both French and German schools, says little about France or Germany as nation states, representing their history as a series of unfortunate conflicts on the way to a Union where conflicts can no longer occur. The textbook is consistently anti-American and equates America with the Soviet Union as joint causes of the cold war and of the tensions that divided Europe. It is also unstinting in its praise for the European Union, as a cosmopolitan project spreading peace and order where the nation states (the last example of which is America) spread only violence, exploitation and distrust.

The book is the work of ten learned professors, five French and five German. And I doubt that any of them believes a word of it. But its purpose is that of historical narratives at every time and in every place: to provide a new myth of the past. The EU cannot create a rival identity to the nation state, unless it can identify itself as something superior to the nation states. It must become a project of *release* from the errors and crimes of nationhood. And this means identifying the nation state as a symptom of the adolescence of mankind, a stage on the way to transnational maturity. And it also involves identifying the last great nation state in the modern world – the United States of America – as an example of what must be overcome, if mankind is to enter into a secure and peaceful possession of its patrimony.

We have heard all that before, of course. It is the message of the socialist internationals, the message with which the Communist Party once seduced the intellectuals of Europe, so that they would lend their weight to the Soviet conquest of their continent. It is the message propounded by the Italian Eurocommunists, who played their own important part in working for a transnational European Union. Like all messages devoted to 'the future of an illusion' it needs an enemy in order to recruit its friends. That this enemy should be

America, the latest and greatest example of the nation state, lies in the logic of the case. We should not be surprised, therefore, if anti-American attitudes now occupy the place in European debates that were previously occupied by the anti-bourgeois posture of the French and Italian leftists, and the anti-Semitic posture of their rightist opponents.

Where does this leave American foreign policy? The first conclusion to draw is that America is destined to be increasingly alone in the world. The 'democracies' with which the US is allied in Europe are no longer true democracies, since their law, their domestic policy and – if things go according to plan – their foreign policy will soon be dictated to them by committees whom they can neither elect nor reject. Those committees will be programmed according to a transnational ideology which is completely at variance with the American vision. Their policy will not be to spread democracy beyond the borders of the European Union, but to extinguish democracy within them. As for the Middle East and Islam, the European machine will continue to appease the Islamists, by denying the religious and cultural tradition of Europe, and abasing itself before the ongoing invasion.

The second conclusion is that the loss will not be America's but Europe's. The European project has imposed upon the nations of Europe a policy of 'free flow' of peoples, which has made it impossible to ensure that the people living in its territories share the loyalty of their immediate neighbours. The inexorable movement towards ethnic, religious and racial conflict has begun, and – without the nation state and a strong ideology of nationhood – there is little hope of preventing it.

The third conclusion is that if, as I have argued, nationhood is a precondition of democracy, it would be better for America to build alliances with genuine or emerging nation states – with Japan, South Korea, Australia, India – than with the European powers. It would be better to work for the democratization of China than for the democratization of the Islamic world. It would be better still to retreat from too much involvement in a world of lunatics, and to build up defences at home. For home is how a nation state defines itself.

6

Should he have Spoken?
(From *The New Criterion*, 2006)

In 1968 the products of the post-war baby boom decided to seize the European future and to jettison the European past. In that same year Enoch Powell delivered to the Birmingham Conservatives the speech known forever after as 'Rivers of Blood': a speech that cost him his political career, and which, on one plausible interpretation, made the issue of immigration undiscussable in British politics for close to forty years. It is a speech that raises in its acutest form the question of truth: what place is there for truth in public life, and what should a politician do when comfortable falsehoods have settled down in government, and their uncomfortable negations seek forlornly for a voice?

'Human kind cannot bear very much reality', said T. S. Eliot. It is not one of his best lines, but he used it twice – in *Murder in the Cathedral* and in *Four Quartets* – and in both places its prosaic rhythmlessness reinforces its sense, reminding us that our exaltations are invented things, and that we prefer inspiring fantasies to sobering facts. Enoch Powell was no different, and his inspiring fantasy of England caused him to address his countrymen as though they still enjoyed the benefits of a classical education and an imperial culture. How absurd, in retrospect, to end a speech warning against the effects of uncontrolled immigration with a concealed quotation from Virgil. 'As I look ahead', Powell said, 'I am filled with foreboding. Like the Roman, I seem to see "the River Tiber foaming with much blood"'. These words were addressed to an England that had forgotten the story of the *Aeneid*, along with every other story woven into its former identity as the 'sweet, just, boyish master' of the world – to borrow Santayana's luminous phrase. It is hardly surprising that Powell's words were instantly converted to 'rivers of blood', and their speaker dismissed as a dangerous madman.

It is, in fact, the Cumaean Sybil who utters that prophecy in Book VI of the *Aeneid*, and although she is foreseeing the troubles that come from immigration, it is to the troubles suffered by an immigrant that she refers. The immigrant in question – Aeneas – travels to Italy at the head of a determined retinue, carrying his household gods and a divine right of residence. His intention to settle is not to be brooked, and if this means 'wars, horrid wars', so be it. Modern immigrants don't, on the whole, behave so badly. They don't need to. They come as the heads of families, and even if the family might comprise four wives and twenty children, it arrives to a red carpet of legal privileges, eagerly unrolled by publicly funded lawyers, and to a welcome trough of welfare benefits that few indigenous citizens can claim, however much they have contributed to the common fund.

Yet, like Aeneas, our immigrants come carrying their household gods. Like Aeneas, they come with an unbrookable intention to make a home for themselves. And if their gods dislike the indigenous rivals, they will soon make this fact known. Such predictions as Powell made in his speech, concerning the tipping of the demographic balance, the ghettoization of the industrial cities, and the growth of resentment among the indigenous working class have been fulfilled. Only the sibylline prophecy has fallen short of the mark. Even so, the Madrid and London bombings and the murder of Theo van Gogh are viewed by many Europeans as a foretaste of things to come. It is now evident to everyone that, in the debate over immigration, in those last remaining days when it could still have made a difference, Enoch Powell was far nearer the truth than those who instantly drove him from office, and who ensured that the issue was henceforth to be discussed, if at all, only by way of condemning the 'racism' and 'xenophobia' of those who thought like Powell. As for the racism and xenophobia of the incomers, it was indiscernible to the liberal conscience, which has never been able to under-stand that liberalism is an *unusual state of mind*.

Liberalism emerges from a long-standing rule of law, shaped by the Enlightenment view of citizenship, and dependent upon the shared customs, shared language, and shared culture of a people who have lived together in a common home and acquired the habit of defending it. But it is virtually unknown among people who are seeking territory, and who have conscripted their gods to fight for it. The book of Joshua tells the story of such a people, and it contains in its bloodthirsty pages not a single liberal sentiment. The one gesture of kindness that the book records towards the indigenous people is bestowed on those who had betrayed their native city to its foes. This reward offered for the basest form of treachery indicates how far the Israelites were, in their need, from any liberal view of the human condition.

At the time when Powell made his speech, British politicians were schooled in the Bible and the Greek and Roman classics; they could dispute the factual basis for Powell's prophecy only by putting out of mind what they had every reason to know, namely that many of the newcomers to Britain would be strangers to liberal values, attached to their own communities, suspicious towards the host culture, and anxious to insulate themselves and their children from its influence. In the face of those manifest truths our political class had recourse to Doublethink. Like the White Queen in *Through the Looking Glass*, they practised the art of believing six impossible propositions before breakfast, including the proposition that pious Muslims from the hinterlands of Asia would produce children loyal to a secular European state.

This flight from reality is not a new feature of political life. It is always easier to bequeath a problem to your successors than to face it yourself, and when the problem is intractable, Doublethink will soon erase it, as Hitler was erased from the thoughts of the appeasers, and the Gulag from the political map of the peaceniks. Nor are American presidents any more realistic than the rest of us. When the embassy in Tehran was invaded and United States' citizens taken hostage, President Carter chose not to notice what was, certainly *de facto* and probably *de jure*, a declaration of war. That may prove to have been the costliest mistake made by America in the Middle East. Likewise, the silencing of Enoch Powell has proved more costly than any other post-war domestic policy in Britain, since it has ensured that immigration can be discussed only now, when it is too late to do anything about it or to confine it to those who come in a spirit of obedience towards the indigenous law.

As I implied, Powell was also in flight from reality – the reality of British society as it was in 1968. The British people had lost their imperial identity without gaining a national identity with which to replace it. There were Scottish nationalists, Welsh nationalists, and Irish nationalists, but no English nationalists and therefore – since England was the core of Britain, the seat of government, and the central fact of our history – no British nationalists either. Powell's invocation of Virgil fell on deaf ears – or rather on ears that pricked up only at the sound of 'blood'. And his punctilious syntax, resounding with the rhythms of the Book of Common Prayer and rich in allusions to a history that was publicly remembered, if at all, only as an object of ridicule, created the impression of a *paterfamilias* in some Edwardian play, strutting at the front of the stage while his disobedient daughter flirts unnoticed in the background.

Moreover, Powell's fantasy vision of Britain was absolutely necessary to him. The truths that he wished to put across were uttered in defence of Old England, and it was unthinkable to him that he might be speaking into the void. Powell's England was a place made sacred by Chaucer and Shakespeare, by the Anglican settlement and the anointed monarch, by the common law and the Great Offices of State. It was the very same England that Churchill had invoked in his wartime speeches: a country whose past was lost in Arthurian mists, whose title was as God-given as that of the Israelites and whose patriotism outshone that of Rome. Those who silenced Powell therefore believed that it was not he but they who were on the side of truth. They were introducing realism and sobriety in the place of dangerous romantic dreams. Not for nothing, they said, did Powell refer to authorities who wrote in dead languages and believed forgotten myths; not for nothing did he choose, when invited onto BBC Radio's 'Desert Island Discs', only episodes from *The Ring of the Nibelung* of Richard Wagner. The man was clearly living in Cloud Cuckoo Land. And

Powell accepted the expression with a wry smile: after all, it comes from Aristophanes.

Truth, Plato believed, is the business of philosophy, but it is rhetoric, not philosophy, that moves the crowd. So how can we protect people from fatal errors, such as those that tempted Athens into conflict with Sparta, or those which, much later, led the Germans, mesmerized by Hitler, into an equally suicidal war? Plato did not believe that philosophers would be listened to: their words would sound strange and ambiguous, and their eyes would be turned from present and time-bound emergencies towards the stratosphere of eternal truths. Nevertheless among the rhetorical devices of politicians, it is still possible to distinguish the noble lies from their ignoble negations. The noble lie is the untruth that conveys a truth, the myth that maps reality. It is thus that Plato justified the stories of the gods and their origins which inspire people to live as though nearer to the source of things, and to discover in themselves the virtues that exist only when we find our way to believing in them.

In the Platonic scheme of things, Powell's vision of England might be seen as a noble lie. He was exhorting his countrymen to *live up to* something, and that thing was an ideal image of their country, shaped by myth in the style of Hesiod. The England of Powell's dream was fashioned from heroic deeds and immemorial customs, from sacred rites and solemn offices whose meaning was inscrutable from any point outside the social context that defined them. By fixing their sights on this vision, the British people would be in some way perfecting themselves, and establishing their right to their ancestral territory. In place of this noble vision, however, they were also being offered an ignoble lie. The emerging multicultural community would make no place for a common obedience, a common loyalty, or a shared history: it would inevitably deprive the British people of their geographical, cultural, and political inheritance. And yet they were being told that it would not harm them, that they would even be improved by it, since it would inject energy, variety, and youth into a tired old way of life.

The problem with Plato's theory of the noble lie is that noble lies have to be believed by the one who utters them.

Otherwise people will see through the deception and withdraw their support. And a lie that is believed is not really a lie. It was impossible to discern, in Powell's steely manner, ancestor-laden syntax, and fixed, expressionless gaze, whether he really believed in the nation that he described with his toneless incantations. He was invoking England in the way that a Professor of Classics (which once he was) invokes Greece – as an idea whose roots are buried deep in the archaeology of consciousness.

Plato's theory of the noble lie was a first shot at describing the role of myth in human thinking. Myths are not falsehoods, nor are they scientific theories: they are attempts to capture difficult truths in symbols. Myths also arm us against realities that are otherwise too fateful or disturbing to bear contemplation. Powell's deep attachment to Wagner went hand in hand with his own desire for a national myth of England. The composer of *The Ring of the Nibelung* was adamant that the work possessed 'the ring of truth'. Myth, for Wagner, was the opposite of fantasy: it was a truth-directed, rather than an illusion-directed, device. He made this observation in connection with the old myths of Greek tragedy, and saw the tragedians as disinterring from those myths the 'concealed deep truths' about the human condition that they symbolized. In the same spirit Wagner wished to use the old myths of the Germanic peoples to explore truths about the modern psyche. His success in this is of less importance than the attempt. Thanks to Wagner, myth-making became a deliberate enterprise, rather than the work of the collective unconscious.

But conscious myth – the noble lie – is a different thing altogether from the myths that emerge from the unconscious fears and longings of a people. Unconscious myth conveys truth because it is the residue of life and the after-image of suffering. Conscious myths, however, are the instruments of human purpose. In the work of a great artist like Wagner they may point towards the truth. Released into the stream of political life, however, they can be directed as easily towards falsehood. Many blame Wagner for that exercise in collective mythopeia which brought the Nazi Party to power in Germany and extinguished the light of civilization across the continent. And many, looking back on Powell's vision of

England, believe that it showed the same dangerous tendency – not towards the truth of the modern condition, but towards a fantasy. Once released from the educated mind in which it was first conceived, this fantasy would run riot in the feelings of ignorant people and there fully justify the charge of 'racism' that was wrongly but understandably directed at Powell.

Such is the controversy as we see it now, forty years on: an ignoble lie against a dangerous myth. Whichever way you look at it, truth was the victim, and while the truth can now be cautiously acknowledged, it is acknowledged too late. Decisions can still be taken, but only in the hope of limiting the damage. And even now, when opinion across Europe is unanimous that immigration must be controlled, and that Muslims must be integrated into the secular culture, liberal politicians are refusing to admit to a problem or to confess that they are the cause of it. They still preach 'multiculturalism' as the sign of our 'vibrant' future; they still condemn 'racism and xenophobia' as the enemy; they still try to state and solve the problem by the promiscuous multiplication of 'human rights'. Their Enlightenment creed makes it all but impossible for them to acknowledge the fundamental truth, which is that indigenous communities have legitimate expectations which take precedence over the demands of strangers. True, indigenous communities may also have duties of charity towards those strangers – or towards some of them. But charity is a gift, and there is no right to receive it, still less to force it from those reluctant to give.

The destructive effects of liberalism are not usually felt by the liberals themselves – not immediately, at least. The first victim of liberal immigration policies is the indigenous working class. When the welfare state was first conceived, it was in order to provide insurance for poorer members of the indigenous community, by taxing their income in exchange for the benefits which they may one day need. The rights involved were quasi-contractual: a right of the state to levy contributions in exchange for a right of the citizen to receive support. The very term used to describe the deal in Britain – 'national insurance' – expresses the old understanding, that the welfare system is part of being together as a nation, of belonging with one's neighbours, as mutual beneficiaries of an ancestral right. The liberal view of rights, as universal possessions which make no reference to history, community, or obedience, has changed all that. Indigenous people can claim no precedence, not even in this matter in which they have sacrificed a lifetime of income for the sake of their own future security. Immigrants are given welfare benefits as of right, and on the basis of their need, whether or not they have paid or ever will pay taxes. And since their need is invariably great – why else have they come here? – they take precedence over existing residents in the grant of housing and income support. Those with a handful of wives are even more fortunate, since only one of their marriages is recognized in European systems of law: the remaining wives are 'single mothers', with all the fiscal advantages which attach to that label. All this has entailed that the stock of 'social housing' once reserved for the indigenous poor is now almost entirely occupied by people whose language, customs, and culture mark them out as foreigners.

It is not 'racist' to draw attention to this kind of fact. Nor is it racist to argue that indigenous people must take precedence over newcomers, who have to earn their right of residence and cannot be allowed to appropriate the savings of their hosts. But it is easier for me to write about these matters in an American intellectual journal than in an English newspaper, and if I tried to write about these things in a Belgian newspaper, I could be in serious trouble with the courts. The iron curtain of censorship that came down in the wake of Powell's speech has not lifted everywhere; on the contrary, if the EU has its way, it will be enshrined in the criminal code, with 'racism and xenophobia' – defined as vaguely as is required to silence unwanted opinion – made into an extraditable offence throughout the Union.

The problem with censorship, as John Stuart Mill pointed out a century and half ago, is that it makes it impossible for those who impose it to discover that they are wrong. The error persists, preventing the discussion that might produce a remedy, and ensuring that the problem will grow. Yet when truth cannot make itself known in words, it will make itself known in deeds. The truth about Hitler burst on the world in 1939, notwithstanding all the pious words of the appeasers.

And the truth about immigration is beginning to show itself in Europe, notwithstanding all the liberal efforts to conceal it. It is not an agreeable truth; nor can we, in the face of it, take refuge in the noble lies of Enoch Powell. The fact is that the people of Europe are losing their homelands, and therefore losing their place in the world. I don't envisage the Tiber one day foaming with much blood, nor do I see it blushing as the voice of the muezzin sounds from the former cathedral of St. Peter. But the city through which the Tiber flows will one day cease to be Italian, and all the expectations of its former residents, whether political, social, cultural, or personal, will suffer a violent upheaval, with results every bit as interesting as those that Powell prophesied.

SECTION 3

SEX AND THE SACRED

7

The Philosophy of Love
(From *Death-Devoted Heart*, 2004)

Much of the literature of courtly love is abstract and allegorical, reflecting in a general way on love, desire and marriage, without attaching these things to concrete individuals and their fate. Such is *Le Roman de la Rose*, for example, and Chaucer's *Parliament of Fowles*. But those works also define erotic love as a predicament of rational beings, who desire each other as individuals, and for whom love is a 'singling out', at one and the same time a choice and a destiny. The high-toned neo-Platonism of Chaucer, Boccaccio, and their contemporaries therefore goes with a new-found interest in the 'heroes of love' – those who have undergone exemplary trials on behalf of their passion. In treating the stories of Tristan and Troilus, poets were consciously placing the particular before the general, and the suffering individual before the fallen kind.

They were also reflecting on a philosophical question, one inherited from neo-Platonism and Avicenna, but a question that the sacramental view of marriage had brought into relief. Succinctly put, the question is this: to what part of the human being does erotic love belong – to the body or to the soul? If to the body, then what part does rational choice play in our sexual emotions, and how can they be disciplined, refined, and controlled? If to the soul, then what part does the body play in the expression of love, and is carnal union really the goal of it? And if carnal union is the goal, is erotic love simply a form of concupiscence, a bodily appetite like hunger or thirst?

These questions were not new. They had troubled Plato, too, and through neo-Platonist writers like Boethius and

Avicenna, Plato's influence was exerted over the entire literature of courtly love. Those who regard this literature as reflecting the parochial concerns of a passing social order often fail to see that its questions are still with us, even if we need another language to express them, and even if Platonic and Christian conceptions of the soul are no longer tenable. We are rational animals; but which part of our being – the rational or the animal – moves us to erotic love? And which part of us, if any, is fulfilled by love, and how?

Such questions had an added force for medieval writers on account of the Christian doctrine of charity. Christ reduced God's commandments to two: love God entirely, and love your neighbour as yourself. But if love can be commanded, then love must be a choice. It must involve voluntary actions and voluntary thoughts. The New Testament word for love – *agape* – is translated as *caritas* in Latin and charity in our own authorized version of the Bible. It is a technical term designed to accommodate the revolutionary idea of love as a duty...

Medieval writers did not suppose that erotic love is divinely inspired; on the contrary, they accepted the New Testament ideal of a love brought down to us from God, a love that comes to us as a duty, which provides the test of virtue here on earth, and which therefore must be separated from every form of sensual longing. But precisely because their world-view was founded in the cult of *agape*, they recognized *eros* as a problem to be solved. And the evident solution was to re-fashion erotic love on the model of the love that we owe to God. Like that other and higher love erotic love is a destiny, both a joy and a burden, and it points beyond the world to a realm of grace. It is surrounded with sacred rites and customs; it imposes a rule of chastity and fidelity; and it transforms the lover into a quasi-supernatural being, capable of virtuous deeds and noble sacrifices beyond the reach of common mortals. The medieval author of *The Pearl* finds this divine inspiration in paternal love for his dead daughter – and he beautifully persuades us that this is possible. But the spiritualization of the father-daughter love in *The Pearl* is plausible only because the daughter is dead, transformed into the angel who brings consolation to her grieving father. That unusual instance apart, it is invariably erotic love, rather than the other loves of human society, that has been re-made by the poets as a Godwards-tending exaltation of the soul. This is true pre-eminently of the medieval tradition from which Wagner drew his inspiration. But it is true too of oriental traditions, and notably that of the Sufi mystics, typified by Hafiz – another of Wagner's enthusiasms – whose odes, written in the form of the *ghazâl* or amorous lyric, seem to be addressed to an earthly beloved, but are in fact addressed to God.

That Christian and Muslim writers should think of erotic love in this way ought, however, to surprise us. Alone among human loves, the erotic can take the form of sin; and the sin of loving in unholy union is compounded by the carnal nature of desire, which imbues erotic love with the character of a bodily temptation. Parental love, sibling love and friendship are not forms of temptation: if they involve sin it is because they may lead you into sin, as when a doting mother shields her criminal son from justice. In themselves, however, these day-to-day loves are always innocent, nor do they have a carnal focus. As Gottfried is at such pains to point out, erotic love can be debased, made vicious and disgusting, by our way of treating it. Prostitution, obscenity, perversion, paedophilia – all these things display the inherently problematic nature of the sexual act, and the need to safeguard its expression by distinguishing virtuous from vicious desire.

So why pick on the erotic, as an icon of the love that aspires to redemption, and which is rewarded through grace? Medieval Christian and Muslim poets were not the first to travel this path, and some understanding of their motives can be gained from Plato, originator of the Neoplatonic cosmologies and erotologies that dominated both medieval and classical Arabic literature. In *The Symposium* Socrates expounds the famous Platonic theory of the soul's ascent, from the desire for carnal union with the beautiful object to the act of serene contemplation of the Form of the Beautiful. This purging away of the base trappings of carnal desire, so as to enjoy love not as a species of concupiscence but as a form of quasi-religious veneration, was, for Plato, the rational solution to an existential predicament. Sexual desire afflicts us as a kind of trouble – an overcoming of the soul by passions whose bodily origin sets them beyond the reach of our intellectual powers.

We are compromised by desire, but also, for that very reason, prompted to overcome its force. We do this by using the principal weapon that reason has provided: the shift of attention from the particular to the universal, and therefore from the time-bound and mortal to the timeless and eternal. The very thing that renders erotic love so dangerous – the carnal attachment which comes to us from a place outside our conscious thought – provides the opportunity for a quasi-religious transcendence, into the unseen realm of the Forms.

Inspiring though that theory is, it is philosophically flawed. Plato holds that one and the same emotion can exist, now as a carnal desire, now as a rational contemplation of the Forms. But this is surely incoherent. What makes love erotic is precisely the carnal desire for the human individual; and no emotion founded in desire for an individual can be identical with another state of mind, in which the object is a universal, and in which desire has been discarded. What Plato is describing is not the ascent of erotic love to a higher level, but the loss of erotic love, and its replacement by something else – a bloodless philosophical passion that has nothing of the erotic about it at all, and which is not even directed towards a human being.

Despite that, to my mind insuperable, difficulty, Plato's image of spiritual ascent has never lost its fascination for poets, theologians and philosophers, and it is important to understand why. The reason, it seems to me, is to be discovered not by examining erotic love, but by turning to the phenomenon in which that love is grounded, and which Plato sought to overcome: sexual desire. Plato's account of love was premised on a particular view of sexual desire, one inherited by Avicenna, by Aquinas, by the poets of courtly love, and by Dante. In desire, he believed, we act and feel as animals. In erotic love, however, it is our nature as rational beings that is primarily engaged – a fact which was made particularly apparent to Plato by his own homosexuality, which seemed to divorce erotic love from animal reproduction, and at the same time to deprive the sexual act of any higher rational purpose. In order to permit the full flowering of erotic love, therefore, Plato considered it necessary to discard the element of desire. The resulting purified love would be a rational state of mind, without any trace of the bodily pollution from which it originated.

This vision of the erotic – as bifurcated between rational love and animal desire, so that the peculiarly human aspect is only accidentally connected to the animal – is founded in a mistake. The intentional object of desire is redescribed in Plato's theory, not as the person desired, but as the act performed with him or her. The resulting mechanistic vision of sex has damaged discussions of this topic from Plato to the present day. In our time it has resurged in two forms: intellectual and practical. The intellectual form is epitomized in the pseudo-scientific studies of sex that have dominated recent discussions of the erotic; the practical form is displayed in pornography, and the (more or less successful) attempt to change the focus of sexual desire, from the individual object to the transferable commodity. Both these developments can be understood once we see human beings as Kant and Wagner saw them, namely as incarnate persons, in whom animal and self exist in an inextricable unity, each both exalted and compromised by the other.

Discussion of the modern, postromantic, attitude to sex must inevitably begin from Freud, whose revelations, introduced as neutral, 'scientific' truths about the human condition, were phrased in the terms which are now more or less standard. According to Freud, the aim of sexual desire is 'union of the genitals in the act known as copulation, which leads to a release of the sexual tension and a temporary extinction of the sexual instinct, a satisfaction analogous to the sating of hunger'. This scientistic image of sexual desire gave rise, in due course, to the Kinsey report, and is now part of the standard merchandise of disenchantment. It seems to me that if it contains any truth, it is because it has been *accepted* as true, and, in being accepted, changed the phenomenon that it set out to describe. Freud's theory is not a theory of human sexual desire in the social conditions which emerge spontaneously between rational beings. It is a description of sexual feelings transformed by a kind of scientistic prurience, and by an obsession with the human object that clouds awareness of the subject.

As soon as we look at things as artists and poets have

described them, we can see how far is the Freudian picture from what was previously known. Consider the phenomenon so bleakly described by Freud – sexual pleasure. This pleasure is unlike the pleasure of eating, in that its object is not consumed. It is unlike the pleasure of a hot bath, in that it involves taking pleasure in an activity, and in the other person who joins you. It is unlike the pleasure of watching your child at play, since it involves bodily sensations and a surrender to physical impulses. Sexual pleasure resembles the pleasure of watching something, however, in a crucial respect: it has *intentionality*. It is not just a tingling sensation; it is a response to another person, and to the act in which you are engaged with him or her. The other person may be imaginary: but it is towards a person that your thoughts are directed, and the pleasure depends on the thoughts.

Pleasure that depends on thought can be mistaken, and it ceases when the mistake is known. Although I would be a fool not to jump out of the soothing bath after being told that what I took for water was really acid, this is not because I have ceased to feel pleasurable sensations in my skin. The pleasure of the hot bath is 'purely physical', without intentionality and detached from thought. Contrast the pleasure you take in seeing your child win the long jump at his school sports day: should you discover that, after all, it was not your child but another who resembles him, your pleasure would instantly cease.

Likewise, in the case of sexual pleasure, the discovery that it is an unwanted hand that touches you at once extinguishes your pleasure. The pleasure experienced until that point could not be taken as confirming the hitherto unacknowledged sexual virtues of some previously rejected applicant. Hence a woman who makes love to the man who has disguised himself as her husband is no less the victim of rape, and the discovery of her mistake will lead to instant revulsion. It is not simply that consent obtained by fraud is not consent; it is that the woman has been violated, in the very act which caused her pleasure, so that the pleasure itself was a kind of error. (Something of this is captured in Benjamin Britten's *The Rape of Lucretia*. More interesting, from the philosophical point of view, is the case of Alcmene, visited by Jupiter in the form of her husband Amphitryon. Does Jupiter really succeed in enjoying Alcmene, is she really unfaithful to her husband, and has Amphitryon genuine grounds for jealousy? Plautus treats this situation as comic, Kleist as tragic, and Giraudoux as fraught with irony. But none of them solves the puzzle.)

Sexual pleasure is dependent on arousal, a condition distinct from, though displayed by, tumescence. Arousal is a 'leaning towards' the other, a movement in the direction of the sexual act, which cannot be fully distinguished either from the thoughts on which it is founded or from the desire to which it leads. Arousal is a response to the thought of the other as a self-conscious agent, who is alert to me and who can have 'designs' on me. This is evident from the caress and the glance of desire. A caress of affection is a gesture of reassurance – an attempt to place in the consciousness of the other an image of one's own warm concern for him or her. Not so, however, the caress of desire, which *outlines* the body of the recipient; it is an exploratory, rather than a reassuring gesture. It aims to fill the surface of the other's body with a consciousness of your interest – interest not only in the body but in the person *as* embodied. This consciousness is the focal point of pleasure in the one who inspires it. Sartre writes of the caress as 'incarnating' the other: as though, by your action, you bring the soul into the flesh (the subject into the object) and make it palpable.

The caress of desire is given and received with the same awareness as the glance is given and received. They each have an epistemic component (a component of anticipation and discovery). It is hardly surprising, therefore, that the face should have such supreme and overriding importance in sexual interest. From the scientist perspective it is hard to explain why the face should have the power to determine whether we will or will not be drawn to seek pleasure in another part. But of course the face is the picture of the other's subjectivity: it shines with the light of self, and it is as an embodied subject that the other is wanted. Perversion and obscenity involve the eclipse of the subject, as the body and its mechanism are placed in frontal view. In obscenity, flesh is represented in such a way as to become opaque to the self that inhabits it: that is why there is an obscenity of violence as well as an obscenity of sex, a torturing of the flesh which extinguishes the light of freedom and subjectivity.

A caress may be accepted or rejected: in either case, it is because it has been 'read' as conveying a message sent from you to me. I do not receive this message as an explicit act of meaning something, but as a process of mutual discovery, a growing to awareness in you which is also a coming to awareness in me. In the first impulse of arousal, therefore, begins that chain of reciprocity which is fundamental to interpersonal attitudes. She conceives her lover conceiving her conceiving him... not *ad infinitum* but to the point of mutual recognition, where the partners are fully identified in each other's eyes with their bodily presence.

Sexual arousal has, then, an intentionality that is not merely epistemic but also inter-personal. In its normal form it is a response to another individual, based in revelation and discovery, and involving a reciprocal and cooperative heightening of the common experience of embodiment. It is not directed beyond the other, to the world at large; nor is it straightforwardly transferable to a rival object who might 'do just as well'. Of course, arousal may have its origin in highly generalized thoughts, which flit libidinously from object to object. But when these thoughts have concentrated into the experience of arousal their generality tends to be put aside; it is then the other who counts, and his or her particular embodiment, as well as I myself and the sense of my bodily reality in the other's perspective. Hence arousal, in the normal case, seeks seclusion in a private place, where only the other is relevant to my attention. Indeed, arousal attempts to abolish what is not private – in particular to abolish the perspective of the onlooker, of the 'third person' who is neither you nor I.

This natural movement is further amplified and idealized in our thinking so as to give sense and meaning to the vision of a chaste and inviolable attachment, such as that described in the tale of Tristan and Isolde. This story, like the companion story of Troilus and Cressida, presents the sexual bond as sacramental in itself, whether or not endorsed by theological doctrine or consecrated by a religious rite. In the romantic fabrication known as the letters of Héloïse and Abelard, the abbess recalls the moments of intense lust that she had enjoyed with her unfortunate lover, and – although he rebukes her for dwelling on them – they form a kind of metaphysical vindication of her love and a spiritual proof of marriage. This late medieval work belongs to the same tradition as the tales of Tristan and Troilus: like them, it is an attempt to come to terms with the inherent paradox of sexual desire – that it is both an attraction between objects and a dialogue of subjects – and to find in passion another and higher kind of action.

People express themselves through their intentional acts. But they *reveal* themselves in what is unintentional and beyond ready control. Hence the importance in sexual relations of those responses which cannot be willed but only predicted, but which are nevertheless peculiar to self-conscious beings. Blushing is a singular instance. Although an involuntary matter, and – from the physiological point of view – a mere rushing of blood to the head, blushing is the expression of a complex thought, and one that places the self on view. My blush is an involuntary recognition of my accountability before you for what I am and what I feel. It is an acknowledgement that I stand in the light of your perspective and that I cannot hide in my body. A blush is attractive because it serves both to embody the perspective of the other and also at the same time to display that perspective as an involuntary response to *me*. Your blush is not merely caused by me but in some way directed at me and establishes a relationship between us. The same is true of unguarded glances and smiles, through which the other subject rises to the surface of his body, so to speak, and makes himself visible. In smiling, blushing, laughing and crying, it is precisely my loss of control over my body and its gain of control over me that create the immediate experience of an incarnate person. In such expressions the face does not function merely as a bodily part but as the whole person: the self is spread across its surface and there 'made flesh'. In blushes, smiles and glances, in short, the body exalts and reveals the person, shows the subject in the object, and makes of that subject an object of desire – of the desire to be united with *this person*, which is also a desire to possess. All this is audible in the Prelude to *Tristan und Isolde*, and in the motive of the Look that provides its inexorable onward motion.

The concepts and categories that we use to describe the embodied person are far removed from the science of the human body. What place in such a science for smiles as opposed to grimaces, for blushes as opposed to flushes, for looks and glances as opposed to mere visual perception? In seeing your colour as a blush, I am also seeing you as a responsible agent and situating you in the realm of embarrassment and self-knowledge. (Hence nonrational animals cannot blush, not even those animals, like pigs, with translucent skin.) If we try to describe sexual desire with the categories of human biology, we miss precisely the intentionality of sexual emotion, its directedness towards the embodied subject. Freud's description of desire is the description of something that we know but shun. An excitement that concentrates on the sexual organs, whether of man or of woman, which seeks, as it were, to bypass the complex negotiation of the face, hands, voice and posture, voids desire of its intentionality and replaces it with a pursuit of the sexual commodity, which can always be had for a price. We have become habituated to forms of sexual interest in which the person, the freedom and the virtue of the other are all irrelevant to the goal. But we should see this not as a gain in freedom but a loss of it, since it involves precisely setting freedom aside as an irrelevant adjunct to the object of desire.

To someone agitated by his desire for Jane, it is ridiculous to say, 'Take Henrietta, she will do just as well'. Thus there arises the possibility of mistakes of identity. Jacob's desire for Rachel seemed to be satisfied by his night with Leah, only to the extent that, and for as long as, Jacob imagined it was Rachel with whom he was lying. (Genesis 29: 22–25; and see the wonderful realization of this little drama in Thomas Mann's *Joseph and his Brothers*.) Our sexual emotions are founded on individualizing thoughts: it is *you* whom I want and not the type or pattern. This individualizing intentionality does not merely stem from the fact that it is persons (in other words, individuals) whom we desire. It stems from the fact that the other is desired as an embodied subject and not as a body ...

The crime against love is the admission of substitutes: for by this means we leave the world of value and enter the world of price. It is for this reason that societies have devoted such attention to the sexual mores of their young. Traditional sexual education may be summarized in anthropological language as an attempt to impart an 'ethic of pollution and taboo'. Children were taught to regard their bodies as subject to pollution by misperception or misuse. The sense of pollution is by no means a trivial side-effect of the 'bad sexual encounter': it may involve a penetrating disgust at oneself, one's body, and one's existential condition, such as is experienced by the victim of rape. Those sentiments express the tension contained within our experience of embodiment. At any moment we can become 'mere body', the self-driven from its incarnation, and its habitation sacked.

The most important root idea of sexual morality is that I am in my body not as a 'ghost in the machine' but as an incarnate person. I do not stand to my body in an instrumental relation: subject and object are merely two aspects of a single thing, and sexual purity is the guarantee of this. Sexual virtue does not forbid desire: rather, it makes true desire possible by reconstituting the physical urge as an interpersonal feeling. Children who learn 'dirty habits' detach their sexuality from themselves, setting it outside themselves as a curious feature of the world of objects; their fascinated enslavement to the body is also a withering of desire, a scattering of erotic energy, and a loss of union with the other. Sexual virtue sustains the subject of desire, making him present as a self in the very act that overcomes him.

Life in the actual world is difficult and embarrassing. Most of all is it difficult and embarrassing in our confrontation with other people who, by their very existence as subjects, rearrange things in defiance of our will. It requires a great force, such as the force of erotic love, to overcome the self-protection that shields us from intimate encounters. It is tempting to take refuge in substitutes that neither embarrass us nor resist the impulse of our spontaneous cravings. The habit easily grows of creating a compliant fantasy world of desire, in which unreal objects become the focus of real emotions and the emotions themselves are withdrawn from personal relations thus impoverishing our social experience. In this process the imagined other, since he or she is entirely the instrument of my will, becomes an object for me, one among many substitutes defined purely in terms of a sexual use. The sexual world of the fantasist is a world without subjects, in which others appear as objects only. And when a person is targeted by a desire nurtured on fantasy – when a real subject is treated as a fantasy object – the result is a sin against love. This is the sin of lust or concupiscence, that Gottfried attributes to King Mark...

This returns us to the great question that troubled Plato, Avicenna, and the poets of courtly love – what has desire to do with love and love with desire? In a celebrated study C.S. Lewis carefully distinguishes the various loves of humankind and draws an interesting contrast between erotic love and friendship. 'Lovers', he writes, 'are normally face to face, absorbed in each other; friends, side by side, absorbed in some common interest'. This suggestive observation finds confirmation in Wagner's drama, in which the side-by-sideness of Isolde and Brangäne, and of Tristan and Kurwenal, are both contrasted with the face-to-faceness of the lovers, not merely in Act 2 but in all that has preceded it. (It is because the lovers are already face to face in Act 1 that Tristan is avoiding Isolde's glance.) Josef Pieper makes a similar point, remarking that lovers talk to each other incessantly about their love whereas friends never mention it. And again Wagner illustrates the point, making it central to Act 2, in which the mutual interrogation of lovers, normally so dull to an outsider, is shown in all its poignant inwardness. That is why Brangäne and Kurwenal are so important to the drama as Wagner conceives it, and not merely (in Brangäne's case) because of the conventional need for a confidante: their loyalty and devotion, belonging to the sphere of friendship, place an isolating frame around Tristan and Isolde's love. Friendship, Wagner shows, means comfort, help and security; erotic love means distress, anxiety and danger. Whereas your friend wants your good, your lover wants *you*; and if he cannot have you, then his love may turn to hate.

Erotic love is therefore not a form of companionship or mutual support, although it may lead in time to those goods. In its initial and defining impulse it is a desire for reciprocal possession, a desire to possess the other by being oneself possessed by him. As such, erotic love envisages no worldly benefits or gains beyond itself. It is therefore irreducible either to charity (*agape*) or to friendship, and the poets of courtly love were deceiving themselves when they represented erotic love as, in Chaucer's words, a 'choice all free'. We may choose to give way to this love or to conceal it; but what we give way to or conceal is not itself a choice.

For the same reason, erotic love cannot be construed as a kind of amalgam of love (conceived either as *agape* or as *philia*, friendship) and sexual desire. Nor can the element of desire be 'refined away' leaving the love itself unaltered. Erotic love is an exaltation of desire itself to the point of complete attachment. Its aim is to possess, to hold, to exclude; and its object is neither the body of the beloved nor the soul. It is the embodied person: the free being bound by flesh.

The distinction between erotic love and friendship is worth dwelling upon, since it casts light on one of Wagner's aims in *Tristan und Isolde*, and also in the *Ring*, which is to tie erotic love to sacrifice, and sacrifice to redemption – in other words to re-cast the Christian message with *eros* in *agape*'s stead. Here, briefly, is how we might state the distinction: erotic love begins from desire and bears the traces of it ever after. Hence erotic love focuses on the embodiment of its object: not on the *body* (since that would involve the perversion of desire), but on the other *as embodied*. The other is present in his flesh; in sexual desire he also *presents* himself and makes of himself a *present*.

Love, like desire, feasts on looks: for it is through the look that this 'presenting' of the self is most immediately accomplished (one reason why beauty has so much to do with it.) But looks are neither necessary (blind people too can desire) nor sufficient. Desire is expressed in arousal and seeks to arouse its object through touching, fondling, and caressing. In arousal the body occupies the foreground; yet it also becomes transparent, exposing the other person as object and subject of desire. Hence desire is dangerous, compromising, the source of existential anxiety. Only in certain circumstances is desire advisable, and only rarely is its expression safe. Institutions exist in order to protect us from the abuse of sexual feeling. There are laws circumscribing the erotic, but none limiting friendship.

A lover may also be a friend, but he is not a friend by virtue of being a lover. On the contrary: love is jealous and at war with every rival – even the rival of whom the friend would approve. Hence those chilling words of Blake:

Love seeketh only self to please,
To bind another to its delight;
Joys in another's loss of ease
And builds a Hell in Heaven's despite.

The lover is focused on the beloved; but he does not really accept the otherness of the beloved – does not accept that the other's life is a life apart and does not place the other's interests above his own interest in being first in the other's affections.

In friendship there is a recognition and acceptance of the otherness of the friend. Friendship involves loyalty not to a cause or a common concern but to an *individual*. This loyalty involves both closeness and distance. The friend seeks the other's company but also seeks the other's completeness as an individual and therefore his full autonomy as another, with a life of his own.

Hence friendship tends to be mutual. Although friendship does not seek a return, it dies if the return is never offered. The reward of friendship is friendship, but it is granted only if it is not sought. At the same time, the one who persistently offers friendship to a person who never returns it is not acting as a friend. In such a case, there is another motive at work – love, for example, like the love of a parent towards an ungrateful child, or desire. The concept of unrequited erotic love causes us no difficulty; the concept of unrequited friendship is less easily understood. We recognize in such an idea no motive to which a rational being might easily succumb.

While friendship may be full of feeling, it is not an emotion. Friendly feelings are no more the essence of friendship than respectful feelings are the essence of respect. Friendship is a complex relation between persons, in which each takes the other into consideration. Love, by contrast, is an emotion, which may exist even without the relation for which it yearns. Hence there is no Platonic ascent, no 'overcoming' of friendship, as there is an overcoming of love. Nor do you bask in your friendship as you do in your love – those writers who try to present friendship as a feeling (Montaigne, for instance, in his immensely misleading account of his attitude to La Boëtie), seem always to be writing of something else: a sublimated erotic love, perhaps, or a passionate attachment such as that between parent and child.

Friendship, unlike love, is not exclusive. A person may have several friends, all equally dear, and all accepting the fact with equanimity and even pleasure. Why erotic love should be otherwise is one of the great mysteries of our condition – for after all, both love and friendship are focused on the individual; both involve a kind of surrender of the self; and the most important difference – the presence or absence of desire – seems hardly to prepare us for so momentous a divide.

Friendship is nevertheless like erotic love in certain respects. For example, it occurs only between rational beings. (Animals are companions but never friends, just as they are mates but never lovers.) Friendship involves dialogue and togetherness – although it may stop short of intimacy (whereas erotic love stops short of intimacy only when thwarted or renounced). Both erotic love and friendship are directed towards the individual and regard him as irreplaceable. There is no other, who would 'do just as well', and to propose a substitute for the object of love or friendship is to mistake the motive of both lover and friend. Love and friendship are both 'everlasting' – they die, but they are never 'satisfied', since they have no goal beyond themselves. (The contrast with contract should here be borne in mind: a contract has terms, and ends when those terms are fulfilled.) Finally, both love and friendship are offered and received as *gifts* and can be offered and received in no other way. (Hence there is no contract in which friendship or love is the subject matter.) Moreover they are expressed through gifts and are manifestations of grace.

Friendship is therefore a form of generosity. Although not exclusive, it cannot be universalized any more than the habit of giving can be universalized. (The person who gives to everyone is the person who has nothing to give.) Friendship must therefore be distinguished from *agape* (the 'love to which we are commanded', as Kant described it). *Agape* is a duty and not a gift (even though giving is sometimes a duty – for instance when our neighbour, through no fault of his own, finds himself destitute). We owe this neighbourly love to those with whom we could never stand side-by-side, and also – for the Christian – to those who hate us and to those whose company we abhor.

The friend commands my special attention: I make an effort on his behalf, and his friendship becomes part of my life, something intrinsically valuable to me. The intrinsic value of the 'neighbour' belongs to him as a rational individual. He is valuable for his own sake but not necessarily for me. The value of the friend is a value for *me*; one of my possessions, and one that has no price. Friendship elevates those who are bound by it; it lifts them above the plateau of *agape* into an illuminated region which is *theirs* and which they have no duty to share.

In friendship, as I have said, we recognize the otherness of the other: we do not regard ourselves as bound to him by any fateful tie, such as that which joins parent to child or lover to lover. This recognition of his otherness means that I am also his judge: I strive to forgive his faults but not to ignore them. I am always in a *chosen* relation with my friend, even when the grounds of choice are hidden from me. I grieve at his moral downfall, but I also condemn it; and if he provokes my moral disapproval, my friendship may be finally withdrawn.

The relation between friendship and virtue is intricate and hard to describe: neither Aristotle nor Kant made proper sense of it. Yet it exists and is one reason why friendship is so important to us. The person with genuine friends (as opposed to the man, like Falstaff, who has only 'boon companions', associates in business or partners in crime), is one whom we trust. We have a prior guarantee of his moral worth, since he will be no stranger to virtue. If we find it difficult to believe that there are still people with *genuine* friends, it is because this implies that there really is virtue in the world.

Nobody qualifies for trust merely by having lovers. Erotic love notoriously by-passes moral judgement, fixing itself on the most bizarre or tawdry objects, and dragging down its victim, as Des Grieux is dragged down by Manon or Swann by Odette. At the same time, erotic love idealizes its object, striving to vindicate its vast investment by believing that the cause is worthwhile. Even in erotic love, therefore, we are dominated by the *image* of virtue: of a human being who is special, precious, and worthy of our exclusive care.

8

Meaningful Marriage
(From *A Political Philosophy*, 2006)

An institution can be looked at from outside, with the eyes of an anthropologist, who observes its social function. Or it can be looked at from inside, with the eyes of a participant, whose life it transforms. And what is observable from one perspective may not be observable from the other. The anthropologist who studies the seasonal war-making of a tribe may understand this institution as a way of securing territory, a way of controlling population, and a way of reaching a renewable equilibrium with neighbours. The warrior understands the institution in quite another way. For him it is a source of brotherhood, a mystical affirmation of identity between himself and the tribe, and a call to his soul from 'ancestral voices'. The concepts used by the anthropologist – social function, solidarity, ideology and so on – make no contact with the warrior's experience. If he were to make use of these concepts in describing what he feels, he would immediately cease to feel it. And the concepts that inform the warrior's self-understanding – brotherhood, destiny, sacred obligation – play no part in the anthropologist's explanation of what the warrior does.

This does not mean that the two people are entirely opaque to each other. Maybe, by an act of *Verstehen*, the anthropologist can enter into the experience of the man he studies, and imagine what it is like to see the world as he sees it. Maybe the tribesman can stand back sufficiently from his situation to envisage how it might be understood and explained by someone who was outside the fold of membership. Nevertheless, the two assign different and incommen-

115

surable values to the institution of seasonal warfare, and criticism offered from one perspective might have no bearing on the values that inform the other. For the anthropologist the institution is justified by its function, and if it becomes dysfunctional, then it loses its rationale. For the warrior the institution is justified by the sacred obligations on which it rests, and only if those obligations are rescinded can it be allowed to decay.

This mismatch between external and internal perspectives has been frequently remarked upon, and not only in the context of anthropology. We encounter it in moral philosophy, in the conflict between consequentialism, which sees ethics as policy directed towards an external goal, and the deontological perspective that sees ethics in terms of absolute rights and duties. We encounter it in literature, in the contrast between the author's perspective and the values and motives of his characters. We encounter a version of it, too, in ourselves. For, as sophisticated modern people, we are in the habit of looking on our own values as though they were not ours at all, but the values of some curious stranger, who needs to be put in context and viewed from some fastidious height. We are all familiar with that Prufrock feeling, which reminds us in the midst of our warmest passions that we are perhaps wrong to presume, wrong to assume.

Indeed, it is arguable that the contrast between the two perspectives lies in the nature of things. A person is both I and he, both free subject and determined object, both rational chooser and predictable animal. We can see ourselves in either way, a possibility from which Kant derived his startling vision of our moral and metaphysical predicament. But it is perhaps a distinguishing mark of the modern condition that we are so easily tempted away from the first-person viewpoint to that other and more alienated posture, that turns self into other and choice into fate.

This has a bearing, I believe, on the current debates over marriage. For marriage is one of those institutions that we spontaneously see both from outside, in terms of its social function, and from inside, in terms of the moral and spiritual condition that it creates. No honest anthropologist can fail to acknowledge the functional importance of marriage. In all observed societies some form of marriage exists, as the means whereby the work of one generation is dedicated to the well-being of the next. Marriage does not merely protect and nurture children; it is a shield against sexual jealousy, and a unique form of social and economic co-operation, with a mutually supportive division of roles that more than doubles the effectiveness of each partner in their shared bid for security. Marriage fulfils this complex function because it is something more than a contract of mutual co-operation, and something more than an agreement to live together. Hence marriage enjoys – or has until recently enjoyed – a distinct social aura. A wedding is a rite of passage, in which a couple pass from one social condition to another. The ceremony is not the concern of the couple only, but of the entire community that includes them. For this is the way that children are made – made, that is, as new members of society, who will, in their turn, take on the task of social reproduction. Society has a profound interest in marriage, and changes to that institution may alter not merely relations among the living, but also the expectations of those unborn and the legacy of those who predecease them.

Wedding guests, therefore, symbolize the social endorsement of the union that they have assembled to witness, and the marriage is a kind of legitimization of the potentially subversive desire between the partners. Society blesses the union, but only at a price. And the price has been, in traditional Christian societies, a heavy one: sexual fidelity 'till death do us part', and a responsibility for the socializing and educating of the children. As people become more and more reluctant to pay that price, so do weddings become more and more provisional, and the distinction between the socially endorsed union and the merely private arrangement becomes less and less absolute and less and less secure. As sociologists are beginning to observe, however, this gain in freedom for one generation implies a loss for the next. Children born within a marriage are far more likely to be socialized, outgoing and able to form permanent relationships of their own, than children born out of wedlock. For their parents have made a commitment in which the children are included, and of which society approves. This fact is part of the deep phenomenology of the marital home. Children of married parents find a place in society already prepared for them, furnished by a regime of parental sacrifice and protected by social norms. Take away marriage and you expose children to the risk of coming into the world as strangers, a condition in which they may remain for the rest of their lives.

An anthropologist will hardly be surprised, therefore, to discover that marriage is regarded, in most simple societies, as a religious condition. Rites of passage are conducted in the presence of the ancestors, and the ancestors are presided over by the gods. Religion is one way in which the long-term interests of society may animate the short-term decisions of its present members. Hence it is natural that marriage should be seen from within as something divinely ordained, with a sacred aura that reinforces the undertaken duties and elicits the support of the tribe. You don't have to be a religious believer to observe this or to see its point. You need only be aware of what is at stake, when people bring children into the world and claim those children as their own.

CIVIL UNION

The institution of civil marriage is not a modern invention. It was already established under Roman law, which regarded marriage as a distinct legal status, protected and defined by a purely secular jurisdiction. However, the law took note of religious precedent, looked severely on those who departed from its edicts, required a kind of commitment that went well beyond any merely contractual tie involving children and property and held both parties to their obligations. The shadow of religion fell across the Roman marriage ceremony, with its meticulous rituals and sacred words, and the household gods watched over the transition, in which they were intimately concerned. True, Roman marriages were not conceived as eternal unions: they were the legal embodiment of an intention to live monogamously together, and could be ended by noting that the *affectio maritalis* had ceased. Legal recognition that the marriage was over could be obtained without difficulty, and although in later Christian times the Emperor Justinian briefly succeeded in penalizing consensual divorce, it is clear that the Roman law did not regard marriage as a radical existential change.

With the growth of the Papacy marriage was recaptured from the secular powers, and reconsecrated as the Church's concern. And so it remained throughout the Middle Ages and the early Renaissance. An uneasy truce was struck between secular jurisdictions and ecclesiastical ceremonies, and the Church's interdiction of divorce ensured that marriage laws would enshrine the idea of a lifelong commitment. Marriage was no longer a complex and rescindable relationship, but a permanent change of status, from which there could be no real return.

When Henry VIII took the English into the Reformation, it was on account of his marital problems. He wanted a divorce and the Church would not grant one. Traditional Catholic teaching holds marriage to be an irreversible change of status, not merely within the community but also before God. Hence a marriage cannot be undone, but only annulled. An annulment does not grant release from an existing marriage but declares that the marriage never was. Naturally enough, the process of annulment has been subject to abuses; but even Henry, Defender of the Faith, could not persuade the Church to take the easy way out of their common problem. When the King took the matter into his own hands it was not in order to break the connection between marriage and the Church. On the contrary, marriage remained Holy Matrimony, and Henry solved the Church's problems by appointing himself as the head of it. It was probably not until the French Revolution that the State declared itself to be the true broker and undoer of marriages, and neither the Catholic nor the Protestant Church has ever accepted this as doctrine or afforded its comforts to those who view their marriages as purely civil affairs.

Since then, however, we have experienced a steady de-sacralization of the marriage tie. It is not merely that marriage is governed now by a secular law – that has been the case since antiquity. It is that this law is constantly amended, not in order to perpetuate the idea of an existential commitment, but on the contrary to make it possible for commitments to be evaded, and agreements rescinded, by rewriting them as the terms of a contract.

From the external perspective this development must be seen as radical. What was once a socially endorsed change of status has become a private and reversible deal. The social constraints that tied man and wife to each other through all troubles and disharmonies have been one by one removed, to the point where marriage is hardly distinct from a short-term agreement for cohabitation. This has been made more or less explicit in the American case by the pre-nuptial agreement, which specifies a division of property in the event of divorce. Partners now enter the marriage with an escape route already mapped out.

CONTRACTS AND VOWS

To understand this change we should recognize that, although divorce has been permitted in Protestant cultures for some time, it has not been seen in contractual terms, even by the secular law of marriage. Divorce has been unlike annulment in recognizing that a marriage once existed and is now being undone. But it has been like annulment in recognizing that the spirit of a marriage survives its material death. There could be no return from the state of marriage, but only a transition to another state *beyond* marriage, in which as many of the marital obligations as possible would be salvaged from the ruin and reinstated as lifetime burdens on the parties. Typically, the divorced husband would be charged with the maintenance of his ex-wife, the education and protection of their children, and such other liabilities as could be imposed upon a man now faced with a self-made enemy.

With the pre-nuptial agreement, however, divorce takes on a new meaning. It becomes in a sense the *fulfilment* of the marriage contract, which henceforth loses its force. Spouses no longer enter a marriage but, as it were, stand outside it, fully equipped to move on. Hence marriage has ceased to be what Hegel called a 'substantial tie', and become one of a lifelong series of handshakes. Among the wealthy and the sexy serial polygamy is now the norm. But the word 'polygamy' already begs the most important question – which is whether such an arrangement is really a marriage. Rescindable civil unions cannot conceivably have the function of marriage as traditionally conceived. They cannot guarantee security to children, nor can they summon the willing endorsement of society, by showing the partners' preparedness to make a sacrifice on the future's behalf. The new kind of civil union exists merely to amplify the self-confidence of the partners. Children, neighbours, community, the world – all such others are strangers to the deal. Not surprisingly, when marriage is no more than an official rubber stamp affixed to a purely private contract, people cease to see the point of it. Why bother with the stamp? Whose business is it anyway?

Official policy is, therefore, already recognizing the effect of official policy, which is to downgrade and ultimately abolish the marriage tie. Government forms in Britain ask for details of your 'partner' where once they would have asked for details of your husband or wife. It is all but politically incorrect to declare yourself married to someone (at least to someone of the opposite sex), and many of my liberal friends now refuse to refer to their lifelong companions in terms that imply any greater commitment than that contained in an agreement to share a roof. Children are no longer part of the arrangement, which is conceived purely as a contract between consenting adults. When Kant described marriage as 'a contract for the mutual use of the sexual organs' he may not have had this in mind. But his words were prophetic, and proof of the extent to which his Enlightenment vision was already reshaping the world.

The traditional marriage, seen from the external perspective as a rite of passage to another social condition, is seen from within as a vow. This vow may be preceded by a promise. But it is something more than a promise, since the obligations to which it leads cannot be spelled out in finite terms. A vow of marriage creates an existential tie, not a set of specifiable obligations. And the gradual vanishing of marital vows is one special case of the transition 'from status to contract' which was discussed, from the external perspective, by that great armchair anthropologist Sir Henry Maine. But there is also more to the change than that. The triumph of the contractual view of marriage represents a change in the phenomenology of sexual union, a retreat from the world of 'substantial ties' to a world of negotiated deals. And the world of vows is a world of sacred things, in which holy and indefeasible obligations stand athwart our lives and command us along certain paths, whether we will or not. It is this experience that the Church has always tried to safeguard, and it is one that has been jeopardized by the State, in its efforts to refashion marriage for a secular age ...

THE VOW OF LOVE

It will be said that the vow of love – conceived one way by the courtly literature, and another way by the subversive response to it – is in both versions a piece of ideology. It is an attempt to present as a permanent and metaphysical truth what is in fact no more than a passing social fashion, useful in securing the property relations of a vanished leisure class, but with no claim to be the enduring truth of the human condition. The myth of the love-vow had a lasting influence on Western culture, leading to the great celebrations of man-woman love in Shakespeare and Milton, to the heroic passions explored by Racine, to the literature of romantic love and to the operas of Bellini, Verdi and Wagner. But all this is culture, not nature. Other societies have viewed love, desire and marriage in other terms, and the idea of marriage as rooted in a personal choice and an existential commitment is as foreign to oriental traditions as the love of counterpoint, the belief in the Incarnation or a taste for *confit d'oie*.

It is hard to disagree with all that. Yet there is something that it overlooks, something which is at the heart of the medieval conception of the love-vow, and of the marital practices that it has been used to authorize. This thing is the peculiar intentionality of human sexual emotion. Sexual desire is not a desire for sensations. It is a desire for a person: and I mean a *person*, not his or her body, conceived as an object in the physical world, but the person conceived as an incarnate subject, in whom the light of self-consciousness shines and who confronts me eye to eye, and I to I. True desire is also a kind of petition: it demands reciprocity, mutuality and a shared surrender. It is, therefore, compromising, and also threatening. No pursuit of a mere sensation could be compromising or threatening in this way.

122

Those are not claims about culture, nor are they claims about the way in which desire has been rationalized, idealized or constrained by institutions. They are claims about a particular state of mind, one that only rational beings can experience, and which, nevertheless, has its roots in our embodiment as members of the human species. There are other states of mind that have a passing resemblance to sexual desire, but which do not share its intentionality – for example, the sexual excitement aroused by pornography, or the excitement that finds relief in fetishism and in necrophilia. There is a whole gamut of perversions, the object of which is not to possess another person in a state of mutual surrender but to relieve oneself on a body, to enslave or humiliate, to treat the other as an instrument through which to achieve some sensory excitement, and so on. But in calling these things perversions we indicate a defect in the intentionality from which they spring. They are no more to be seen as expressions of sexual desire than the desire to eat your child is to be seen as an expression of love, even when love, of a perverted kind, is the cause of it. Such is the complexity of the human condition that the mental forces that erupt in us can find just such peculiar outlets. But in describing them as perversions we convey the idea that a state of mind has a normal object, a normal fulfilment, and a normal course towards its goal. In the case of sexual desire the norm can be seen externally, in terms of its social function, and also internally, as a feature of the intentional object and of the description under which he or she is desired ...

STATE AND FAMILY

To what point does this bring us, in the contemporary discussions over marriage? My tentative conclusion is this: that the view of marriage as a sacrament is an accurate, if theologically loaded, account of how marriage has been experienced, of why it is wanted and of what it inwardly does to those who enter it. Marriage is not a contract of cohabitation, but a vow of togetherness. Its foundation is erotic, not in the sense that all marriages begin in or exist through desire, but in the sense that, without desire, the institution would rest on nothing in the human condition. At the same time, looked at from outside, with the eye of the anthropologist, marriage has a function, which is to ensure social reproduction, the socializing of children and the passing on of social capital. Without marriage it is doubtful that those processes would occur, but when they occur they provide both a fulfilment of sexual union and a way to transcend its scant imperatives, into a realm of duty, love and pride. The inner, sacramental, character of marriage is therefore reinforced by its external function. Together they endow marriage with its distinctive character, as an institution that is normal and sublime in equal measure.

When the State usurped the rite of matrimony, and reshaped what had once been holy law, it was inevitable that it should loosen the marital tie. For the State does not represent the Eternal, nor does it have so much regard for future generations that it can disregard the whims of the merely living. The State is always and inevitably the instrument of its current members; it will respond to their pressures and try to satisfy their demands. It has therefore found it expedient to undo the sacrament, to permit easy divorce, to reduce marriage from a vow to a contract and – in the most recent act of liberalization – to permit marriage between people of the same sex. None of this has been done with evil motives, and always there has been, in the back of people's minds, a memory of the sacred and existential ties that distinguish people from animals and enduring societies from madding crowds. The desire has been to retain the distinctiveness of marriage, as the best that we can hope for by way of a lasting commitment, while escaping from its more onerous demands – demands that people are no longer prepared to recognize. As a result marriage has ceased to be a rite of passage into another and higher life, and become a bureaucratic stamp, with which to endorse our temporary choices. I would not call this a gain in freedom – for those choices have never been denied to us, and by dignifying them with the name of marriage we merely place another obstacle before the option to which humanity has devoted so much of its idealizing fervour. Of course, we are still free to dedicate our lives to each other, to our home and to our children. But this act is rendered the more difficult, the less society recognizes the uniqueness, the value and the sacrificial character of what we do. Just as people are less disposed to assume the burdens of high office when society withholds the dignities and privileges which those offices have previously signified, so are they less disposed to enter real marriages, when society acknowledges no distinction between marriages that deserve the name, and relationships that merely borrow the title.

Ordinary conjugal people, who marry and raise children in the traditional way, and who believe that these acts point beyond the present moment to an indefinite future and a transcendental law, have a voice in law-making, and will tend to vote for legislators who uphold the sacramental view of marriage and who pass laws endorsing the normal way of marital sacrifice. From the external point of view, that is what an anthropologist would expect. For societies endure only when they are devoted to future generations, and collapse like the Roman Empire when the pleasures and fancies of the living consume the stock of social capital. In the United States, however, there is another way to legislation, through the Supreme Court, and this way is the way of the State and of the elites who control it. And because the US Supreme Court can override any merely democratically elected body, and will – as the case of *Roe v. Wade* amply demonstrates – use any measure of sophistical argument if it sees the need to do so, Americans are increasingly aware that – in many of the most important matters, the matters that govern the life and death of society – it is the State, not the people, that decides. The attitude of the State to marriage should, therefore, be set beside its attitude to sex education and the bearing of children. The burden of State-sponsored sex education, I have suggested, is to turn the sexual urge away from erotic passion, marital commitment and dutiful child-bearing, towards disposable pleasures. This attitude is reinforced by the State's support for abortion, and its 'discovery', in *Roe v. Wade*, that the unborn have no rights under the Constitution and therefore no rights at all. Put all this together with the State's constant tendency to erode the tie of marriage, and you will be tempted to believe that the State has set itself against the goal of reproduction. This has not been a conscious decision. Nevertheless, it reflects a vast movement in the modern world, towards the confiscation of hereditary rights.

Some will see this attitude as involving a kind of collective infanticide: such, I suspect, is the response of the Roman Catholic Church. Others, however, welcome it, even under the somewhat bleak description that I have offered. Thus Richard Rorty, in *Achieving Our Country*, ostensibly a critique of the anti-patriotism of the left establishment, sees the emergence of the easygoing culture of promiscuity, and the political correctness which is well on the way to censoring out every alternative, as positive steps towards the only thing that matters, which is an 'Enlightenment utopia' in which complete equality of condition will have at last been achieved. To get there you need the Supreme Court, if only to extinguish those exclusive passions and loyalties which are the source of local privilege. The fact that the resulting Utopia will be unable to reproduce itself is not a fact that pragmatists like Rorty are equipped to notice. And what a pragmatist doesn't notice is in any case not a fact...

GAY MARRIAGE

Heterosexual union is imbued with the sense that your partner's sexual nature is strange to you, a territory into which you intrude without prior knowledge and in which the other and not the self is the only reliable guide. This experience has profound repercussions for our sense of the danger and the mystery of sexual union, and these repercussions are surely part of what people have had in mind in clothing marriage as a sacrament, and the ceremony of marriage as a rite of passage from one form of safety to another. Traditional marriage was not only a rite of passage from adolescence to adulthood; nor was it only a way of endorsing and guaranteeing the raising of children. It was also a dramatization of sexual difference. Marriage kept the sexes at such a distance from each other that their coming together became an existential leap, rather than a passing experiment. The intentionality of desire was shaped by this, and even if the shaping was – at some deep level – a cultural and not a human universal, it endowed desire with its intrinsic nuptiality, and marriage with its transformatory goal. To regard gay marriage as simply another option within the institution is to ignore the fact that an institution shapes the motive for joining it. Marriage has grown around the idea of sexual difference and all that sexual difference means. To make this feature accidental rather than essential is to change marriage beyond recognition. Gays want marriage because they want the social endorsement that it signifies; but by admitting gay marriage we deprive marriage of its social meaning, as the blessing conferred by the unborn on the living. The pressure for gay marriage is, therefore, in a certain measure self-defeating. It resembles Henry VIII's move to gain ecclesiastical endorsement for his divorce, by making himself head of the Church. The Church that endorsed his divorce thereby ceased to be the Church whose endorsement he was seeking.

That does not alter the fact that gay marriage furthers the hidden tendency of the postmodern State, which is to rewrite all commitments as contracts between the living. It is a near certainty, therefore, that the American State, acting through the Supreme Court, will 'discover' a constitutional right to gay marriage just as it discovered constitutional rights to abortion and pornography, and just as it will discover, when asked, a right to no-fault divorce.

Those who are troubled by this, and who wish to register their protest, will have to struggle against powerful forms of censorship. People who dissent from what is fast becoming orthodoxy in the matter of 'gay rights' are now routinely accused of 'homophobia'. All over America there are appointment committees intent on examining candidates for suspected homophobia and summarily dismissing them once the accusation has been made: 'You can't have that woman pleading at the Bar, she is a Christian fundamentalist and a homophobe'; 'No, even if he is the world's authority on second dynasty hieroglyphs, you can't give him tenure, after that homophobic outburst last Friday'. This censorship will advance the cause of those who have made it their business to 'normalize' the idea of homosexual union. It will not be possible to resist it, any more than it has proved possible to resist the feminist censorship of the truth about sexual difference. But maybe it will be possible to entertain, between consenting adults in private, the thought that homosexual marriage is no such thing.

9

The Return of Religion

(From *Axess Magazine*, 2008)

Faced with the spectacle of the cruelties perpetrated in the name of faith, Voltaire famously cried 'Ecrasez l'infâme!'. Scores of enlightened thinkers followed him, declaring organized religion to be the enemy of mankind, the force that divides the believer from the infidel and which thereby both excites and authorizes murder. Richard Dawkins is the most influential living example of this tradition, and his message, echoed by Dan Dennett, Sam Harris and Christopher Hitchens, sounds as loud and strident in the media today as the message of Luther in the reformed churches of Germany. The violence of the diatribes uttered by these evangelical atheists is indeed remarkable. After all, the Enlightenment happened three centuries ago; the arguments of Hume, Kant and Voltaire have been absorbed by every educated person. What more is to be said? And if you must say it, why say it so stridently? Surely, those who oppose religion in the name of gentleness have a duty to be gentle, even with – especially with – their foes?

There are two reasons why people start shouting at their opponents: one is that they think the opponent is so strong that every weapon must be used against him; the other is that they think their own case so weak that it has to be fortified by noise. Both these motives can be observed in the evangelical atheists. They seriously believe that religion is a danger, leading people into excesses of enthusiasm which, precisely because they are inspired by irrational beliefs, cannot be countered by rational argument. We have had plenty of proof of this from the

Islamists; but that proof, the atheists tell us, is only the latest in a long history of massacres and torments, which – in the scientific perspective – might reasonably be called the pre-history of mankind. The Enlightenment promised to inaugurate another era, in which reason would be sovereign, providing an instrument of peace that all could employ. In the eyes of the evangelical atheists, however, this promise was not fulfilled. In their view of things, neither Judaism nor Christianity absorbed the Enlightenment even if, in a certain measure, they inspired it. All faiths, to the atheists, have remained in the condition of Islam today: rooted in dogmas that cannot be safely questioned. Believing this, they work themselves into a lather of vituperation against ordinary believers, including those believers who have come to religion in search of an instrument of peace, and who regard their faith as an exhortation to love their neighbour, even their belligerent atheist neighbour, as themselves.

At the same time, the atheists are reacting to the weakness of their case. Dawkins and Hitchens are adamant that the scientific worldview has entirely undermined the premises of religion and that only ignorance can explain the persistence of faith. But what exactly *does* modern science tell us, and just *where* does it conflict with the premises of religious belief? According to Dawkins (and Hitchens follows him in this), human beings are 'survival machines' in the service of their genes. We are, so to speak, by-products of a process that is entirely indifferent to our well-being, machines developed by our genetic material in order to further its reproductive goal. Genes themselves are complex molecules, put together in accordance with the laws of chemistry, from material made available in the primordial soup that once boiled on the surface of our planet. How it happened is not yet known: perhaps electrical discharges caused nitrogen, carbon, hydrogen and oxygen atoms to link together in appropriate chains, until finally one of them achieved that remarkable feature, of encoding the instructions for its own reproduction. Science may one day be able to answer the question how this occurred. But it is *science*, not religion, that will answer it.

As for the existence of a planet in which the elements abound in the quantities observed on planet earth, such a thing is again to be explained by science – though the science of astrophysics rather than the science of biology. The existence of the earth is part of a great unfolding process, which may or may not have begun with a Big Bang, and which contains many mysteries that physicists explore with ever increasing astonishment. Astrophysics has raised as many questions as it has answered. But they are scientific questions, to be solved by discovering the laws of motion that govern the observable changes at every level of the physical world, from galaxy to supernova, and from black hole to quark. The mystery that confronts us as we gaze upwards at the Milky Way, knowing that the myriad stars responsible for that smear of light are merely stars of a single galaxy, the galaxy that contains us, and that beyond its boundaries a myriad other galaxies slowly turn in space, some dying, some emerging, all forever inaccessible to us – this mystery does not call for a religious response. For it is a mystery that results from our partial knowledge and which can be solved only by further knowledge of the same kind – the knowledge that we call science.

Only ignorance would cause us to deny that general picture, and the evangelical atheists assume that religion *must* deny that picture and therefore must, at some level, commit itself to the propagation of ignorance or at any rate the prevention of knowledge. Yet I do not know a religious person among my friends and acquaintances who *does* deny that picture, or who regards it as posing the remotest difficulty for his faith. Dawkins writes as though the theory of the selfish gene puts paid once and for all to the idea of a creator God – we no longer need that hypothesis to explain how we came to be. In a sense that is true. But what about the gene itself: how did that come to be? What about the primordial soup? All these questions are answered, of course, by going one step further down the chain of causation. But at each step we encounter a world with a singular quality: namely that it is a world which, left to itself, will produce conscious beings, able to look for the reason and the meaning of things, and not just for the cause. The astonishing thing about our universe, that it contains consciousness, judgement, the knowledge of right and wrong, and all the other things that make the human condition so singular, is not rendered less astonishing by the hypothesis that this state of affairs emerged over time from other conditions. If true, that merely shows us how astonishing those other conditions were. The gene and the soup cannot be less astonishing than their product.

Moreover, these things would cease to astonish us – or rather, they would fall within the ambit of the comprehensible – if we could find a way to purge them of contingency. That is what religion promises: not a purpose, necessarily, but something that removes the paradox of an entirely law-governed world, open to consciousness, that is nevertheless without an explanation: that just *is*, for no reason at all. The evangelical atheists are subliminally aware that their abdication in the face of science does not make the universe more intelligible, nor does it provide an alternative answer to our metaphysical enquiries. It simply brings enquiry to a stop. And the religious person will feel that this stop is premature: that reason has more questions to ask, and perhaps more answers to obtain, than the atheists will allow us. So who, in this subliminal contest, is the truly reasonable one? The atheists beg the question in their own favour, by assuming that science has all the answers. But science can have all the answers only if it has all the questions; and that assumption is false. There are questions addressed to reason which are not addressed to science, since they are not asking for a causal explanation.

One of these is the question of consciousness. This strange universe of black holes and time warps, of event horizons and non-localities, somehow becomes conscious of itself. And it becomes conscious of itself in *us*. This fact conditions the very structure of science. The rejection of Newton's absolute space, the adoption of the space-time continuum, the quantum equations – all these are premised on the truth that scientific laws are instruments for predicting one set of observations from another. The universe that science describes is constrained at every point by observation. According to quantum theory, some of its most basic features become determinate only at the moment of observation. The great tapestry of waves and particles, of fields and forces, of matter and energy, is pinned down only at the edges, where events are crystallized in the observing mind.

Consciousness is more familiar to us than any other feature of our world, since it is the route by which anything at all becomes familiar. But this is what makes consciousness so hard to pinpoint. Look for it wherever you like, you encounter only its objects – a face, a dream, a memory, a colour, a pain, a melody, a problem, but nowhere the consciousness that shines on them. Trying to grasp it is like trying to observe your own observing, as though you were to look with your own eyes at your own eyes without using a mirror. Not surprisingly, therefore, the thought of consciousness gives rise to peculiar metaphysical anxieties, which we try to allay with images of the soul, the mind, the self, the 'subject of consciousness', the inner entity that thinks and sees and feels and which is the real me inside. But these traditional 'solutions' merely duplicate the problem. We cast no light on the consciousness of a human being simply by re-describing it as the consciousness of some inner homunculus – be it a soul, a mind or a self. On the contrary, by placing that homunculus in some private, inaccessible and possibly immaterial realm, we merely compound the mystery.

It is this mystery which brings people back to religion. They may have no clear conception of science; no theological aptitude, and no knowledge of the arguments, down the ages, that have persuaded people that the fabric of contingency must be supported by a 'necessary being'. The subtleties of the medieval schools for the most part make little contact with the thinking of believers today. Modern people are drawn to religion by their consciousness of consciousness, by their awareness of a light shining in the centre of their being. And, as Kant brilliantly showed, the person who is acquainted with the self, who refers to himself as 'I', is inescapably trapped into freedom. He rises above the wind of contingency that blows through the natural world, held aloft by Reason's necessary laws. The 'I' defines the starting point of all practical reasoning and contains an intimation of the thing that distinguishes people from the rest of nature, namely their freedom. There is a sense in which animals too are free: they make choices, do things both freely and by constraint. But animals are not accountable for what they do. They are not called upon to justify their conduct, nor are they persuaded or dissuaded by dialogue with others. All those goals, like justice, community and love, which make human life into a thing of intrinsic value, have their origin in the mutual accountability of persons, who respond to each other 'I' to 'I'. Not surprisingly, therefore, people are satisfied that they understand the world and know its meaning, when they can see it as the outward form of another 'I' – the 'I' of God, in which we all stand judged, and from which love and freedom flow.

That thought may be poured out in verse, as in the *Veni Creator Spiritus* of the Catholic Church, in the rhapsodic words of Krishna in the *Baghavad Gita*, in the great Psalms that are the glory of the Hebrew Bible. But for most people it is simply there, a dense nugget of meaning in the centre of their lives, which weighs heavily when they find no way to express it in communal forms. People continue to look for the places where they can stand, as it were, at the window of our empirical world and gaze out towards the transcendental – the places from which breezes from that other sphere waft over them. Not so long ago, God was in residence. You could open a door and discover him, and join with those who sang and prayed in his presence. Now he, like us, has no fixed abode. But from this experience a new kind of religious consciousness is being born: a turning of the inner eye towards the transcendental and a constant invocation of 'we know not what'.

Distrust of organized religion therefore goes hand in hand with a mourning for the loss of it. We are distressed by the evangelical atheists, who are stamping on the coffin in which they imagine God's corpse to lie and telling us to bury it quickly before it begins to smell. These characters have a violent and untidy air: it is very obvious that something is missing from their lives, something which would bring order and completeness in the place of random disgust. And yet we are uncertain how to answer them. Nowhere in our world is the door that we might open, so as to stand again in the breath of God.

Yet human beings have an innate need to conceptualize their world in terms of the transcendental, and to live out the distinction between the sacred and the profane. This need is rooted in self-consciousness and in the experiences that remind us of our shared and momentous destiny as members of Kant's

'Kingdom of Ends'. Those experiences are the root of human as opposed to merely animal society, and we need to affirm them, self-knowingly to possess them, if we are to be at ease with our kind. Religions satisfy this need. For they provide the social endorsement and the theological infrastructure that will hold the concepts of the transcendental and the sacred in place. The insecurity and disorder of Western societies comes from the tension in which people are held when they cannot attach their inner awareness of the transcendental to the outward forms of religious ritual. People have turned away from organized religion, as they have turned away from organized everything else. But the atheists who dance on the coffin of the old religions will never persuade them to live as though the thing inside were dead. God has fled, but he is not dead. He is biding his time, waiting for us to make room for him. That, at least, is how I read the growing obsession with religion and the nostalgia for what we lost when the congregations shut their Bibles and their hymn books, broke asunder and went silently home.

SECTION 4

Culture

10

The Aesthetic Gaze

(From *Modern Culture*, 2000)

What exactly does the word 'aesthetic' mean? The question is not just one of definition – it is one of discovery, identification and description. There is a state of mind, an attitude, a stance towards the world, for which we have borrowed, under the influence of Enlightenment philosophers, a Greek word that means something quite different. (*Aesthesis* denotes sensation or perception.) Why have we singled out this state of mind (if that is what it is)? What is important about it, and why should it have been ennobled by so many artists and thinkers, to sit on a throne archaically devoted to the gods?

Those questions are among the most difficult that philosophers have to confront – which perhaps explains why no philosophers now confront them. You cannot expect an impregnable theory of the aesthetic in two pages. Nevertheless, we need a theory of *some* kind, and what follows is the best I can do.

Rational activity involves both ends and means. In a technological age we acquire an increasing grasp of the means to our goals, and a decreasing grasp of the reasons why we should pursue them. The clarity of purpose that I observed in Homer's Odysseus is not a clarity about means: it is a clarity about ends, about the things that are worth doing *for their own sake*, like grieving and loving and honouring the gods. The mastery of means that emancipated mankind from drudgery has brought with it a mystery of ends – an inability to answer, to one's own satisfaction, the question what to feel or do. The mystery deepens with the advent of the consumer society, when all the channels of social life are devoted to consumption. For consumption, in its everyday form, is not really an *end*. It destroys the thing consumed and leaves us empty-handed: the consumer's goals are perpetually recurring illusions, which vanish at the very moment they loom into view, destroyed by the appetite that seeks them. The consumer society is therefore phantasmagoric, a place in which the ghosts of satisfactions are pursued by the ghosts of real desires.[1]

In the world of religion all things appear in two guises: as instruments for our uses, and as creations, earthly manifestations of some higher design. The myths and sacred stories shine through their earthly instances, and the ordinary world is transfigured into a realm of miracles. Everything is what it is, while representing something else – the higher form of itself that is narrated in the myth. The world of Odysseus has not been 'instrumentalized'; it has not yet been enslaved by the imperatives of human desire. Still less is it a world of consumables, to be devoured by relentless and ultimately purposeless appetites. Objects in this world are both instruments and signs: and, in their semantic aspect, they reflect back to the observer a vision of his social life. He confronts in them not objects only, but the eyes of the gods, who remind him of his duties and offer comforting, socially endorsed instructions. In modern jargon, the Greek hero is not *alienated* from the things he uses, but lives with them on terms of respect, finding in the midst of means, the ends which make them useful.

Take away religion, however, and this easy path to comfort is at once overgrown with doubt and fear and selfishness. Add technological mastery, and nature begins to lose all trace of the divine; the old mysteries and myths give way to the new mystery – the mystery of ends in a world of means. In such a predicament people experience a deep-down need for the thing that is not just desired but valued; the *unconsumable* thing, wanted not as a means but for its own sake, as an end. The idea of the sacred satisfies that need – but only by requiring faith and devotion. Besides, it is not the sacred object which is the end but the god who shines through it. The peculiarity of the sacred object is that it is a *necessary means*, one that cannot be replaced or discarded, without fundamentally changing the character of the god to which it is the avenue. Hence sacred objects are filled with an aura of meaning – they are places where calculation stops, where the endless pursuit of means is measured against a value which is not instrumental but intrinsic.

Imagine a sacred statue of the god, placed within its shrine, visited by worshippers who lay their gifts before it. Among the visitors is an enlightened philosopher. He does not worship since he no longer believes in the god; but he is moved by the reverential atmosphere, by the sublime stillness of the sculpture, and the serene belief to which it testifies. He does not address the image with religious feeling as his neighbours do; he does not treat it as an avenue through which another and higher being can be approached and mollified. His emotion attaches to the image itself. The signifier has become the signified. It is *this* thing, the statue, which is or contains the meaning of the shrine. The enlightened visitor directs his attention to the stone, to the way it is worked and finished, to the expression on the face of the god, and the breathing limbs of marble. It is an image of the divine, replete with a more than human tenderness and concern. These epithets describe not the god but the statue. The enlightened visitor does not believe the sacred story; so far as he is concerned, the god is a fiction. His awe is not religious, but aesthetic. To put it another way: he rejoices in the statue, not for the god's sake, but for its own sake. Every meaning that he finds in this marble figure resides, for him, in the figure itself. To the believer the statue is a means to the god; to the philosopher the god is a means to the statue. Yet neither is guilty of idolatry.

I have described there a paradigm case of aesthetic interest. The visitor is interested in the sculpture not as an instrument or a document, but for its own sake. The interest is essentially visual, and bound up with the appearance of what is seen. Aesthetic interest is not cut off from intellectual or spiritual concerns: for these too affect the experience. The god's face has a serene appearance, and this serenity, which invades the face and shines from it, is part of the way the statue looks. In aesthetic interest appearances become signs – signs of themselves.

Kant described aesthetic interest as 'disinterested'. This is what I take him to mean: all animals have interests. They are interested in satisfying their needs and desires, and in gathering the information required for their well-being. Rational beings have such interests, and use their reason in pursuing them. But they also have 'interests of reason': interests which arise from their rationality, and which are in no clear way related to desires, needs and appetites. One of these, according to Kant, is morality. Reason motivates us to do our duty, and all other ('empirical') interests are discounted in the process. That is what it *means* for a decision to be a moral one. The interest in doing right is not an interest of mine, but an interest of reason *in* me.

Reason also has an interest in the sensuous world. When a cow stands in a field ruminating, and turning her eyes to view the horizon, we can say that she is interested in what is going on (and in particular, in the presence of potential threats to her safety), but not that she is interested in the *view*. A rational being, by contrast, takes pleasure in the mere sight of something: a sublime landscape, a beautiful animal, an intricate flower, or a work of art. This form of pleasure answers to no empirical interest: I satisfy no bodily appetite or need in contemplating the landscape, nor do I merely scan it for useful information. The interest is disinterested – an interest in the landscape for its own sake, for the very thing that it is (or rather, for the very thing that it appears). Disinterestedness is a mark of an 'interest of reason'. We cannot refer it to our empirical nature, but only to the reason that transcends empirical nature, and which searches the world for a meaning that is more authoritative and more complete than any that flows from desire.

On this account, we should hardly be surprised to discover that the aesthetic is a realm of *value*. We perceive in the objects of aesthetic interest a meaning beyond the moment – a meaning which also *resides* in the moment, incarnate, as it were, in a sensory impression. The disinterested observer is haunted by a question: is it right to take pleasure in *this*? Hence arises the idea of taste. We discriminate between the objects of aesthetic interest, find reasons for and against them, and see in each other's choice the sign and expression of moral character. A person who needs urgently to cut a rope and therefore takes up the knife that lies beside him, does not, in choosing that instrument, reveal his character. The knife is a means, and it was the best means to hand. The person with no such use for the knife, who nevertheless places it on his desk and endlessly studies it, thereby shows something of himself. Aesthetic interest does not stem from our passing desires: it reveals what we are and what we value. Taste, like style, is the man himself.

The same is true of all experiences and activities in which something is treated not as a means, but as an end in itself. When I work, my activity is generally a means to an end – making money, for example. When I play, however, my activity is an end in itself. Play is not a means to enjoyment; it is the very thing enjoyed. And it provides the archetype of other activities that penetrate and give sense to our adult lives: sport, conversation, socialising, and all that we understand by art. Schiller noticed this, and went so far as to exalt play into the paradigm of intrinsic value. With the useful and the good, he remarked, man is merely in earnest; but with the beautiful he *plays*. (*Letters on the Aesthetic Education of Man.*)

There is an element of paradoxism in Schiller's remark. But you can extract from it a thought that is far from paradoxical, namely this: if every activity is a means to an end, then no activity has intrinsic value. The world is then deprived of its sense. If, however, there are activities that we engage in for their own sake, the world is restored to us and we to it. For of these activities we do not ask what they are *for*; they are sufficient in themselves. Play is one of them; and its association with childhood reminds us of the essential innocence and exhilaration that attends such 'disinterested' activities. If work becomes play – so that the worker is fulfilled in his work, regardless of what results from it – then work ceases to be drudgery, and becomes instead 'the restoration of man to himself'. Those last words are Marx's, and contain the core of his theory of 'unalienated labour' – a theory which derives from Kant, via Schiller and Hegel.

Consider conversation: each utterance calls forth a rejoinder; but in the normal case there is no direction towards which the conversation tends. The participants respond to what they hear with matching remarks, but the conversation proceeds unpredictably and purposelessly, until business interrupts it.

Although we gain much information from conversation, this is not its primary purpose. In the normal case, as when people 'pass the time of day', conversation is engaged in for its own sake, like play. The same is true of dancing.

These paradigms of the purposeless can be understood only if we take care to distinguish purpose from function. A socio-biologist will insist that play has a function: it is the safest way to explore the world, and to prepare the child for action. But function is not purpose. The child plays in order to play: play is its own purpose. If you make the function into the purpose – playing for the sake of learning, say – then you cease to play. You are now, as Schiller puts it, 'merely in earnest'. Likewise the urgent person, who converses in order to gain or impart some information, to elicit sympathy or to tell his story, has ceased to converse. Like the Ancient Mariner, he is the death of dialogue.

The same is true of friendship. This too has a function. It binds people together, makes communities strong and durable, brings advantages to those who are joined by it and fortifies them in their endeavours. But make these advantages into your purpose, and the friendship is gone. Friendship is a means to advantage, but only when not treated as a means. The same applies to almost everything worthwhile: education, sport, hiking, fishing, hunting and art. If we are to live properly, therefore – not merely consuming the world but loving it and valuing it – we must cultivate the art of finding ends where we might have found only means. We must learn when and how to set our interests aside, not out of boredom or disgust, but out of disinterested passion for the thing itself.

Of the greatest importance in our lives, therefore, are festive occasions, when we join with other people in doing purposeless things. Sport – and spectator sport in particular – provides a telling instance of this. Look back to the first flowering of our civilization in ancient Greece, and you will find sport already in the centre of social life, a focus of loyalties, a rehearsal of military prowess and a pious tribute to the gods. Pindar wrote in praise of winners at the pan-Hellenic games. But his odes are not records of the fleeting victories of the various contestants. They are descriptions of the gods and their stories, invocations of the divine presence in a place and a time, and an exalted celebration of what it means to be a Hellene among Hellenes, sharing language, history, divinities and fate. They show us the spectator as another participant. His excited cheers, we recognize, are brought up from the very depths of his social being, as a contribution to the action and a kind of recreation of the religious sense. Where there is a true common culture, sport is always a central part of it; and the joyful abundance of religious feeling floods over the event: the gods too are present in the hippodrome, eagerly encouraging their favourites.

A modern football match differs from the ancient chariot race in many ways, the most important being the lack of a religious focus. Nevertheless there are important analogies, most readily observable in the American case, with its great hulks fighting each other like armoured knights for every inch of the field, its roaring crowds in their Sabbath humour, its cheer-leaders bouncing and bobbing with choreographed movements and girlish shouts, its jazz groups and marching bands in uniform, its swirling banners and hand-held vacillating flags. In such events we see a kind of collective exultation which is also an exaltation of the community of fans.

The interest in sport is not yet an aesthetic interest: for there is the unpredictable outcome, the partisanship, the triumph and disaster, towards which all the action is subservient. But it is proximate to the aesthetic, just as it is proximate to the religious. The shared and festive exultation lifts the event high above the world of means, and endows it with a meaning. The game has some of the representational quality of the aesthetic object. It both is itself and stands for itself; once played it becomes a mythic narrative in the annals of the sport, and a tale of heroes. The surplus of interest in the world which spills over in sport is the mark of rational beings, who are satisfied only by supremely useless things.

Still, there is something transient and unfulfilling in even the most exciting football match: the narrative of the match, the myth, can be repeated; but the match, once played, is gone. In aesthetic contemplation, however, we finally step out of the world of perishable things, and find the *unconsumable object*, which is a value in itself. Such things offer visions of the end of life, emancipated from the means. Some of these objects – landscapes, seascapes and skies – are found. But others are made – and when we make them we are consciously addressing what is most attentive, most searching and most responsive in our nature. When the aesthetic becomes a human goal, therefore, it situates itself of its own accord at the apex of our communicative efforts. We make objects replete with meaning, which present human life in its permanent aspect, through fictions and images that enable us to set aside our interests and take stock of the world.

That brief account of aesthetic interest enables us to cast light on high culture. A high culture is a tradition, in which objects made for aesthetic contemplation renew through their allusive power the experience of membership. Religion may wither and festivals decline without destroying high culture, which creates its own 'imagined community', and which offers, through, the aesthetic experience, a 'rite of passage' into the kingdom of ends.[2]

Aesthetic objects, when made, invite us to an 'interest of reason' – a self-conscious placing of ourselves in relation to the thing considered, and a search for meaning which looks neither for information nor practical utility, but for the insight which religion also promises: insight into the why and whither of our being here. Fiction is of the greatest significance in high culture, for the reason that fictional objects are creatures of the imagination. Hence, by pondering them, we free ourselves from our ordinary interests, and enter a realm where practical questions are not mine or yours or anyone's, but the imaginary questions of imaginary beings. Myth is the province of religion; but myth is not fiction, since it does not deal in imaginary worlds. It is received as a narrative of *this* world, but on a higher plane, in which individual characters are dissolved into archetypes, and accidents subsumed by fate. In the mythic narrative everything is typified, and both characters and actions lose their individuality. When the subject of the drama is individualized, myth becomes fiction – the presentation of *another* world, with all the specificity of this one.

Despite these differences, myth and high culture have much in common. Each is concerned to idealize the human condition, to lift it free from contingencies, and to reveal the inner logic of our passions. Fictional characters are not archetypes but individuals: nevertheless, their characters are filtered through the screen of drama, and only what is typical stands out – typical of that individual, in that predicament. In fiction the dross of contingency is purged, and human life becomes a sign whose meaning is itself. In a high culture, fictional situations and characters are topics of meditation and instruction, as Odysseus was. They create a commentary on this world through thoughts of other worlds, where sympathy runs free. Yet the object of interest is always also here and now – the particular words, sounds, sights and gestures that are brought before us by the work of art. It is scarcely surprising, therefore, that there should attach to the products of a high culture the same sense of profound mystery and ineffable meaning that is the daily diet of religion. Our lives are transfigured in art, and redeemed of their arbitrariness, their contingency and littleness. This redemption occurs with no leap into the transcendental, no summoning of the god of the shrine, but simply in a purposeless encounter with a useless object. It therefore haunts us with its familiarity, its this-worldliness, its human pathos.

It seems to me that the art of our high culture – and not only of ours – has drawn upon and amplified the experiences which are given in less conscious form by religion: experiences of the sacred and the profane, of redemption from sin and the immersion in it, of guilt, sorrow and their overcoming through forgiveness and the oneness of a community restored. Art has grown from the sacred view of life. And that is why art suddenly leapt into prominence at the Enlightenment, with the eclipse of sacred things. Thereafter art became a redeeming enterprise, and the artist stepped into the place vacated by the prophet and the priest. People began to dispute passionately over the difference between good art and bad, and to construct curricula whose sole contents were the masterpieces of a literary, musical or artistic tradition.

At this point you might object to the direction of my argument. Surely, you will say, to place art and religion in such proximity is to ignore their essential rivalry. Religion involves the expression and enforcement of a shared belief. It is a matter of faith and obedience. Art requires no common belief, but only an imaginative involvement with situations, characters, ideas and life-styles that may have no independent appeal. We can find beauty in works which grow from false religions, which express other cultures, and which reflect worldviews remote from ours. Indeed, on one plausible view, it is part of the value of art, that it causes us to widen our emotional horizons, by inducing imaginative sympathy with forms of life that run counter to our expectations. And you might go further, offering as one justification for Western civilization that – thanks to the Enlightenment – it has emancipated art from religious usage, set it against the reign of prejudice, and created, by means of the imagination, a moral space – a place of freedom and experiment – that has never existed elsewhere.

You might also take exception to my argument from the religious perspective. To narrow the distance between art and religion, you might say, is to run the risk of aestheticizing religion, so voiding it of faith and worship. It is to make an idol of art, and to demote the supremely important matter, which is faith and its moral sequel, to a subordinate position in the scheme of things. It is, to borrow Tom Paine's metaphor, to pity the plumage and forget the dying bird.

Two considerations might neutralise those objections. Faith and worship are the goals of religious practice, and for the believer they are ends in themselves. But to the anthropologist, looking on religion from a point of view outside it, faith and worship are means, not ends. Religion has a twofold social function: to establish the motives on which a community depends; and to teach the art of feeling. By sacralizing the core experiences of society, religion eternalises our commitments, makes us admirable to one another, elevates the human person to the summit of creation, and gives sense and direction to our lives. It does this in a unique way, by offering to all-comers, whatever their education, the experience of sacred words and rituals. This experience transfigures human life, and imbues it with a long-term dutifulness. But it is available only through faith. It is outside the reach of the anthropologist, whose knowledge of the function of religion sets him at a distance from its doctrines. The function is fulfilled only by those who are ignorant of it, and who devote their attention to the gods.

Art too has a function – and it is closely related. Art ennobles the human spirit, and presents us with a justifying vision of ourselves, as something higher than nature and apart from it. It does this, not as a religion does, by demanding belief and worship. For it engages our sympathies without compelling any doctrine. We are not *aware* of this function, unless subliminally. Nevertheless it informs our judgements, and causes us to evaluate works of art as more or less moving, more or less compelling, more or less serious. When a work of art conveys a view of things, our interest is not in the truth of that view, but in the extent to which it can be incorporated into a life of lasting commitment and serious feeling.

The point was made in other terms by T.S. Eliot, in an early essay on Shelley, and later, in *The Use of Poetry and the Use of Criticism*, where he tries to justify his low opinion of Shelley as a poet. Eliot criticizes Shelley not for the atheistical views expressed in his poems – much as Eliot disapproved of them – but because these views are entertained in a puerile way. They are not put to the test, not given the kind of poetic examination which would show how a life of serious feeling could be built on them. They lack the seriousness and sincerity that would make them worthy of imaginative endorsement. Such, in a nutshell, is Eliot's answer to the problem of 'poetry and belief', and it seems to me to be the right one.

Furthermore, to say that the function of art lies close to that of religion is not to aestheticize religion. It is merely to notice – what is all-important to us, who live in a cynical age – that for those blessed by a high culture it is possible, though with ever-increasing difficulty, to retain the consoling vision which religion grants to all its supplicants. It is possible, through the complicitous web of feeling that a culture keeps in place, to look on the human spirit as a thing redeemed.

If those thoughts are true, then they help to explain the importance of tradition, and of its complement, originality. An artistic tradition is a constantly evolving system of conventions, allusions, cross-references and shared expectations. Themes, forms, ornaments and styles are things both inherited and invented, and the inheritance is part of what makes the invention possible. The successful work of art presents exemplary content in exemplary form; its character as an end implies that it is irreplaceable – there is no other work that will 'do just as well', since what it does is itself. Hence it is always there, never surpassed or replaced, always to be revisited. Inevitably, therefore, a high culture involves a repertoire, an accumulation of works of art and exemplary utterances, which create the common ground in which the new and the surprising are planted.

Words in a language owe their meaning to conventions, and we learn the language by internalizing the rules. It is a convention of English that chickens are denoted by the word 'chicken', and not by 'poule' or 'dajajah'. Once in use, however, a word acquires meaning in another way, through the association of sound and sense, through colliding and consorting with other words in a language, through the literary works which exploit its expressive potential, and so on. Hence the English 'chicken' has an aura distinct from Arabic 'dajajah', and poems about chickens cannot be translated without loss of meaning from one language to the other.

Meaning in art does not arise from conventions or rules. On the contrary, conventions and rules arise from meaning. The meaning of a chord in music is not arbitrarily assigned like the meaning of a word, but attached by the magnetic force of context. Gradually, as chords are used and re-used, their musical potential becomes standardized; they become mossed over with allusions and reminiscences. It is only then that artistic conventions (like that of the twelve-bar blues) make sense: by exploiting and standardizing a meaning that is achieved in another way. Moreover, art, unlike language, is intrinsically suspicious of this standardizing process. Convention is tolerable only as a background to other and more individual meanings: if it becomes the foreground of the artistic enterprise, the result is cliché. The constant lapse into cliché, and the fastidious fear of it, are marks of a high culture in decline.

Allusion and elusiveness are as important in high culture as they are in the language and rites of a religion. To explain is to alienate: it is to show something as 'outside', observed but not internalized. It is to place conception above experience, as in science or historical research. Nothing is significant aesthetically, unless embodied in, and revealed through, experience. Hence the need for allusion, which imports a reference without describing it, so leaving the thread of pure experience unbroken. Moreover, allusions, unlike explanations, create a social context: common knowledge, common references, common symbols, embodied in an experience assumed also to be common. In grasping an allusion we enter a shared experience and an implied community.

An allusion is designed to be noticed: it expressly summons one work into the orbit of another. Allusions exploit familiarity and also create it, binding the high culture into a many-stranded web. Literary forms are themselves allusive: heroic couplets point the English reader to Pope and Dryden, as does the sonnet to Shakespeare, Donne and Wordsworth, while the unrhymed pentameters of Tennyson stand in the shadow of Wordsworth, looking constantly upwards to that source. The intentions of the author play with the expectations of the reader, and it is thus that a literary culture arises – a complex and communal game, but one of the highest seriousness, whose subject-matter is a shared experience of life.

The self-conscious act of sharing is essentially *critical* – it both idealizes human emotion and also elicits sympathy; it therefore cannot escape judging and being judged. It is right to sympathize, for example with Othello's final grief over the woman he has murdered (and in any case, it is really *grief* over *her?*)? An artistic tradition is an exercise of imagination; it is also an exercise of taste, which is in turn a meditation on human experience and an attempt to build a shared conception of what is worthy of our concern. The disgusting, the morbid, the banal and the sentimental are avoided, or not avoided only because unnoticed – which itself bespeaks a decline of taste. It is in epochs of cultural decline that criticism becomes important. Criticism is a last ditch attempt to be part of the artistic tradition, to retain the internal perspective on an inherited culture, and to fight off the corruption of sentiment that comes about when cliché and sentimentality are mistaken for sincere expression. By eliciting sympathy towards empty forms, the cliché impoverishes the emotional life of those who are drawn to it. Hence the extreme vigilance with which modern critics try to draw the line between the genuine and the fake emotion.

Although artists borrow procedures, forms and repertoires, although they are contributing to a continuous and publicly validated enterprise, they can make no impact merely by copying what has already been done. The encounter with the individual is what makes art so supremely interesting: we, the audience, have set our interests aside, in order to open ourselves to what another person is, says and feels. It need not be new; but it must at least be *his*. A work is original to the extent that it *originates* in its creator. It shows us the world from his or her perspective, draws us into spheres which are not our own, and enables us to rehearse the possibilities of feeling on which an ideal community – a community of sympathy – is founded. Without originality the high culture will die, drooping into tired gestures and imitative rituals, like the worn-out ceremonies of a religion that is no longer believed.

Originality is not an attempt to capture attention come what may, or to shock or disturb in order to shut out competition from the world. The most original works of art may be genial applications of a well-known vocabulary, like the late quartets of Haydn, or whispered meditations like the Sonnets of Rilke. They may be all but unnoticeable amid the fanfares of contemporary self-advertisement, like the trapped interiors of Vuillard or the tucked-away churches of Borromini. What makes them original is not their defiance of the past or their rude assault on settled expectations, but the element of surprise with which they invest the forms and repertoire of a tradition. Without tradition, originality cannot exist: for it is only against a tradition that it becomes perceivable. Tradition and originality are two components of a single process, whereby the individual makes himself known through his membership of the historical group.

Although the aesthetic experience is central to high culture, it is not the only source upon which a culture draws. Any social in which we strive to give meaning to something as an end attracts to itself the community of sentiment for which we spontaneously hunger. Two significant instances of this are costumes and manners. In a flourishing high culture people dress not only for the utility of dressing, but also as a part of social display, signalling through their costumes their place in an idealized community, and representing their character and their social valency in the forms and colours of their clothes. Manners have a similar meaning: they too are part of representation, and although manners have a function, in binding communities together and smoothing the edges where friction occurs, the function is not the purpose. Only when manners are cultivated for their own sake, for the grace and good nature that are intrinsic to them, do they fulfil their function of oiling the social wheels. And when the function becomes the purpose, as in much modern business, manners become a thin pretence.

Still, it is the work of art which has, since the Enlightenment, provided our paradigm of high culture; and there is a reason for this. When a common culture declines, the ethical life can be sustained and renewed only by a work of the imagination. And that, in a nutshell, is why high culture matters.

NOTES

1. That which is, to my mind, most enduring in Marx's contribution to the study of political economy, is his recognition of the hallucinogenic character of a money-economy, as exemplified by what he called 'commodity fetishism'; see *Capital*, vol. 1, ch. 1, section 4.

2. I take the term 'imagined community' from Benedict Anderson, whose book is devoted to another but closely related question – the question of nationalism.

11

Knowledge and Feeling
(From *Culture Counts*, 2007)

It is one of the most deeply rooted superstitions of our age that the purpose of education is to benefit those who receive it. What we teach in school, what subjects we encourage in universities, and the methods of instruction are all subject to the one over-arching test: what do the kids get out of it? And this test soon gives way to another, yet more pernicious in its effect, but no less persuasive in the thinking of educationists: is it relevant? And by 'relevant' is invariably meant 'relevant to the interests of the kids themselves'. From these superstitions have arisen all the recipes for failure that have dominated our educational systems: the proliferation of ephemeral subjects, the avoidance of difficulties, methods of teaching that strive to maintain interest at all costs – even at the cost of knowledge. Whether we put the blame on Rousseau, whose preposterous book *Émile* began the habit of sentimentalizing the process whereby knowledge is transferred from one brain to another, on John Dewey, whose hostility to 'rote learning' and old-fashioned discipline led to the fashion for 'child-centred learning', or simply on the egalitarian ideas which were bound to sweep through our schools when teachers were no longer properly remunerated – in whatever way we apportion blame, it is clear that we have entered a period of rapid educational decline, in which some people learn masses, but the masses learn little or nothing at all.

THE GOAL OF KNOWLEDGE

The superstition that I referred to is, in a certain measure, the opposite of the truth. True teachers do not provide knowledge as a benefit to their pupils; they treat their pupils as a benefit to knowledge. Of course they love their pupils; but they love knowledge more. And their over-riding concern is to pass on that knowledge by lodging it in brains that will last longer than their own. Their methods are not 'child-centred' but 'knowledge-centred', and the focus of their interest is the subject, rather than the things that might make that subject for the time being 'relevant' to matters of no intellectual concern. Any attempt to make education relevant risks reducing it to those parts that are of relevance to the uneducated – which are invariably the parts with the shortest life-span. A relevant curriculum is one from which the difficult core of knowledge has been excised, and while it may be relevant now it will be futile in a few years' time. Conversely irrelevant-seeming knowledge, when properly acquired, is not merely a discipline that can be adapted and applied; it has a knack of being exactly what is needed, in circumstances that nobody foresaw. The 'irrelevant' sciences of Boolean algebra and Fregean logic gave birth, in time, to the digital computer; the 'irrelevant' studies of Greek, Latin and ancient history enabled a tiny number of British graduates to govern an Empire that stretched around the world, while the 'irrelevant' paradoxes of Kant's *Critique of Pure Reason* caused the theory of relativity to dawn in the mind of Albert Einstein.

It is worth saying all that, not only because the superstitions to which I refer are so deeply rooted in our modern ways of thinking, but also because those who adopt them will never see the educational value of culture, and will never have a clue as to how it might be taught. What does it benefit ordinary children that they should know the works of Shakespeare, acquire a taste for Bach or develop an interest in medieval Latin? All such attainments merely isolate a child from his peers, place a veil between his thinking and the only world where he can apply it, and are at best an eccentricity, at worst a handicap. My reply is simple: it may not benefit the child – not yet, at least. But it will benefit culture. And because

153

culture is a form of knowledge, it is the business of the teacher to look for the pupil who will pass it on.

TYPES OF KNOWLEDGE

To make good that reply, however, I must say a little about knowledge. When we say that Mary knows something, we imply that her way of thinking and acting is responsive to the way things are, so that her judgement is reliable and her actions blessed with success. Thus if I say, 'She really knows this stuff', patting a book of physics, you can take it that Mary is someone who could tell you the facts about physics. Likewise, when I point to her in the dressage arena and say, 'She really knows what she is doing', you will infer that, if you follow her example, you too will ride a horse. The topic of knowledge is hotly disputed among philosophers, but that much at least is agreed. And it explains why knowledge is important, and why human beings have developed procedures and institutions for acquiring it and passing it on. Knowledge gained is a gain for all of us; knowledge lost, a loss that all must bear. It does not matter who possesses the knowledge: the important thing is that it should be there, publicly available, and that human beings should know how to recuperate it from the common fund. That is what education does for us: it keeps knowledge alive, by endowing people with the ability to summon it, either because they have internalized it like Mary, or because they have learned to unlock the books and records in which it is sequestered. That textbook of physics may contain all the knowledge that we need about its subject matter, but without Mary and people like her this knowledge will be lost – and maybe lost forever. You and I have a key to that knowledge, which is: 'Ask Mary'. But unless someone really 'knows this stuff', books and records are no better than the book of nature, which stares at us mutely until we rediscover the spell that makes it speak.

It is sometimes said that we now live in a 'knowledge economy', and that 'information technology' has vastly increased the extent and accessibility of human knowledge. Both claims are false. 'Information technology' simply means the use of digital algorithms in the transference of messages.

The 'information' that is processed is not information *about* anything, nor does it have its equivalent in knowledge. It treats truth and falsehood, reality and fantasy, as equivalent, and has no means to assess the difference. Indeed, as the Internet reveals, information technology is far more effective in propagating ignorance than in advancing science. For, in the conquest of cyberspace, ignorance has a flying start, being adapted to the habits of idle minds. Similarly, the claim that we exist in a 'knowledge economy' is entirely unfounded. The effect of information technology is to give images precedence over thought and to multiply a thousand-fold the noise that fills the space in which ideas are conceived and brokered. Hence when it comes to the great decisions, noise drowns out, the still small voice of understanding. It was knowledge that enabled those 1,000 British civil servants to govern the vast subcontinent of India, or a comparable number of Roman citizens to bring law and order to the entire civilized world. It was knowledge painfully acquired from books and acquired in silence – and it was acquired because the competing noise had been carefully filtered out by educational institutions that created a common frame of reference among those who attended them. America today has several million civil servants, engaged in multiplying and perpetuating each others' mistakes, and the cause of this is information.

There is another reason for distrusting the easy equation of information with knowledge, which is that it represents knowledge as a single kind of thing. The paradigm proposed is that of factual knowledge, the kind of knowledge that can be contained in a textbook and deployed by the person who understands what the textbook says. But that is only one kind of knowledge, and a comparative late-comer to the scene of human instruction. There is also practical knowledge – the knowledge that shows itself in the skills of the hunter-gatherer or the soldier, and equally in the ability to nurse, to support and to console. Greek philosophers distinguished, in this connection, *theoria* from *praxis*, arguing that both are exercises of the rational mind. For just as there are reasons for believing, so are there reasons for action, and while the first count towards the truth of what is believed, the second count towards the rightness of what is done. The person with knowledge is the one who can be relied upon to guide us towards reason's goal, which is truth in the one case, rightness in the other.

In ordinary language we make a distinction between knowing *that* and knowing *how*, and the philosopher Gilbert Ryle pinpointed this fact as a kind of warrant for the ancient distinction. I know that the earth goes round the sun, and I know how to ride a bicycle. The first is knowledge of a fact, the second knowledge of a technique. And clearly I can know how to ride a bicycle even if I haven't the faintest idea of the theory which explains why bicycles stay upright when ridden. Conversely I can be entirely conversant with the theory, and have no ability to stay aloft on a bicycle.

ENDS AND MEANS

If that were all that the distinction between theoretical and practical knowledge amounted to, we should be hard-pressed to find a place for culture in the curriculum. We should have on the one hand the hard sciences – like physics, chemistry, and math – together with history and geography, all of which deal in facts. And, on the other hand, we should have technical disciplines – engineering, craft, and sports. Languages, which involve both factual knowledge and practical skills, would form a kind of intermediate zone, but culture would be nowhere on the curriculum. What facts do you learn from Chaucer other than the fact that he wrote those poems? And what skills has a medieval Englishman to communicate through his poetry, to the busy children of today?

Surely, however, there is more to practical knowledge than skills and techniques. Someone who has mastered the military arts may use them for good ends or bad, and the same is true of any skill. Yet there is something more to be learned, when we learn a skill, which is how to make proper use of it. The good soldier, as this character was drawn in literature, was not merely someone who had mastered the arts of warfare; he was someone for whom the sense of honour and duty governed all that he did, in whom impatience with insults and challenges was tempered by chivalry and the desire to protect. In short, he was someone with a specific set of military virtues – virtues that might very well lead him into danger or into other kinds of trouble, but which attracted to him the admiration and affection of those who depended upon his courage and his skills.

Some philosophers speak, in this connection, of a distinction between knowledge of means, and knowledge of ends; for Aristotle the distinction was that between skill and virtue. Whichever language we choose, we find ourselves embroiled in the deepest philosophical controversy. Can there really be such a thing as practical knowledge, when what is at stake is not technique or skill, but the purposes to which we apply them? Is there really such a thing as aiming in ignorance, and such a thing as aiming knowledgeably? And is *that* the difference between the bad person and the good, namely a difference in *knowledge*?

Cutting through this knot is not easy. But ordinary language offers us another clue. We recognize not only knowledge *that* and knowledge *how*, but also knowledge *what*, and this idiom seems to be irreducible to either of the others. You are sitting in your office and a colleague storms in and baselessly accuses you of insulting her. Reporting the episode afterwards you say 'I didn't know what to do'. What kind of ignorance are you referring to? You come home from your husband's funeral, sweep with desolate eyes the house that you had shared with him, sit empty and forlorn on the couch, and then suddenly you 'know what to do': there are friends to write to, tasks to complete, and the string quartet you were rehearsing for a concert.

This 'knowing what to do' looks very like what philosophers have had in mind in referring to knowledge of ends. It is not just a matter of knowing how to go about some existing purpose; it is a matter of having the right purpose, the purpose appropriate to the situation in hand. Of course, there is a difficulty presented by that word 'appropriate'. But we are not without intuitions as to what it means. The inappropriate action is marked by a certain kind of failure: it peters out, stumbles into confusion, makes the situation worse than it might have been. Conversely, the appropriate action is the one that rescues what can be rescued, which brings success where success is feasible, leads on from one affirmative to another, so that the agent is never nonplussed or thwarted in his aims. In short, this kind of 'knowing what' has to do with success in action. The one who 'knows what to do' is the one on whom you can rely to make the best shot at success, whenever success is possible.

KNOWING WHAT TO FEEL

But there is another application of the phrase 'knowing *what*', which is even more pertinent to my theme: knowing what to feel. When your colleague burst in to your office that day to plaster you with gratuitous insults, you didn't know what to feel – anger, puzzlement, fear, pity, all 'crossed your mind', but none took possession of it. When, coming home from the walk which had begun when you stormed out in anger from a marital quarrel, you find your husband dead on the living room floor – then too, perhaps, you don't know what to feel. And maybe for days afterwards you remain numb, cold, barely sentient with the shock of it. Even people whose responses are entirely normal can find themselves, in such a situation, not 'knowing what to feel', and looking for a way forward that will help them.

There are forms of 'knowing how' which involve 'knowing what'. Knowing how to console another is not simply a matter of skill. It involves knowing what to feel, as well as knowing how to express that feeling in words and gestures. It means being able to sympathize, while retaining sufficient distance to judge just how much sympathy would be right, and towards what aspect of the other's predicament. In general it is in the workings of sympathy that our emotions undergo their severest test: the temptation is to retreat from the spectacle of suffering, or else to sentimentalize and so to deny the reality. Learning what to feel in the face of another's grief or distress is one of the hardest aspects of moral education.

I shall take for granted this idea of knowing what to feel, and hope that subsequent arguments will persuade you that there really is such a thing, and that it is critical to moral education. The two kinds of 'knowing what' are not as distinct as I have implied. Knowing what to do means being rightly motivated, and right motivation means right feeling. The connections here are deep, and it was Aristotle who first tried to spell them out, arguing that right action springs from virtue, and that virtue is a habit in which a distinctive motive is embedded. That motive requires, in turn, a kind of order in one's emotions, an ability to feel rightly, towards the right object in the right degree. Thus the good-tempered person is one who is 'angry at the right things and with the right people, and further, as he ought, when he ought, and as long as he ought'. In general, to teach virtue we must educate the emotions, and this means learning 'what to feel' in the various circumstances that prompt them. The virtuous person, in Aristotle's understanding, does not merely know what to do and what to feel: his life and actions are imbued with the kind of success which is the reward of rational beings, and which Aristotle described as *eudaimonia*, a term normally translated as happiness or fulfilment.

TEACHING VIRTUE

How is virtue taught? Aristotle's answer is simple: by imitation. But the answer is too simple. For we can imitate virtuous actions only if we are in a position that calls for them. Rudimentary justice, rudimentary courage, and the day-to-day forms of prudence and temperance are, of course, constantly called for. But the testing experiences, the difficult temptations, the human complexities which may one day beset us are things that we encounter only when it is too late to acquire the virtues that will see us through. Maybe, by practising virtue in our small corner of the world, we will be more ready to practise it in the great field of human conflict. Even if that is not so, we can nevertheless gain the knowledge *what to feel*, in those testing circumstances. We cannot be sure, when the time comes, that we shall feel as we ought: but we can rehearse in imagination the knowledge that we might one day require.

For instance we can read stories of the heroes and their adventures; we can study narratives of historical exploits, and look at pictures of the life that we share. We can listen to homilies and rehearse in ritual form the joys and sufferings of revered and exemplary people. In all kinds of ways the emotions and motives of other people 'come before us' in works of art and culture, and we spontaneously sympathize, by recreating in imagination the life that they depict. It is not that we imitate the characters depicted, but that we 'move with' them, acquiring an inner premonition of their motives, and coming to see those motives in the context that the writer or artist provides. Through imagination we reach emotional knowledge, and maybe this is the best way, in the advance of the crucial tests, of preparing ourselves for the joys and calamities that we will some day encounter.

Much of this imaginative education is conducted through religion. Rationalists tend to think of religious education as involving the transmission of doctrines about God, man and creation – doctrines, they believe, that do not stand up to scientific examination, and which in any case hardly fit those who accept them for membership of a sceptical modern community. In fact religious education down the ages has been very little concerned with doctrine. Its main message has been contained in rituals, maxims and stories, and the goal of all three is moral education – teaching what to do, and more importantly, what to feel, in the circumstances of ordinary human life. The goal of religious education is, on the one hand, the cultivation of the heart, not the head, and the doctrines make sense of that other knowledge, a knowledge that we acquire more easily through ritual, and through holy words and examples, than through any form of theory. On the other hand – and here lies the deep difference between religion and culture – the education of the emotions through religion occurs only when the doctrines are believed. That is why culture cannot be a religion substitute, even though, in a sense, religion is a culture substitute in the lives of those who lack 'aesthetic education'.

CONSERVING PRACTICAL KNOWLEDGE

Let us return now, to the thoughts from which this chapter began. I emphasized that we make a mistake in believing that education exists primarily to benefit its recipient. I suggested, rather, that the goal of education is to preserve our communal store of knowledge, and to keep open the channels through which we can call on it when we need to. This may seem a more plausible suggestion when referring to knowledge *that* than when referring to knowledge *how* or *what*. Practical knowledge seems far more intimately bound up with the circumstances of its use than theoretical knowledge. Nevertheless, it is true of practical knowledge, too, that we educate people in order to conserve it, and if we ever lose sight of this truth, then we are sure to lose what practical knowledge we have. If ever we think that we teach skills merely to benefit those who acquire them, skills will rapidly decline to the rudimentary forms that are most easily bestowed on all comers. If, however, we believe that we teach skills in order to *keep those skills alive*, then we shall go on stretching ourselves, singling out those best able to acquire the skills in question, encouraging them to build on what they have acquired and to enhance it. This we do as much in engineering and information technology as in sport, and it is the principal argument for introducing a competitive element into education – that we thereby single out those best fitted to receive it, to enhance it, and to pass it on.

The same is true of that other form of practical knowledge – not knowledge of means, but knowledge of ends, which betokens success in action and the right feelings that engender it. Teachers who wish to impart this knowledge are not interested only in the distribution of its embryonic forms: like teachers of physics, they wish to perpetuate a communal human acquisition, that will be lost if it is never passed on. Of course, they can pass on the rudiments of virtue and sympathy in the traditional way: through the stories and maxims of a religion, and the education in manners and morals that religion facilitates. But they are aware of the vast range and abundance of human sympathy, and of its embodiment and refinement in works of art and reflection. By inducing the love of those things, they perpetuate the knowledge of the human heart. Ideal visions of the human condition, not only of what we are, but of what we are capable of, are distilled in the works of our culture. From these visions we acquire a sense of what is intrinsically worthwhile in the human condition, a recognition that our lives are not consumed in the fire of means only, but devoted also to the pursuit of intrinsic values. The reader of Wordsworth's *Prelude* learns how to animate the natural world with pure hopes of his own; the spectator of Rembrandt's *Night Watch* learns of the pride of corporations, and the benign sadness of civic life; the listener to Mozart's *Jupiter* symphony is presented with the open floodgates of human joy and creativity; the reader of Proust is led through the enchanted world of childhood and made to understand the uncanny prophecy of our later griefs which those days of joy contain. Such experiences are intrinsically valuable to us, and they are part of that inimitable knowledge of life which is the gift of culture.

In short, we should see culture as Schiller and other Enlightenment thinkers saw it: the repository of emotional knowledge, through which we can come to understand the meaning of life as an end in itself. Culture inherits from religion the 'knowledge of the heart' whose essence is sympathy. But it can be passed on and enhanced, even when the religion that first engendered it has died. Indeed, in these circumstances, it is all the more important that culture be passed on, since it has become the sole communicable testimony to the higher life of mankind . . .

12

Classicism Now
(Previously Unpublished)

A time-traveller from the past, asked to assess the achievements of modernism in architecture, would surely conclude that, judged as a whole, the movement has been a failure. Modernist housing is synonymous with alienation, vandalism and decay. Modernist factories and warehouses are universally received as blots on the landscape, whose raw functionality is profoundly at odds with the natural environment. Modernist buildings violate the skyline, the street-line, and the urban texture of downtown areas, with few if any compensating advantages. Within thirty years all modernist buildings lose their original use without gaining another, thereafter to become wasting assets, which can be neither repaired nor demolished without enormous expense. Most important of all, modernism – despite its handful of acknowledged masterpieces – has produced no monumental style. There is no common language, agreed principles, or polite discourse of modernism, which would permit the designers of public spaces to endow them with the cheerful pageantry of an Italian piazza or the unassuming dignity of Bath. The modernist public building is self-centred; it may, like Boston Town Hall, draw attention to the architect and his skills, but it usually pays scant respect to the surrounding fabric. (Boston Town Hall looks like the enormous packing case from which the neighbouring Faniel Hall has been lifted.) Like London's South Bank, or New York's Lincoln Center, modernist monuments soon begin to stand out, not for their merits, but for their defects – crumbling dysfunctional survivals from the age of ill-considered and temporary things.

The time-traveller, observing all this, would surely be tempted to conclude that modernism was not just a failure but a mistake. What was wrong, he might ask, with the classical tradition, which had been the common language of architecture down the centuries, and which had lent itself to every conceivable use, and adapted itself to every historical change? Why throw away this precious legacy of practical wisdom, if the result is so obviously ill-suited to survive? Why do architects no longer follow the example of Michelangelo on the Campidoglio, building not so as to stand out but so as to fit in, and expressing their originality not in defiance of the surrounding context but by means of it? The classical language enabled Michelangelo not just to build, but to *compose*, fitting detail to detail in his own Palazzo del Senatore, while matching his work to the other buildings of the square. The strength of his composition is of a piece with the humility through which it was achieved. So why not continue in this vein, not slavishly imitating the past, but nevertheless using its language, so as to stay in communication, as Michelangelo did, with the other builders of the city? After all, isn't that what a city is about – the dialogue across generations, which brings past, present and future together in a shared commitment to a place and its meaning?

Having voiced such thoughts, our time-traveller would be astonished by the critical orthodoxy that would immediately rise up to oppose him. Architects, the critics will say, should be true to their time, to their materials and to themselves. Imitation, rule-following, and stylistic formalities are a threat to creativity. Originality, sincerity and self-expression are the only standards by which a building should be judged. In any case it is no longer possible to return to the classical tradition, which was part of a vanished climate of ideas. To design with columns, entablatures, mouldings and capitals would be to produce copies – pastiche versions of ancient monuments. Instead of real, affirmative buildings which claim space for human uses, we should end up with stage sets. And this is not just an aesthetic failing. It is a moral failing too. For it constitutes a subtle denial of the real and vital experience of the modern city. Stage sets are suitable only for imaginary life, not for real life. At best they are charming invocations of a nostalgically embellished past. At worst they are an outright denial of the modern city.

The critical orthodoxy which established modernism in architecture took its inspiration from impressionist painting, symbolist poetry, and atonal music – in other words, from artistic movements addressed to an élite. The modern architect was likened to the modern painter – dedicated to re-shaping the language of his art, so as to explore new regions of the human psyche and new possibilities of expression. Aesthetic freedom and experiment were held to be, in architecture as in the other arts, the pre-conditions of authentic utterance. Classical architecture was therefore seen in the same light as figurative painting and tonal music: the last gasp of a culture from which the life had fled. The fact that the classical tradition was popular, functional and pleasing to the eye did not deter the modernist critics: on the contrary this was simply the final proof that classicism was kitsch.

This attitude to architecture is what has enabled the modernists to ignore the general public, and to build in defiance of popular taste. Indeed, a favourable judgement from the man in the street would be a warning sign – a sign that those old desires for form, order, cosiness and human scale have been respected. Hence major planning decisions in our cities, in both Europe and America, are seldom if ever submitted to popular vote, and are either pushed through by direct lobbying of the city council or submitted to a panel of experts chosen for their modernist orthodoxy.

It is here that our time-traveller might begin his reply. The classical tradition arose, he might argue, because cities were built by the people who live in them, in order to protect and celebrate their communal life. Modernism and post-modernism wrongly identify the task of the architect in terms appropriate to the private arts of painting, poetry and music, where endless experiment, and the élite culture which endorses it, are entirely natural. Nobody can object to Schoenberg's experiments in atonality or to Boulez's crystalline sound-effects, since nobody has to listen to them. But this experimental and defiant outlook is not acceptable in a public art like architecture: indeed, it violates the fundamental premise from which all good architecture begins, which is the connection between building and settlement. Cities arise from the human determination to dwell in a place, not for a day or a year; not even for thirty years; but forever. Urban architecture – and urban monuments in particular – ought to be invocations of the permanent. It is this which makes the classical styles not only agreeable to every age but also adaptable to every use. They are adaptable because they are marked by the will to endure, the collective decision to stand above the tide of appetite and history, and to make a permanent claim to space. This is why we admire the Parthenon, and why architects ever since have returned to it as a model for their work.

In place of this reverence for the permanent, the critics offer us what the early propagandist for modernism, Sigfried Giedion, called 'the eternal present': in other words buildings attached to the moment of their birth, which is simultaneously the moment of their death. Consider Norman Foster's Law Faculty in Cambridge: a building that reaches neither forwards nor backwards in time, and that relates to nothing that is permanent in our nature or our aspirations. Modernist buildings now have a dépassé and expensive shabbiness, like the Lincoln Center in New York, which already, after only four decades, requires a multi-billion dollar face-lift. Unlike Michelangelo's Campidoglio, the Center remains fixed in the moment of its creation. It is not, as is the Campidoglio, a place of study, wonder and pilgrimage. By striving to be 'of its time', and 'relevant', the building was no sooner built than outmoded, carrying into the future only its burden of maintenance costs – a burden inescapably connected with the modernist styles and the materials that they necessitate.

Moreover, our time-traveller might add, it is entirely absurd to believe that by using the classical language you are sacrificing originality, life and expression. The history of Western architecture is a history of classical revivals, each one bringing a new note of freshness, a new conviction, and a new endorsement of contemporary life. The revolution in architecture that was led by Brunelleschi and continued in the work of Michelangelo was animated by a conscious desire to learn from Roman architecture, to understand and internalize its rules and details, and at the same time to produce forms and structures that would be suitable to the life of an Italian city. And what Brunelleschi and Michelangelo did was done also by their successors: by Palladio, Wren, Hawksmoor and Soane; by Cockerell and Barry; by McKim, Mead and White – and by countless other architects with the sense, modesty and respect for their fellow citizens that placed permanent values ahead of transient fashions in their thinking.

To the time-traveller familiar with the discussions, projects and movements from which the fabric of our modern cities arose, the classical tradition will have another, and more political, merit. Unlike modernism, the classical tradition has provided examples, rules and precedents that were the starting point equally for the highest aesthetic endeavours, and for ordinary and unassuming buildings. It was a tradition available to everyone, regardless of talent, and able to create a spontaneous urban harmony incorporating the humblest residences and the grandest public buildings side by side. Architecture, it should be remembered, is first and foremost a vernacular art, like dance and clothing. Although there are the great projects, and the great architects who succeed in them, both are exceptions. We build because we need to, and for a purpose. Most people who build have no special talent, and no high artistic ideals. For them, aesthetic taste is important not because they have something special or entrancing to communicate, but precisely because they do not. Being decent and alert to their neighbours, they nevertheless want to do what is right. Hence repeatability and rule-guidedness are vital architectural resources. Style must be so defined that anyone, however uninspired, can make good use of it, and add thereby to the public dwelling space that is our common possession. That is why the most successful period of Western architecture – the period in which real and lasting towns of great size were envisaged and developed – was the period of the classical vernacular, when pattern books guided people who had not fallen prey to the illusion of their own genius.

The failure of modernism, our time-traveller might say, lies not in the fact that it produced no great or beautiful buildings – the Chapel at Ronchamp, and the houses of Frank Lloyd Wright abundantly prove the opposite. It lies in the absence of any reliable patterns or types, which can be used in awkward or novel situations so as spontaneously to harmonize with the existing urban decor, and so as to retain the essential nature of the street as a common home and dwelling-place. The degradation of our cities is the direct result of the emphasis on the architect, as innovator and visionary, guided by an artistic idea. As a result of this emphasis, ordinary functional buildings acquired, during the twentieth century, no aesthetic guidelines: certainly no guidelines comparable to those laid down by the classical tradition. Buildings arose in our streets as by-products of engineering, rather than as contributions to the urban décor. The result was the 'modernist vernacular', whose principal device is the stack of horizontal layers, with jutting and obtrusive corners, built without consideration for the street, without a coherent façade, and without an intelligible relation to its neighbours.

Of course, this does not rule out the possibility of a modernist monument – and indeed, if Frank Lloyd Wright had had his way, America would consist of nothing else: one vast ocean-to-ocean suburb of automobile-fed dream-houses, each a self-contained aesthetic masterpiece, each expressing the individuality of both architect and owner, and each surrounded by its isolating plot of land. But this just means that, for Frank Lloyd Wright, architecture is not concerned to build cities, but to destroy them – and to destroy their natural settings too. The real challenge to modernism is to conceive a monument which will also be an integrated part of the urban fabric – in the manner of the Campidoglio or the Piazza San Marco. And that is what our time-traveller cannot discover. Comparisons between modernist and classical attempts at monumental architecture suggest that the up-to-dateness and iconoclasm of the former promote the sense of their temporary and provisional nature. The super-modernist capital of Brasilia was soon deserted, having proved impossible to work in and unfitting as a home. And Le Corbusier's monumental modernist town of Chandigar in India is now an unhappy slum, deserted by the middle classes and devoid of civic pride.

At the very moment when Le Corbusier was planning Chandigar, however, Lutyens was at work on the Viceroy's house in New Delhi. And while our time-traveller will experience the first as a dull, dispiriting work of routine

planning, he will welcome the second as a striking, vigorous
and original monument, whose originality is all the more
exalted for the fact that it arises from millenia of tradition,
subtly adapted by Lutyens to the climate and the native art-
forms of the place where his building was to stand. Of course,
Lutyens' building was designed for an imperial arrangement
that was soon to vanish. But then Le Corbusier's town was
designed for a socialist society that never materialized. And not
only is Lutyens' building still functioning half a century after
the end of Empire, you can be certain that it will be standing
when Chandigar has crumbled to dust. It is of the essence of
the classical idiom that it is not tied to a transient function.
Classical buildings endure because they are loved, admired
and accepted, and enjoy an innate adaptation to human needs
and purposes that fits them to every normal social and political
change.

The modernists have a reply to all this. The Viceroy's house,
they will say, is dishonest, untruthful, part of the ideology of
empire which, by borrowing and adapting the monumental
language of the classical tradition, tries to represent a crumbling
political dominion as a permanent and unassailable fact. That,
they will say, is why the classical language is no longer available.
It expresses a political project, based on hierarchy, tradition,
order and control, which we moderns have repudiated, not only
in our buildings, but also in our souls.

Such an argument was already used by Frank Lloyd
Wright, when insisting that the old classical houses of the
Americans '*lied* about everything', having 'no sense of space as
should belong to a free man among a free people in a free
country'. In place of such houses, Wright proposed a
democratic architecture for a 'morally strong and simple-
hearted people'. Yet Wright's houses are quintessentially
aristocratic. They are expressions of belligerent sovereignty,
capturing far more space than their owners need, and
requiring an enormous outlay in capital and running costs,
with no concern whatsoever for neighbours, the environment
or future generations. And it is quite wrong to suppose, as
Wright supposed, that the classical styles are uniquely suited to
aristocratic and imperial forms of life. Boullée and Ledoux saw
a revised and monumental classicism as the way to capture the

new spirit of the French Revolution; American architects, from Jefferson to Greenberg, have seen the classical as the true democratic style. Mussolini appropriated the classical for fascism, Hitler for national socialism, Stalin for communism, and the architects of Victorian London and Manchester for the society based on trade. In short, classicism has no one ideological function. For what it signifies is not the triumph of this or that political system, but the universal human need for permanence, for a present that melds with the past and the future, and for building which is a monument to our brief existence here.

That is all very well, the modernists say, but architecture must be true to itself, to its materials, and to the spirit of the times. Classical architecture, however, is a fake, a way of encrusting modern buildings with stucco, from an age whose values we have discarded. To this our time-traveller might reply that so it has always been. Humane and considerate architecture has to do with concealing as well as revealing things. Much of the built work of the great Alberti in the fifteenth century consisted in the partial transformation of existing buildings. His Tempio Malatestiana in Rimini was a shell to encase the old church of San Francesco; at the Palazzo Rucellai, Florence, his façade was a separate project unrelated to the interiors, which had been built by others before his arrival. And at Santa Maria Novella in Florence Alberti again contributed merely a façade, incorporating one partially executed in about 1300 as part of a Gothic church, the nave of which he did not alter. Hanging like a giant piece of ornamental embroidery, his work at Santa Maria Novella, if it were built today, would be condemned as both 'facadism' and 'pastiche', not in keeping with its age; for Alberti based it stylistically on a much earlier building from a much earlier experiment in classicism, the twelfth-century church of San Miniato al Monte. One of the most admired and famous buildings of the Renaissance, Palladio's basilica at Vicenza (1549–80), also turns out to be a brilliant essay in 'facadism', a casing melded into an existing medieval structure of totally different style, materials and configuration. Wren's St Paul's Cathedral similarly exhibits at every turn the art of concealment.

But what the modernist would dismiss as 'facadism' and untruth is shown by such examples to be a deeper kind of truth – truth to the life and needs of a human community. As citizens we are concerned with the public appearance of buildings, and wish to find our life endorsed and given permanence by the artefacts that grow in our midst. What Alberti undertook at Santa Maria Novella was a task that many architects now share, faced by the bleak discarded wrecks of the modernist period, and endeavouring to re-integrate them as 'built citizens', so to speak, in the urban way of life. And they can succeed, as Allan Greenberg succeeded with the abandoned supermarket in Manchester Connecticut, now a dignified courthouse, and as John Outram succeeded, with the Harp Heating Headquarters in Swanley, Kent.

So what remains of the modernist dogma that tells us to turn our back on a tradition that has proved itself, and adopt a fashion that has not? Our time-traveller may rest his case with examples: there are enough of them, and the evidence is overwhelming. But in fact, if he belongs to the intellectual tradition of Vitruvius, Alberti, Palladio and Chambers, he has much more than examples to offer. He has a vision of architecture that is universal in its aim, and comprehensive in its understanding of the relation between buildings and people. According to this vision the goal of architecture is *fittingness*: buildings must fit to each other and to the urban context; and part must fit to part in the composition of the whole. This demand for fittingness stems from a deep human need. We seek to be at home in the world – to come in from our wandering, and to settle in the place that is ours. Hence we need to match and to harmonize, projecting thereby our common commit-ment to the peaceful settlement of a common place.

The classical tradition took, as its central idea, the column, symbol of standing, bearing the architrave with a visible upthrust of rooted strength. The column can be repeated; it has an internal grammar, derived from base, shaft and capital; and also an external grammar, derived from the relations between vertical and horizontal sections, and the correspon-dence of part with part in a colonnade. This grammar, expressed through engaged column and pilaster, can be seen on all the humble warehouses of Lower Manhattan, and it is one reason why those buildings are still there, despite having lost their original use and the many uses that have succeeded it. It is the common root of almost all styles that have had lasting appeal to urban residents. The Romanesque and the Gothic, the Islamic mosque and medreseh, the Hindu temple and palace, all give emphasis to the load-bearing vertical, and embellish those points of interaction where arch and architrave are supported. It is surely no accident that the most loved and visited public building recently erected in Greater London is the Hindu Temple in Neasden.

This embellishment of visible junctions is central to the classical tradition. It enables us to divide a building into self-dependent parts, and therefore to see the façade not as assembled merely, but as *composed*, in the way that a work of music is composed. This is the significance of the Orders, not only in their original Greek and Roman deployment, but also in all the subsequent revivals, when architects reached again for the true principles of their craft. The Order is the primary unit of classical design, a complete vertical element, all the details of which are visually comprehended within the upward movement. Plinth, cornice, entablature, column, capital and mouldings serve not merely to mark out the proportions of the walls and to bear the structure of the roof: they also divide the unit into intelligible sections, investing it with light, shade and contrast, so that proportions become visible and relations defined. The Order outlines and explores a posture, imitating the human frame and answering to our ways of seeing it; at the same time it establishes a grammar, so that part can be matched with part, and a relation of 'fittingness' established between them, as it is established by Michelangelo in the casing that he provided for the Palazzo del Senatore.

The discipline contained in an Order brings an immense gift of freedom: the Order can be extended sideways into colonnades, courtyards and façades; along straight lines or curves; through squares, streets or crescents. In each new arrangement its orderliness and posture are preserved. This flexibility is common to all idioms that share the vertical emphasis, which is why they fit so well into pre-existing streets and townscapes. By contrast, the horizontally-composed building always clears a space around itself, refuses to align itself, and is seen as a violation of the surrounding urban fabric. It is therefore no accident that, when people think seriously about the city and how it should look to its residents, they again and again return to the classical style. This is not dishonesty, but, on the contrary, a recognition of real human needs. If we must speak of dishonesty in architecture, the term should be applied to those clean, featureless walls of glass and steel, from which mouldings and verticals have been banished, which face in no direction, and which pose as visions of the future, in order to disguise the fact that they are premonitions of decay.

The Orders identify particular junctures in the wall or colonnade as points of drama and transition. Here the movement is gathered up, arrested and then passed on with a renewed impetus. Base, capital, architrave and cornice; string courses, plinths and attic storeys – all are picked out with shadows and given their specific character. The geometry of the building is made perceivable, since the lines have beginning, middle and end, and are integrated into a composition, which arises out of them with the kind of logical flexibility that is characteristic of a fugue in music.

That is one reason why the classical idiom lends itself (as the modernist idiom does not) to the construction of façades, and therefore to the creation of monumental spaces. Modernist, and to a lesser extent post-modernist, buildings face in no particular direction, and offer no coherent aspect, no over-mastering composition, from whatever angle they may be viewed. Modernist doors are tucked out of the way, meaninglessly and invisibly. The buildings contain no real apertures, since the distinctions between window, wall-space and door have been virtually abolished, or at any rate confused, by the use of glass screens that incorporate all of them and elide them into a single movement. The result is a street without thresholds, where the distinction between private and public is no longer set in stone.

It is in this monumental use that the virtues of the classical Orders, and their undying relevance to our cities, are most clearly perceivable. A century ago New Yorkers had no doubt about this. The great railway stations of McKim, Mead and White, the clubs, museums and public library, were all conceived in classical terms, not so as to create a pastiche version of ancient Rome, but so as to dignify and embellish a modern city, and to make it friendly, open and accessible to the citizens who live and work in it. We get an inkling of the effect from Grand Central Station – an unhurried, dignified interior, whose effect is to soothe the haste of city life, and to celebrate the moments of arrival and departure. Such a building clearly shows the way in which a space is marked out as public by its architectural shell. There is no need for signs to state this in words: it is an immediate quality of the experience itself, as the visitor enters the vestibule and senses the gravitational pull of the colossal Order.

Grand Central Station is not a great building by any means. But it trenchantly illustrates the falsehood of the dogma that the classical language, used in a modern context, is anachronistic. The language of classical building is a living language, packed with historical reference, but nevertheless constantly developing in response to changing human needs. It lends itself naturally to the most important task of city planning, which is the creation of public buildings and public spaces that are perceived as such, and enjoyed as a common possession. And it is the repository of 3,000 years of problem solving, in all the circumstances that urban people have encountered. Surely, then, our time-traveller would be right, when he tells us that no argument has been given him for thinking that the Lincoln Center could not be rebuilt in the classical style, using materials and forms that have shown their ability to last, to inspire and to comfort, and which will be accepted by everyone save the modernists as an embellishment to America's greatest city.

13

Music

(From *Philosophy: Principles and Problems*, 2005)

Music is, or resides in, sound. But that is not a helpful thing to say, if we do not know what sound is. It is tempting to divide the world into things (tables, chairs, animals, people) and their properties. But sounds don't fit into either category. Sounds are not properties of the objects that emit them: they do not *inhere* in objects, as colours, shapes and sizes do. But nor are they things. Sounds, unlike things, *occur*; they do not fill physical space in the way that things do, nor do they have boundaries. A sound occurs only if it is produced in some way, and it ceases when the mode of production ceases. In a nutshell, sounds are not things or properties, but events, standing in relations of cause and effect to other events.

However, they are events of a peculiar kind. In most other cases we identify events by observing the changes in things. A car crash is an event, in which a car changes in respect of its properties and position. We understand the event, by understanding the change. In the case of sound, however, nothing changes. The sound occurs – but it is not a property of anything. It is self-sufficient, and we may hear it while having no knowledge of its cause. It is, so to speak, an event in which no *thing* participates – a 'pure event'. This is a very odd kind of entity, for a variety of reasons. Suppose you observe a car crash, and I ask you, 'How many events are you witnessing?' You would probably be stuck for a reply. The crash is one event, if you mean to refer merely to the change in the car: but there is much more that happens – to the people inside, to the road, to the wheels of the car, the headlights; you could go on forever. There are as many events as there are changes in things. But you don't have to count them. Events do not exist *over and above* the changes in things, and the only items in the world that you need to identify in order to refer to events are the things in which they occur.

In the case of sounds, however, we have no such easy way of answering the question 'How many?' When a violin and a flute sound in unison, it is arbitrary whether we say there is one sound or two: we have only the vaguest concept of the 'individual' sound, and seem to get by without settling questions of identity and difference. But sounds are objective: they are part of reality, and not to be confused with the auditory experiences through which we perceive them. Imagine that you enter a room and hear the first bars of Beethoven's Fifth Symphony. You leave the room and return a minute later to hear the start of the development section. Would it not be natural to conclude that the symphony had been sounding in your absence – that the sounds of the work had persisted unheard in the room where first you encountered them? In other words, is it not natural to distinguish the sound – which really exists out there – from the experience of hearing it, which exists only in me?

Not all sounds are music. There are noises, shouts, words and murmurings which, while they may occur in music, are not in themselves music. When does sound become music? Pitch is not the decisive factor: there are pitched sounds which are not music (sirens, peals of bells, tonic languages), and music which involves no pitched sounds (African drum music, for example). Nor is rhythm the decisive factor, if you mean by rhythm the regularity of a sound-pattern: for this is a feature of all normal machines. Nor is harmony decisive: whenever I switch on this computer it emits an A minor chord, with added seventh and ninth, which is about as far from music as anything that occurs in my study.

The question is best approached by asking another: what is it to *hear* a sound as music? Sounds heard as music are heard in a special kind of relation to one another. They appear within a musical 'field of force'. The transformation is comparable to that which occurs when we hear a sound as a word. The word 'bang' consists of a sound. This sound could occur in nature, yet not have the character of a word. What makes it the word that it is, is the grammar of a language, which mobilizes the sound and transforms it into a word with a specified role: it designates a sound or an action in English, an emotion in German. When hearing this sound as a word, I hear the 'field of force' supplied by grammar. Likewise, to hear a sound as music is not merely to hear it, but also to *order* it, in a certain kind of relation to other actual and possible sounds. A sound, ordered in this way, becomes a 'tone'.

When we hear tones we hear their musical implications in something like the way we hear the grammatical implications of words in a language. Of course, we probably don't know the theory of musical organization, and cannot say in words what is going on when the notes of a Haydn quartet sound so right and logical. We have only *tacit* knowledge of the musical grammar (if grammar is the word for it), just as we have a tacit knowledge of the grammar of English. Our knowledge of the principles of musical organization is expressed not in theories but in acts of recognition.

Tones in music are heard is a space of their own. They do not mingle with the sounds of the world around them, although they may be drowned by them. Music exists in its own world, and is lifted free from the world of objects. Nor do we hear tones in music as belonging to the causal order. The middle C that we hear does not strike us as the effect of someone blowing on a clarinet; rather it is a response to the B that preceded it, and calls in turn for the E that follows. When Brahms hands the second theme of the last movement of the B-flat piano concerto from orchestra to piano and back again, we hear a single melody jump electrically across these poles. Each note follows in sequence as though indifferent to the world of physical causes, and as though responding only to its predecessor and to the force that it inherits from the musical line. There is a 'virtual causality' that generates tone from tone in the musical line, even when the tones themselves are produced by quite different physical means. The physical world here sinks away into the background.

The virtual causality of the melodic line operates in a virtual space. The pitch spectrum for us has a 'high' and a 'low'. Music rises and falls in a one-dimensional space, and we have a clear impression both of the rapidity of the music, and of the distance through which it passes. Pitches define locations, and intervals measure distances. Chords can be filled, hollow, stretched, packed, or dense: and these spatial descriptions capture what we hear, when we hear the chords as music.

As soon as you examine the matter with a philosophical eye, however, you will see that those spatial descriptions are deeply mysterious. Suppose a melody begins with the clarinet playing middle C, and moves upward to E on the trumpet. You hear a movement through musical space, and also a change of timbre. But what exactly moves? Obviously C does not move to E, since C is always and essentially the pitch which it is. Nor does the clarinet 'move' to the trumpet. Besides, in the musical experience, 'clarinet' is the description of a colour, not a cause. The more you look at it, the harder it is to find anything in the musical space that actually *moves*: the melody itself does not move, being a sequence of discrete pitches, each of which is fixed forever at the 'place' where it is heard. The 'useless space' of Rilke's sonnet is indeed useless, for it is not a space at all, but only the appearance of a space.

Nevertheless, we hear it as a space, and the experience of movement is ineliminable. Moreover it is a space which is very like a one-dimensional physical space in other ways. We have already seen that there is a virtual causality which operates between events in this space: the tones of a melody are responses to the tones which precede them, and causes of the tones to come. It is also a space through which forces exert themselves: gravitational and magnetic forces, which bend tones in different directions and with different strengths. When music cadences from a dominant seventh onto the tonic, with the seventh leading, the dominant in the bass pulls the seventh down onto the third of the tonic. At the beginning of the *Rite of Spring*, after the bassoon has played in A minor for a bar, the horn enters on C-sharp, and you hear the melody push this C-sharp away from it and out of the musical line. The bassoon has established a field of force, which is exerting itself against the intruder. Tones become lighter and easier to carry as they rise, while those in the bass are heavy and, when filled with close harmony, painful to lift – so that cellos, bassoons and basses, at the end of Tchaikovsky's Sixth Symphony, collapse under the burden, and the music breaks and dies. Melodies sink and soar, they push against barriers and enter into places of rest and repose. Music is activity and gesture, and as we listen we move along with it, with no consciousness that the forces and fields against which we exert ourselves are not present in the music too.

How is this 'useless space' organized? It is normal to suggest that the crucial components in musical organization, apart from pitch, are three: rhythm, melody and harmony. But how are these defined? When you hear a rhythm, what exactly do you hear? If sounds occur in a regular sequence, you may hear them as organized rhythmically – but you may equally not do so (as when overhearing the clicking of the wheels of a railway carriage). And sounds arranged irregularly might by immensely rhythmical, like the last movement of the *Rite of Spring*. It seems that, when we hear a rhythm, we group the sounds into measures, and again into beats within each measure, in such a way as to allow stresses and accents to ride on the surface of a wave. This wave is not there, in the sounds – for they could be grouped in countless contrasting ways. But it is there in the way that we hear the sounds, imbuing them in our perception with a force that ties them together, and induces a constantly fluctuating force.

What now of melody? This phenomenon too, which seems so easy to recognize, is immensely hard to pin down. When we hear a melody we hear something begin, at a definite point in time. But what begins? And where exactly? A melody introduced by an upbeat, like the main theme of the last movement of Brahms' First Symphony, can be heard as beginning either on the upbeat, or on the down beat to which it leads. For many people it begins somewhere between those two, in mid-air, so to speak. Once begun a melody proceeds through musical space – but not necessarily to a definite ending (think of the melody that opens Rachmaninov's Second Piano Concerto). Nor, while it lasts, does the melody require there to be *sound*. The main theme of the last movement of Beethoven's *Eroica* symphony consists largely of silences: but the melody continues uninterrupted through these silences, quite indifferent to the presence or absence of orchestral sound. It is almost as though the sounds *point* to the melody, which exists elsewhere, in a 'useless space' of its own. Here is a striking illustration of the distinction between the physical world of sounds, and the 'intentional' world of music.

The difficulties that we have in defining melody are duplicated in the case of harmony. Both melodies and chords are 'unities': musical entities with distinct parts, which are nevertheless heard as *one*. Yet they are unities of different kinds: the one a unity across time, the other a unity of simultaneous tones. Not every sequence is a melody, and not every 'simultaneity' a chord. Both diachronous and synchronous unity in music admit of many varieties. Thus we distinguish, among diachronous unities, between melodies, phrases, motifs and themes. A phrase is heard as incomplete, while a motif is heard as a living, moving 'building block' – a 'palpitating stone'. Themes may be melodic or merely 'architectonic', like the theme built from fifths that opens Berg's Violin Concerto, and which could hardly be described as a melody (a 'tune').

Likewise chords exist in many varieties: consonant and dissonant, open and closed, saturated and unsaturated. Some 'demand resolution', while others stand complete in themselves. What makes a chord the chord that it is depends not merely on the tones and the intervals that compose it, but also on the musical context in which it occurs. What in Mozart would be described as a 'half diminished seventh', appears in Wagner as the famous 'Tristan chord' – the difference being not in the pitched sounds from which it is composed, but in the musical syntax which subsumes it. Tones may sound together, without forming a chord, even if they are, from the acoustic point of view, part of a single harmony. In classical counterpoint we seldom hear the simultaneities as chords, since each voice is, so to speak, running through them without pause. The unity of a chord seems to be *sui generis*: it is a unity that we 'hear in' the tones, but which is not reducible to their physical concurrence.

The critical feature of melodies, motifs and phrases is the presence of one or more 'boundaries': events which constitute a beginning and end, and which may be more or less permeable, more or less resistant to outside invasion, more or less definitive in bringing the musical movement to a close. Phrases may be open at both ends, like the three-note phrase that opens

Mozart's 40th Symphony. (And here is an interesting question: when exactly does the melody 'take off': when does the upbeat end and the downbeat begin?) Or they may be closed at the beginning (i.e. not heard as a continuation of the phrase before), like the opening motif of Beethoven's Fifth Symphony; or closed at the end, like the descending scale motif in the last movement of Ravel's Concerto for the Left Hand. This phenomenon of 'closure' is often singled out by musicologists as the root of musical structure in the Western classical tradition; but the attempt to explain it in other terms invariably runs into the ground, when it is discovered that we cannot describe it, except by using metaphors borrowed from contexts which are profoundly different from the context of music.

However difficult it may be to *describe* what we hear in music, however, there is no doubt that we hear it, that it is utterly immediate and intelligible to us, and of consuming interest. In the useless space of music we hear those musical unities – the palpitating stones of melody and harmony – built into living temples in which we wander freely, released from earthly constraints. The individuals in this musical space – harmonies and melodies – are not like individuals in physical space. For one thing, they can occur simultaneously at two difference places, as when one and the same melody sounds in canon. Melodies are events, whose inner structure is one of movement, but in which nothing literally moves. Harmonies too are events, whose inner structure is one of force and tension, creating valencies to which other harmonies congregate and cohere.

Music, so conceived, is not just a pleasant sound. It is the intentional object of a musical perception: that which we hear *in* sounds, when we hear them as music. The musical perception involves an imaginative grouping of tones into phrases, measures and chords; and this grouping is subject to emendation as we listen to and study what we hear. Hence music may be both understood and misunderstood: to understand is to hear an order that 'makes sense of' the sounds. By drawing someone's attention to features that he has not heard, or has not attended to, I can make the music 'click into place' for him, and the order that was previously inaudible now becomes heard. This order is not part of the world of sounds: only rational beings can perceive it, since its origin is in the self-conscious mind. When I hear music with proper understanding, I am in some sense putting myself *into* it, imbuing it with a life that originates in me. At the same time this life, projected outwards from its human prison, takes on another character: it moves freely in a useless space of its own, where bodily objects can no longer encumber it. Music therefore offers an image of the subject, released from the world of objects, and moving in response to its own caprice. It does not describe the transcendental subject: but it *shows* it, as it would be, if it *could* be shown.

The space of music is incommensurate with physical space; the time of music is likewise incommensurate with physical time. One and the same melody can be played fast or slow; the 'pure events' of music can be reversed, as when a theme is played in retrograde, or a passage runs backwards to its starting point (like the film music in Berg's *Lulu*); a motif can be played now as a melody, now as a chord – like the Curse motif in Wagner's *Ring*. Although music cannot break free of the prison of time, the temporal order that it reveals stands in no clear relation to the order of physical time. A vast ocean of musical time lies between the great drum strokes of Mahler's Tenth Symphony: but only a few seconds separate the physical sounds; time moves slowly and sluggishly in the opening measures of Haydn's *Creation*, but rapidly, tightly and with the greatest alertness in the last movement of Mozart's *Jupiter* Symphony; time is fragmented in Webern's *Konzert* op. 24, and scattered like stars. In these and countless other ways, we find it impossible to hear music simply as a series of events in physical time, related by before and after to the events in the surrounding physical world. Each work of music occurs in its own time, built from those 'palpitating stones' that can be shifted freely in both directions. Hence we have the experience, in music, of individuals which 'take up' the time in which they occur, and exclude other individuals from being there: as the final tonic chord of a classical symphony drives all rival tones from the place it occupies. In all these respects musical time resembles space: it is a 'spatialized' representation of temporal order.

Of course, not every work of music provides these strange experiences in equal measure. It is only the greatest labour of style and architecture that can place the freely moving subject in this useless space and build there its 'godly home'. The masterpieces of music may, however, lift us from our time and space into an ideal time and space, ordered by an ideal causality, which is the causality of freedom. From the ideal time of music it is, so to speak, a small step to eternity. Sometimes, listening to a Bach fugue, a late quartet of Beethoven, or one of those infinitely spacious themes of Bruckner, I have the thought that this very movement which I hear might have been made known to me in a single instant: that all of this is only accidentally spread out in time before me, and that it might have been made known to me in another way, as mathematics is made known to me. For the musical entity – be it melody or harmony – is only a visitor to *our* time; its individuality is already emancipated from real time, and remains undamaged by all those transformations of musical time to which I referred. We may therefore come to think of this very individual as emancipated from time entirely, and yet *remaining an individual*. In the experience of music, therefore, we can obtain a glimpse of what it might be, for one and the same individual, to exist in time and in eternity. And this encounter with the 'point of intersection of the timeless with time' is also an encounter with the pure subject, released from the world of objects, and moving in obedience to the laws of freedom alone.

SECTION 5

Homecomings

14

Conserving Nature

(From *A Political Philosophy*, 2006)

Environmentalism has recently tended to recruit from people on the left, offering ecological rectitude as part of a comprehensive call for 'social justice'. However, concern for the environment is shared by people of quite the opposite temperament, for whom constitutions and procedures are more important than social goals, and who regard the egalitarian project with scepticism. The appropriation of the environmental movement by the left is in fact a relatively new phenomenon. In Britain the movement has its roots in the nineteenth-century reaction to the Industrial Revolution, in which Tories and radicals played an equal part, and the early opposition to industrial farming joins guild socialists like H. J. Massingham, Tories like Lady Eve Balfour and eccentric radicals like Rolf Gardiner, who borrowed ideas from left and right and who has even been identified (by Patrick Wright) as a kind of fascist. Moreover, contemporary environmentalists are aware of the ecological damage done by revolutionary socialism – as in the forced collectivization, frenzied industrialization and gargantuan plans to shift populations, rivers and whole landscapes that we have witnessed in the Soviet Union and China. Left-wing thinkers will not regard those abuses as the inevitable result of their ideas. Nevertheless, they will recognize that more work is needed, if the normal conscience is to be persuaded that socialism contains the answer to the growing ecological problem. At the same time, they seldom recognize any affinity with 'the right', and often seem to regard 'conservatism' as a dirty word, with no semantic connection to the 'conservation' that they favour.

The explanation, I believe, is that environmentalists have been habituated to see conservatism as the ideology of free enterprise, and free enterprise as an assault on the Earth's resources, with no motive beyond the short-term gains that animate the market. Those who have called themselves conservatives in the political context are in part responsible for this misperception. For they have tended to see modern politics in terms of a simple dichotomy between individual freedom on the one hand and state control on the other. Individual freedom means economic freedom and this, in turn, means the freedom to exploit natural resources for financial gain. The timber merchant who cuts down a rain forest, the mining corporation that ransacks the subsoil, the motor manufacturer who churns out an unending stream of cars, the cola merchant who sends out a million plastic bottles each day – all are obeying the laws of the market, and all, unless checked, are destroying some part of our collective environment. And because in a market economy the biggest actors do the most damage, environmentalists turn their hostility on big businesses, and on the free economies that produce them.

Abolish the market economy, however, and the normal result is enterprises that are just as large and just as destructive but which, because they are in the hands of the State, are usually answerable to no sovereign power that can limit their predations. It is a plausible conservative response, therefore, not to advocate economic freedom at all costs, but to recognize the costs of economic freedom and to take all steps to reduce them. We need free enterprise, but we also need the rule of law that limits it. When enterprise is the prerogative of the State, the entity that controls the law is identical with the entity that has the most powerful motive to evade it – a sufficient explanation, it seems to me, of the ecological catastrophe of socialist economies.

However, there is another and better reason for thinking that conservatism and environmentalism are natural bed-fellows. As I argue, conservatism is an exercise in social ecology. Individual freedom is a part of that ecology, since without it social organisms cannot adapt. But freedom is not the sole or even the central goal of politics, even if it is the attribute that, at a deep level, makes politics both necessary and possible. Conservatism and conservation are in fact two aspects of a single long-term policy, which is that of husbanding resources. These resources include the social capital embodied in laws, customs and institutions; they also include the material capital contained in a free, but law-governed, economy. The purpose of politics, on this view, is not to rearrange society in the interests of some overarching vision or ideal, such as equality, liberty or fraternity. It is to maintain a vigilant resistance to the entropic forces that erode our social and ecological inheritance. The goal is to pass on to future generations – and if possible to enhance – the order and equilibrium of which we are the temporary trustees.

The conservative understanding of political action is there-fore formulated, as a rule, in terms of trusteeship, rather than enterprise, of conversation rather than command, of friendship rather than solidarity. Those ideas lend themselves readily to the environmental project, and it always surprises me that so few environmentalists seem to see this. It is obvious to a conservative that our reckless pursuit of individual gratifica-tion jeopardizes the social order just as it jeopardizes the planet. And it is obvious too that the wisest policies are those that strive to protect and keep in place the institutions that place a brake on our appetites, and which renew the sources of social contentment.

The major difficulty, from the environmental point of view, is that social equilibrium and ecological equilibrium are not the same idea, and not necessarily in harmony. Two examples illustrate the problem. Democracies seem to achieve equili-brium only in a condition of economic growth. Periods of stagnation, rapid inflation or impoverishment are also periods of radical discontent, in which envy, resentment and anger lead to instability. Hence the first concern of democratic governments is to encourage economic growth, regardless of the environmental costs of it. We see this in the present British Government's attitude to airports, business parks and roads, the environmental impact of which is put out of mind, once these things are seen as economic assets. We see it, too, in the American response to the Kyoto accords. It is not big business that puts the real pressure on the American House of Representatives not to ratify such agreements, but the desire of its members to be re-elected.

Nor is democracy the only problematic case. Other forms of social equilibrium may equally pose a threat to the environment, not because they depend on economic growth, but because they depend on population growth, or on the consumption of some finite resource like a rain forest. The conservative response to this kind of problem is to recognize that environmental equilibrium is a part of any durable social order. The conception put before us by Burke is in fact one that ought to appeal to environmentalists. Burke's response to Rousseau's theory of the social contract was to acknowledge that political order is like a contract, but to add that it is not a contract between the living only, but between the living, the unborn and the dead. In other words, to speak plainly, not a contract at all, but a relation of trusteeship, in which inherited benefits are conserved and passed on. The living may have an interest in consuming the Earth's resources, but it was not for this that the dead laboured. And the unborn depend upon our restraint. Long-term social equilibrium, therefore, must include ecological equilibrium.

This thesis, which environmentalists are apt to express in terms of 'sustainability', is better expressed in Burke's way. For Burke reminds us of a motive that arises naturally in human beings, and which can be exploited for the wider purpose of environmental and institutional conservation: namely, love. This motive leads people both to create good things and to destroy them. But it turns of its own accord in a direction that favours conservation, since human love extends to the dead and the unborn: we mourn the one and plan for the other out of a natural superfluity of good will. True social equilibrium arises when the institutions are in place that encourage that superfluity and channel it towards the maintenance of the social organism. The principal danger is that those institutions might be destroyed in the name of present emergencies, present appetites and the egregious needs of the merely living.

This emphasis on small-scale, observable and believable human motives is one of the strong points of conservative political thinking. Socialists place before us ideals of equality and social justice. But they seldom trouble to ask whether anyone – still less whether everyone – is motivated to pursue those things. The same problem arises with the environmentalists' goal of sustainability. It may be my goal and yours: but what about Jill, John and Marianne? Liberals are on safer ground with their ruling concept of liberty: it can be assumed that rational beings will aim for liberty, since liberty is the precondition of aiming for anything. On the other hand, my liberty may be your servitude; the pursuit of liberty does not guarantee that liberty will be available to all. And while it is true that people often surrender part of their liberty, the principal cause of their doing so is the emotion – namely, love – that conservatives wish to place at the heart of the social organism.

It seems to me that the greatest weakness in radical environmentalism has been its failure to explore the question of human motivation. There is one overwhelming reason for the degradation of the environment, and that is human appetite. In the wealthier parts of the world people are too many, too mobile, too eager to gratify their every desire, too unconcerned about the waste that builds up in their wake, too ready, in the jargon of economics, to externalize their costs. Most of our environmental problems are special cases of this general problem. And the problem can be more simply described as the triumph of desire over restraint. It can be solved only when restraint prevails over desire, in other words, only when people have re-learned the habit of sacrifice. For what do people make sacrifices? For the things that they love. And when do these sacrifices benefit the unborn? When they are made for the dead. Such was the core sentiment to which Burke and de Maistre made appeal.

There is a tendency on the left to single out the big players in the market as the principal culprits: to pin environmental crime on those – like oil companies, motor manufacturers, logging corporations, agribusinesses, supermarkets – who make their profits by exporting their costs to future generations. But this is to mistake the effect for the cause. In a free market these ways of making money emerge by an invisible hand from choices made by all of us. It is the demand for cars, oil, cheap food and expendable luxuries that is the real cause of the industries that provide these things. Of course it is true that the big players externalize their costs whenever they can. But so do we. Whenever we travel by air, whenever we visit the supermarket, whenever we consume fossil fuels, we are exporting our costs to future generations. A free economy is one that is driven by individual demand. The solution is not the socialist one, of abolishing the free economy, since this merely places massive economic power in the hands of unaccountable bureaucrats, who are equally in the business of exporting their costs. The solution is to rectify our demands, so as to bear the costs of them ourselves. In short, we must change our lives. And we can change our lives only if we have a motive to do so – a motive that is strong enough to constrain our appetites.

When Burke invoked our feelings towards the dead he was placing in the centre of political order a universal emotion which, he believed, could safeguard the long-term interests of society. But this motive extends no further than our local and contingent attachments. Through institutions of membership and the 'little platoons' that shape our allegiances we can extend our social concern beyond our immediate family. Nevertheless, the sense of a shared inheritance does not extend to all mankind, and the respect for the dead – which is a respect for *our* dead, for those who have made sacrifices on *our* behalf – peters out at the social horizon, where 'we' shades into 'they'. Modern societies are societies of strangers. And one of the underlying conservative projects in our times has been to discover the kind of affection that can bind such a society together across generations, without risking fragmentation along family, tribal or mafia lines.

Conservatives are not in the business of conserving just any law, institution or custom. Their desire is to conserve the institutions that embody collective solutions to recurring problems, and which pass on socially generated knowledge. In Burke's view (and mine) the common law is such an institution; so are political institutions like representative government, and social institutions like marriage and the family. These are institutions that foster the habit of sacrifice, and which therefore generate the motive on which the husbanding of resources depends.

Now there is a real cost involved in upholding such institutions and defending them from predation – a cost that imbues Burke's *Reflections on the French Revolution* with its air of solemn melancholy. For entropy can beset even the most settled form of human engagement. The social conservative who, for example, defends the family in modern conditions attracts the anger of those who have liberated themselves from this particular institutional constraint. It does no good to follow Charles Murray and James Q. Wilson in pointing out the social costs of single-parenthood and divorce. For that is simply to speak for future generations, people who don't yet exist, and who have been dropped from the equation.

Something similar happens when we consider questions of ecology. To defend slow food, slow transport and low energy consumption in a society addicted to fast food, tourism, luxury and waste is to risk the anger of those who need to be converted. Not only are there no votes to be won by seeking to close airports, to narrow roads or to return to a local food economy, there is the serious risk of making matters worse, by representing environmental protection as the cause of nostalgic cranks. All environmental activists are familiar with this reaction. But I am surprised that they do not see that it is a version of the very same reaction that is directed towards social conservatives, when they defend the beleaguered moral order that was – until a few decades ago – passed from generation to generation as a matter of course. Environmentalists and conservatives are both in search of the motive that will defend a shared but threatened legacy from predation by its current trustees ...

What is needed is a non-egotistic motive that can be elicited in ordinary members of society, and relied upon to serve the long-term ecological goal. Burke proposed 'the hereditary principle', as protecting important institutions from pillage or decay, and believed that people have a natural tendency to accept the limits that this principle places on their desires. Hegel argued for the priority of non-contractual obligations, of the kind that sustain the family, and believed that similar obligations could be recuperated and exercised at the political level. In similar vein, de Maistre gave a central place to piety, as a motive that puts divinely ordained traditions and constitutions above the temptations of self-interest.

None of those suggestions is likely to carry complete conviction today, though each tries to frame a picture of human motivation that does not make rational self-interest the sole ground for collective decision-making. Burke's invocation of the hereditary principle is of particular interest, however, since it engages directly with what he predicted (rightly as it happened) would be the outcome of the French Revolution – namely a squandering of inherited resources and a wholesale loss of what is now called 'social capital', including law, educational institutions and public or quasi-public endowments.

Burke's model of inheritance was the English hereditary estate, which removed assets from the market, protected them from pillage and erected in the place of absolute ownership a kind of trusteeship, with the life-tenant as beneficiary. This institution, protected by law, withheld land and natural resources from exploitation, and endowed tenants for life with a kind of sovereignty on condition that they passed the land unencumbered to their heirs. No environmentalist can be insensible of the enormous ecological benefit of 'settled land', so conceived. This was a resource that could not be exploited for all it was worth. It had to be used for the benefit of the 'successors in title' – in other words, sustainably ...

Burke saw the hereditary principle as a psychological obstacle before those who had wished to lay their hands on the estates, the endowments, the church-owned and institution-owned buildings and treasuries that had safeguarded the national assets of France from generation to generation. And he foresaw that, once the principle was rejected, restraint would have no motive, and the assets would be seized and squandered. But to respect the hereditary principle means to accept unequal holdings, hereditary status and the influence of family over individual fortunes. It is impossible to combine this state of mind with the modern demand for equality, which loudly affirms the rights of the living over the paper claims of the dead.

We cannot return to the kind of social motivations that Burke called upon: people don't think that way any more. But we should take a lesson from Burke, Hegel and de Maistre. We should recognize that environmental protection is a lost cause if we cannot find the human motive that would lead people in general, and not merely their self-appointed representatives, to advance it. And here, I think, is where environmentalists and conservatives can and should make common cause. And that common cause is local – specifically national – loyalty.

Many environmentalists on the left will acknowledge that local loyalties and local concerns must be given a proper place in our decision-making, if we are to counter the adverse effects of the global economy. But they will tend to baulk at the suggestion that local loyalty should be seen in national, rather than communitarian, terms. However, there is a very good reason for emphasizing nationality. For nations are communities with a political shape. They are predisposed to assert their sovereignty, by translating the common sentiment of belonging into collective decisions and self-imposed laws. Nationality is a form of territorial attachment. But it is also a proto-legislative arrangement. And it is through developing this idea, of a territorial sentiment that contains the seeds of sovereignty within itself, that conservatives make their distinctive contribution to ecological thinking ...

Rather than attempt to rectify environmental and social problems on the global level, conservatives seek local controls and a reassertion of local sovereignty over known and managed environments. This means affirming the right of nations to self-government, and to the adoption of policies that will chime with local loyalties and sentiments of national pride. The attachment to territory and the desire to protect that territory from erosion and waste remain powerful motives, and ones that are presupposed in all demands for sacrifice that issue from the mouths of politicians. For this motive is the simple and powerful one, of love for one's home.

It is only at this local level that I believe it is realistic to hope for improvement. For there is no evidence that global political institutions have done anything to limit the global entropy. On the contrary, by encouraging communication around the world and by eroding national sovereignty and legislative barriers, they have fed into that global entropy and weakened the only true sources of resistance to it. I know many environmentalists who seem to agree with me that the WTO is now a threat to the environment, not merely by breaking down self-sufficient and self-reproducing peasant economies, but also by eroding national sovereignty wherever this places an obstacle before the goals of multinational investors. And many seem to agree with me that traditional communities deserve protection from sudden and externally engineered change, not merely for the sake of their sustainable economies, but also because of the values and loyalties that constitute the sum of their social capital. The odd thing is that so few environmentalists follow the logic of this argument to its conclusion, and recognize that we too deserve protection from global entropy; that we too must retain national sovereignty as our greatest political asset in the face of it; and that we too must retain what we can of the loyalties that attach us to our territory, and make of that territory a home. Yet, in so far as we have seen any successful attempts to reverse the tide of ecological destruction, these have issued from national or local schemes, to protect territory recognized as 'ours' – defined, in other words, through some inherited entitlement. I am thinking of the recycling initiatives that are gradually freeing Germany from the plague of plastic bottles, the legislation that freed certain states of the United States from polythene bags, the clean-energy initiatives in Sweden and Norway, the Swiss planning laws that have enabled local communities to retain control over their environments and to think of those environments as a shared possession, and so on. These are small-scale achievements, but they are better than nothing. Moreover, they are successful because they make appeal to a natural motive – which is love of country, love of territory and love of that territory as home.

That, it seems to me, is the goal towards which serious environmentalism and serious conservatism both point – namely, home, the place where we are, the place that defines us, that we hold in trust for our descendants and that we don't want to spoil. Many of those who have seen this connection between conservatism and environmentalism have also been suspicious of it. And local environmentalism between the wars – especially in Germany – was undeniably part of the collectivist frame of mind, even if only circumstantially connected to the Nazi and Communist frenzy. However, I think it is time to take a more open-minded and imaginative vision of what conservatism and environmentalism have to offer each other. For nobody seems to have identified a motive more likely to serve the environmentalist cause than this one, of the shared love for our home. It is a motive in ordinary people. It can provide a foundation both for a conservative approach to institutions and a conservationist approach to the land. It is a motive that might permit us to reconcile the demand for democratic participation with the respect for absent generations and the duty of trusteeship. It is, in my view, the only serious recourse that we have, in our fight to maintain local order in the face of globally stimulated decay. And it is worth adding that, in so far as thermodynamics has a story to tell, it is this one.

This is why I think conservatives are likely to dissociate themselves from currently fashionable forms of environmental activism. Radical environmentalists are heirs to the leftist suspicion of nations and nationhood. They repudiate old hierarchies, and strive to remove the dead form their agenda, being largely unmoved by Burke's thought that, in doing so, they also remove the unborn. They define their goals in global and international terms, and support NGOs and pressure groups which they believe will fight the multinational predators on their own territory and with weapons that make no use of national sovereignty.

Conservatives dislike this approach for two reasons. First, the NGOs and pressure groups that are favoured by the activists are as unaccountable and unrepresentative as the predators they oppose. Second, they recruit their following through hatred and demonization – hatred of the big businesses, the big polluters, the apologists for capitalism and so on, against whom they see themselves pitted as David against Goliath. In other words, they put politics on a war footing, in the manner of St Just and Lenin. This runs totally counter to the conservative desire to found politics in friendship and conversation, and to resolve conflicts wherever possible through dialogue. Conservatives tend to see the environmental NGOs, like Greenpeace, as threats to social equilibrium, on account of their desire to pin on the big actors blame which should in fact be distributed across us all. And by casting the conflict in the form of a zero-sum game between themselves and the enemy, they obscure what it is really about, which is the accountability of both.

The point can be illustrated in the remarkable case of Greenpeace versus Shell, over the matter of the Brent Spar oil rig, which Shell had proposed to dispose of by sinking it in the sea. Greenpeace weighed in with a massively orchestrated hate campaign against Shell, involving boycotts, advertising, leaflets and pressure on shareholders, in order to prevent the sinking of the oil rig. The reason given was that the rig contained many thousand tonnes of oil and would be an environmental hazard for years to come: a reason that turned out to be false. No suggestion was made that Greenpeace and Shell should sit down together and discuss the problem. This was a fight to the death, between the forces of light and the forces of darkness. Greenpeace won and the rig is now rusting in a Norwegian fjord, an unsightly wreck costing many millions to dismantle, a process that will certainly be far more polluting than the one originally proposed by the corporation. Having cost Shell millions of dollars and unjustly damaged its reputation, Greenpeace, on proof that the rig after all contained no oil, offered an airy apology and went on to its next campaign.

In such examples we see how environmental activism, divorced from national sentiments that can carry the people with it, and expressed through unaccountable bodies that follow self-chosen global agendas, does little or nothing to further the environmental cause. And conservatives will see this as an inevitable result of the radical mindset. Radicals prefer global ideals to local loyalties, and rather than making bridges to their opponents, prefer to demonize them (as Bjorn Lomborg, for example, has been demonized in recent assaults on his work). Institutions like Greenpeace bypass national governments, while exerting force that need never account for its misuse. They exhibit the exultant self-righteousness that Burke discerned in the French Revolution, and which he believed would lead not merely to the disenfranchizing of ordinary citizens, but to the squandering of their inheritance.

My own hope is that environmentalists will grow out of the witch-hunting mentality that has alienated conservatives, and that conservatives will cease to be defensive about their true agenda, which is the one implied in their name. I would like to see an *Ecologist* magazine that makes room, in its scheme of things, for old Tory values of loyalty and allegiance. For it seems to me that the dominance of international decision-making by unaccountable bureaucracies, unaccountable NGOs and corporations accountable only to their shareholders (who may have no attachment to the environment which the corporations threaten) has made it more than ever necessary for us to follow the conservative path. We need to retreat form the global back to the local, so as to address the problems that we can collectively identify as ours, with means that we can control, from motives that we all feel. And that means being clear as to who *we* are, and why we are in it together and committed to our common survival . . .

15

The Philosophy of Wine
(From *The World of Fine Wine*, Issue 6, 2005)

Philosophers have probably drunk more than their fair share of
wine; but they have not had a fair share in the words written
about it. In particular, they have largely avoided discussing
the most important philosophical issue with which wine
acquaints us, which is that of intoxication. What exactly is
intoxication? Is there a single phenomenon that is denoted by
this word? Is the intoxication induced by wine an instance of
the same general condition as the intoxication induced by
whisky say, or that induced by cannabis? And is 'induced' the
right word in any or all of the familiar cases?

It is important to distinguish intoxication from drunkenness.
The first is a state of consciousness, whereas the second is a
state of unconsciousness – or which tends towards unconsciousness. Although the one leads in time to the other, the
connection between them is no more transparent than the
connection between the first kiss and the final divorce. Just as
the erotic kiss is neither a tame version nor a premonition of
the bitter parting to which it finally leads, so is the intoxicating
taste of the wine neither a tame version nor a premonition of
drunkenness: they are simply not the 'same kind of thing', even
if at some level of scientific theory they are discovered to have
the same kind of cause.

It is also questionable to speak of the intoxication that we
experience through wine as 'induced by' the wine. For this
implies a separation between the object tasted and the
intoxication felt, of the kind that exists between drowsiness
and the sleeping pill that causes it. When we speak of an

intoxicating line of poetry, we are not referring to an effect in the person who reads or remembers it, comparable to the effect of an energy pill. We are referring to a quality in the line itself. The intoxication of Mallarmé's *abolit bibelot d'inanité sonore* lies there on the page, not here in my nervous system.

I don't say that the case of wine is exactly like that of poetry. The one is a sensory experience, the other in part intellectual; the one is available whatever the state of your education, the other depends upon knowledge, comparison and culture; the one is strictly tied to the senses of taste and smell, while the other engages the contemplative senses of sight and hearing. And all those comparisons point towards a deep and philosophically highly significant distinction, between sensory and aesthetic pleasures.

Still, there is no doubt that the intoxicating quality that we taste in wine is a quality that we taste in *it*, and not in ourselves. True, we are raised by it to a higher state of exhilaration, and this is a widely observed and very important fact. But this exhilaration is an effect, not a quality bound into the very taste of the stuff, as the intoxication seems to be. At the same time, there is a connection between the taste and the intoxicating effect, just as there is a connection between the exciting quality of a football game and the excitement that is produced by it. However, the intoxication that I feel is not just caused by the wine: it is, to some extent, *directed at* the wine, and has a quality of 'relishing' which makes it impossible to describe in the abstract, as though some other stuff might have produced it. The wine lives in my intoxication, as the game lives in the excitement of the fan: I have not swallowed the wine as I would a tasteless drug; I have taken it into myself, so that its flavour and my mood are inextricably bound up with each other.

Our experience of wine depends upon its nature as a drink – a liquid which slides smoothly into the body, lighting the flesh as it journeys past. This endows wine with a peculiar inwardness, an intimacy with the body of a kind that is never achieved by solid food, since food must be chewed and therefore denatured before it enters the gullet. Nor is it achieved by any smell, since smell makes no contact with the body at all, but merely enchants without touching, like the beautiful girl at the other end of the party. An intoxicating drink, which both slides down easily and warms as it goes, is a symbol of – and also a means to achieve – an inward transformation, in which a person *takes something in* to himself. Hence you find wine, from the earliest recorded history, alloted a sacred function. It is a means whereby a god or daemon enters the soul of the one who drinks it, and often the drinking occurs at a religious ceremony, with the wine explicitly identified with the divinity who is being worshipped: witness the cult of Dionysus, the Eleusian mysteries, the Athenian festivals such as the Thesmophoria, the mystery cults of Diana and the Egyptian child Horus. For the anthropologist the Christian Eucharist, in which the blood of the sacrificed lamb is drunk in the form of communion wine, is downstream from the mystery cults of antiquity, which are in turn downstream from those ceremonies that accompanied the vinification of the grape among the great heroes who first discovered how to do it and believed, with commendable piety, that it was done by a god.

This symbolic use of wine in religious cults is reflected too in art and literature, in which magic drinks are conceived as mind-changing and even identity-changing potions, which slide down the gullet taking their spiritual burden into the very source of life. Wagner makes potent use of this symbolism, for example in the celebrated *Sühnetrank*, or drink of atonement, which dedicates Tristan to Isolde and Isolde to Tristan forever. We find this symbolism easy to understand, since it draws on the way in which intoxicating drinks, and wine pre-eminently, are 'taken into oneself', in a way that tempts one almost to a literal interpretation of that phrase. It is as though the wine enters the very self of the person who drinks it. The symbolism of the drink, and its soul-transforming effect, reflects the underlying truth that it is only rational beings who can appreciate things like wine. Animals can be drunk; they can be high on drugs and fuggy with cannabis; but they cannot experience the kind of directed intoxication that we experience through wine, since relishing is something that only a rational being can exhibit, and which therefore only a rational being can do.

The effect of wine is understood, by the observer as much as the consumer, as a temporary possession, a passing alteration, which is not, however, an alteration that changes the character of the one in whom it occurs. Hence you can go away and sleep it off; and the ancient characterizations of Silenus are of a creature alternating drink and sleep, with a crescendo of drunkenness between them. Moreover, and more importantly, alcohol in general, and wine in particular, has a unique social function, increasing the garrulousness, the social confidence and the goodwill of those who drink together, provided they drink in moderation. Many of the ways that we have developed of drinking socially are designed to impose a strict regime of moderation. Buying drinks by round in the pub, for example, has an important role in both permitting people to rehearse the sentiments that cause and arise from generosity (yet without bearing the real cost of them), while controlling the rate of intake and the balance between the inflow of drink and the outflow of words. This ritual parallels the ritual of the Greek symposium, and that of the circulation of wine after dinner in country houses and Oxbridge common rooms.

To understand the social nature of wine we must recognize that wine is not simply a shot of alcohol, and wine must never be confused in its effect with spirits or even with cocktails. Wine is not a mixed drink but a transformation of the grape. The transformation of the soul under its influence is merely the continuation of another transformation that began maybe fifty years earlier when the grape was first plucked from the vine. (That is one reason why the Greeks described fermentation as the work of a god. Dionysus enters the grape and transforms it; and this process of transformation is then transferred to us as we drink.)

When we raise a glass of wine to our lips, therefore, we are savouring an ongoing process: the wine is a living thing, the last result of other living things, and the progenitor of life in us. It is almost as though it were another human presence in any social gathering, as much a focus of interest and in the same way as the other people there. This experience is enhanced by the aroma, the taste and the simultaneous impact on nose and mouth. The whole being of the drinker rushes to the mouth and the olfactory organs to meet the tempting meniscus, just as the whole being of the lover rises to the lips in a kiss. It would be an exaggeration to make too much of the comparison, ancient though it is, between the erotic kiss and the sipping of wine. Nevertheless, it is not an exaggeration, but merely a metaphor, to describe the contact between the mouth and the glass as a *face to face* encounter between you and the wine. And it is a useful metaphor. Whisky may be *in* your face, but rarely is it *face to* face as wine is. The shot of alcohol as it courses through the body is like something that has *escaped from* the flavour. The alcoholic content of the wine, by contrast, remains part of the flavour, in something like the way that the character of an honest person is revealed in his face. Spirits are comparable in this respect to cordials and medicinal drinks: the flavour detaches itself readily from the effect, just as the face and gestures of a shallow person detach themselves from his long-term intentions. The companionship of wine resides in the fact that its effect is not underhand or concealed but present and revealed in the very flavour. This feature is then transmitted to those who drink wine together, and who adapt themselves to its quintessential honesty.

The ancient proverb tells us that there is truth in wine. The truth lies not in what the drinker perceives but in what, with loosened tongue and easier manners, he reveals. It is 'truth for others', not 'truth for self'. This accounts for both the social virtues of wine and its epistemological innocence. Wine does not deceive you, as cannabis deceives you, with the idea that you enter another and higher realm, that you see through the veil of Maya to the transcendental object or the thing-in-itself. Hence it is quite unlike even the mildest of the mind-altering drugs, all of which convey some vestige, however vulgarized, of the experience associated with mescalin and LSD, and recorded by Aldous Huxley in *The Doors of Perception*. These drugs – cannabis not exempted – are epistemologically culpable. They tell lies about another world, a transcendental reality beside which the world of ordinary phenomena pales into insignificance or at any rate into less significance than it has. Wine, by contrast, paints the world before us as the true one, and reminds us that if we have failed previously to know it then this is because we have failed in truth to belong to it, a defect that it is the singular virtue of wine to overcome.

Hence wine, when drunk in company, induces an opening

out of the self to the other, a conscious step towards asking and offering forgiveness: forgiveness not for acts or omissions, but for the impertinence of existing. Although the use of wine in the Christian Eucharist can be explained as a survival of the pagan cults that Christianity absorbed under the Roman Empire, and although it has authority in the Last Supper, as recorded in the New Testament, there is another reason for the centrality of wine in the communion ceremony, which is that it both illustrates and in a small measure enacts the moral posture that distinguishes Christianity from its early rivals, and which is summarized in the prayer to 'forgive us our trespasses, as we forgive them that trespass against us'. That remarkable prayer, which tells the Christian that he can obtain forgiveness only if he offers it, is one that we all understand in our cups, and this understanding of the critical role of forgiveness in forming durable human societies intrudes too into the world of Islam, in the poetry of Hafiz, Rumi and Omar Khayyam, wine drinkers to a man.

This returns us to our original point, which is that the pronounced mental effects of wine are, so to speak, read back into their cause, so that the wine itself has the taste of them. Just as you savour the intoxicating flavour of the wine, so do you savour its reconciling power: it presents you with the taste of forgiveness. That is one way of understanding the Christian doctrine of transubstantiation, itself a survival of the Greek belief that Dionysus is actually *in* the wine and not just the cause of it. The communicant does not taste the wine with a view to experiencing reconciliation and forgiveness as a subsequent effect. He savours forgiveness in the very act of drinking. This is what reconciliation, mercy and forgiveness *taste like*.

What I have called the 'epistemological innocence' of wine – its disposition to direct our thoughts and feelings to realities – means that, in attempting to describe the knowledge that wine imparts, we look for features of our actual world, features that might be, as it were, epitomized, commemorated and celebrated in its flavours. Hence the traditional perception of fine wine as the taste of a terroir: where that means not merely the soil, but the customs and ceremonies that had sanctified it and put it, so to speak, in communion with the drinker. The use of theological language here is, I believe, no accident. Although wine tells no lies about a transcendental realm, it sanctifies the immanent reality, which is why it is so effective a symbol of the incarnation. In savouring it we are knowing – by acquaintance, as it were – the history, geography and customs of a community.

Since ancient times, therefore, wines have been associated with definite places, and been accepted not so much as the taste of those places, as the flavour imparted to them by the enterprise of settlement. Wine of Byblos was one of the principal exports of the Phoenicians, and old Falernian was made legendary by Horace. Those who conjure with the magic names of Burgundy, Bordeaux and the Rhine and Moselle are not just showing off: they are deploying the best and most reliable description of a cherished taste, which is inseparable from the idea and the history of the settlement that produced it.

And here we should again return to the religious meaning of wine. At the risk of drastically oversimplifying, I suggest that there are two quite distinct strands that compose the religious consciousness, and that our understanding of religion has suffered from too great an emphasis on one of them. The first strand, which we over-emphasize, is that of belief. The second strand, which is slipping away from modern thought (though not from modern reality) is that which might be summarized in the term 'membership', by which I mean all the customs, ceremonies and practices whereby the sacred is renewed, so as to be a real presence among us, and a living endorsement of the human community. The pagan religions of Greece and Rome were strong on membership but weak on belief. Hence they centred on the cult, as the primary religious phenomenon. It was through the cult, not the creed that the adept proved his religious orthodoxy and his oneness with his fellows. Western civilization has tended in recent centuries to emphasize belief – in particular the belief in a transcendental realm and an omnipotent king who presides over it. This theological emphasis, by representing religion as a matter of theological doctrine, exposes it to refutation. And that means that the real religious need of people – a need planted in us, according to some, by evolution and according to others by God – seeks other channels for its expression: usually forms of idolatry that do not achieve the refreshing humanity of the cult.

Far from supposing the cult to be a secondary phenomenon, derived from the theological beliefs that justify it, I take the opposite view, and believe that I have modern anthropology, and its true founder Richard Wagner, on my side. Theological beliefs are rationalizations of the cult, and the function of the cult is membership. It is through establishing a cult that people learn to pool their resources. Hence every act of settling and of turning the earth to the common needs of a community, involves the building of a temple and the setting aside of days and hours for festivity and sacrificial offering. When people have, in this way, prepared a home for them, the gods come quietly in to inhabit it, maybe not noticed at first, and only subsequently clothed in the transcendental garments of theology.

Now it seems to me that the act of settling, which is the origin of civilization, involves both a radical transition in our relation to the earth – the transition known in other terms as that from hunter-gatherer to farmer – and also a new sense of belonging. The settled people do not belong only to each other: they belong to a place, and out of that sense of shared roots there grow the farm, the village and the city. Vegetation cults are the oldest and most deeply rooted in the unconscious, since they are the cults that drive out the totemism of the hunter-gatherer, and celebrate the earth itself, as the willing accomplice in our bid to stay put. The new farming economy, and the city that grows from it, generate in us a sense of the holiness of the planted crop, and in particular of the staple food – which is grass, usually in the form of corn or rice – and the vine that wraps the trees above it. The fruit of the vine can be fermented and so stored in a sterilized form. It provides a place and the things that grow there with a memory.

At some level, I venture to suggest, the experience of wine is a recuperation of that original cult whereby the land was settled and the city built. And what we taste in the wine is not just the fruit and its ferment, but also the peculiar flavour of a landscape to which the gods have been invited and where they have found a home. Nothing else that we eat or drink comes to us with such a halo of significance, and cursed be the villains who refuse to drink it.

16

Thoughts on Hunting
(From *Animal Rights and Wrongs*, 2000)

Nature and culture used be seen as contrasting elements in our
human constitution. But nature is now a product of culture.
Not only does human society shape the environment; it is
human choice that marks off what is 'natural', and which
elevates the distinction between the natural and the artificial
to its sovereign place in the moral order. The natural world
now depends on our efforts to conserve it and therefore on our
judgement as to what belongs to it. Moreover, our very
perception of this world as 'natural' is an artefact, formed and
nurtured by religion, literature, art and the modern media.
When we seek our consolation in nature we are looking in a
mirror that we created for this purpose. Nature smiles back at
us with human features, since we have carefully ensured that it
has no other. All that is truly threatening, alien and mysterious
has been cut from the picture: what remains is a work of art.
We strive to preserve it from that other and artificial world –
the world of machinery, spoliation, production, consumption
and waste. But both worlds are our creation and we can fight
only for the boundary between them, hoping that the part
which consoles us does not dwindle to the point where
consolation becomes a memory.

Nature, as we have invented it, is a source of the beautiful;
but it has ceased to be a source of the sublime. For we meet the
sublime only when we are confronted with our own littleness
and are troubled by forces that we cannot control. The
experience of the sublime vanished at the moment when Burke
and Kant defined it: their descriptions were a kind of

valediction, inspired by the premonition of a world entirely subject to human mismanagement.

None of that alters the fact that the contrast between the natural and the artificial is an immovable part of our worldview and one of the cultural values to which we cling. We need this contrast because we need to see our actions in terms of it. We need to distinguish those impulses which belong to Mother Nature from those which involve bids for freedom. And we need to relate to other creatures for whom there is no such contrast: creatures whose behaviour stems from nature alone. It matters to us that we should be in constant relation to animals – and wild animals especially. For we seek an image of innocence, of the world before our own depredations, the world *without* man, into which man comes as an intruder. The burden of self-consciousness is lightened by this image: it shows us that we walk on firm ground, where the burden may from time to time be set down and upon which we may rest from our guilt. All this is beautifully captured in the opening pages of Genesis and the vision of Paradise – absurd though it may be from the Darwinian perspective – is the perfect symbol of the natural world as it would be, had we been able to produce it unaided, and without relying on the raw material of evolution.

The desire for the natural order is perhaps unknown to those who are truly part of it. But it is an immovable given in the lives of all civilized beings and, even if it cannot be satisfied, it will exert its power over our thinking and make itself known both in the life of the mind and in the life of the body. It burst upon us in the writings of Rousseau, and his egregiously sentimental vision of the state of nature has exerted its charm over many subsequent writers. But it appeared in a more moderate and intriguing form in the writings of the German romantics, three of whom – Schelling, Hegel and Hölderlin – helped to forge the picture of our condition which has since proved most persuasive and to which I pay tribute in what follows.

According to this picture, human history shares the structure of human consciousness; the individual life is a microcosm of the species, which is in turn, for Hegel, a microcosm of the universal *Geist*. The human soul and human society are both founded in a condition of innocence or 'immediacy', in which they are at one with the world and with themselves. And each grows away from this oneness through a process of sundering and alienation, as it comes to recognize the otherness by which it is surrounded and upon which it depends. Finally each attains its redemption, as it is restored to the wholeness from which it began, but at a higher plane – the plane of understanding. Just as the individual self is realized by transcending its self-alienation and becoming fully and completely known to itself, so is society fulfilled when the primitive unity with others is rediscovered, but in the form of a self-conscious and law-guided order.

Wherever we look in the modern world, we find this image of our condition actively colonizing people's plans and projects. Almost everything that is believed in, almost everything for which a real sacrifice is made, has the character of a *Heimkehr* – a return from alienation, destruction and despair, to an image of home. But not home in its innocence. Rather home transfigured, become conscious of itself, and emancipated from the taint of bondage. It is this image which dominates the thinking of the environmental movements of our time and also of the campaigners for animal rights who are so often in conflict with them. Both are haunted by the idea of a primitive unity between man and nature, in which other species have an equal weight to our own. Both are appalled by the accelerating presumption which has alienated man from nature and set him at odds with the order upon which he nevertheless depends. And both look forward to a restored unity with the natural world – a unity achieved not by innocence but by understanding, and by the self-knowledge and self-discipline which comes from accepting our limitations.

Myths are necessary to human life and are part of the price we pay for consciousness. Moreover, even if they give a distorted view of history, they frequently give insight into the human psyche. Planted in us too deep for memory, and beneath the layers of civilization, are the instincts of the hunter-gatherer, who differs from his civilized descendants not only in making no distinction between the natural and the artificial order, but also in relating to his own and other species in a herd-like way. The hunter-gatherer is acutely aware of the distinction between men and women; he quickly unites with his fellows in a common enterprise and is focused by nothing so much as the chase. He is a spontaneously cooperative being, who cooperates not only with his own species but also with those that are most readily adapted to join in his hunting: with horse, hound, falcon and ferret. Towards his prey he takes a quasi-religious attitude. The hunted animal is hunted as an individual – and the instinct to hunt in this way has an obvious ecological function. (Buffalo Bill was the very antithesis of the hunter-gatherer, a degenerate by-product of the civilizing process). But the hunted species is elevated to divine status as the totem and a kind of mystical union between the tribe and its totem seals a pact between them. The experience of the hunter involves a union of opposites – absolute antagonism between individuals resolved through a mystical identity of species. By pursuing the individual and worshipping the species, the hunter guarantees the eternal recurrence of his prey. Totemism is part of the natural ecology of the tribe and its ubiquity is far better explained by its ecological function than by the far-fetched ideas of Freud and Malinowski ...

Why should people wish for this primordial relation with other species and are they justified in pursuing it? To answer these questions it is not enough merely to trace the evolutionary sediment which is stirred by hunting. Nor is it enough to recast the myth from which I began – the myth of man's fall and redemption, and of the homeward journey out of alienation. However suggestive this myth has been to philosophers, artists and writers in the romantic tradition, the fact remains that there is no way back and that the only homecoming that we are offered is a religious one, which promises an *Aufhebung* not here and now but in the unknowable beyond.

As I see the matter, hunting (by which I mean the pursuit of individual animals to the death, as exemplified in angling, ferreting or hunting with hounds) brings into focus the real differences between humans and other animals, and at the same time lifts some of the burden which those differences create. Human beings differ from animals *systematically*. Unlike the other animals with which we come into regular contact, we are self-conscious; our thoughts involve 'I'-thoughts, 'you'-thoughts and 'he, she, we and they' –thoughts. Unlike the animals, we have moral, aesthetic and religious experience; we pray to things visible and invisible; we laugh and grieve; we are indignant, approving and dismayed. And we relate to each other in a special way, through the give and take of practical reason and its associated concepts of justice, duty and right. Human beings are actual or potential members of a moral community, in which each member enjoys sovereignty over his own affairs so long as he accords an equal sovereignty to others. The concepts of right and duty regulate such a community and ensure that disputes are settled in the first instance by negotiation and not by force. And with all this comes an immense burden of guilt. Morality and self-consciousness set us in judgement over ourselves, so that we see our actions and characters constantly from outside, judged by ourselves as we are by others. (It is part of the function of moral dialogue and the concepts of duty, right and justice to generate this external point of view.) We become cut off from our instincts, and even the spontaneous joy of fellowship is diminished by the screen of judgement through which it first must pass.

The hunter-gatherer faces and overcomes the guilt of his condition more easily than we do. The willed identity between the hunter and his tribe, and between the tribe and the universal prey, affirms, for the hunter, his primal innocence. Just as there is no guilt attached to killing when lion kills goat, so are we released from guilt when acting from the imperatives of the species. At the same time, considered as species, the prey is identical with the tribe. Hence this guiltless killing is also a purging of guilt – of the guilt that attaches to the murder of one's kind. The prey becomes a sacrificial victim: the individual pays with his life for the continuity of the tribe, by attracting the accumulated aggression between the hunters which is the price of their mutual dependence.

Although the conditions no longer obtain, in which totemism could be a real moral force, the desire for guiltless killing endures and attracts to itself a powerful residue of social emotion. Hunting, shooting and fishing are forms of social life. Even when conducted alone – as shooting and fishing might be conducted – they are the focus of clubs, outings, parties, contests and festivals. And those who are familiar with the

English countryside will know that hunting is not merely the occasional sport of the wealthy, but an elaborate social artefact, in which all country people from all walks of life participate, and which spills over into horse trials, point-to-points, the pony club, the hunt ball, hunt breakfasts and fun-rides, charity events, puppy shows and farmers' lunches – in short, every available form of social communion. Hunting is also a rehearsal of social instincts and a reaffirmation of our mutual dependence.

It is this, I believe, which explains the extraordinary hold of 'field sports', as they are euphemistically called, over the lives of those who participate in them. There is, in the contest between man and his prey, an inherent social meaning, a summoning into consciousness of the misremembered life of the tribe. Even in angling this is so and, if angling also has its solitary aspect, this is in part because the crucial transition, in which the species becomes incarnate in the individual, can occur only at the end of a single line. It is nevertheless the case that ordinary coarse fishing is a social affair. Much of the joy of angling resides in the concentrated silence of people working side by side along the bank, confident in their neighbours and bound by a common enterprise.

There is another aspect to hunting, however, which also bears on its significance for us, in our attempts to conserve the boundary between the natural and the artificial worlds. Hunting is a territorial activity, and to hunt land and waterways is to exert a claim of ownership. The hunter-gatherer is at no time more attached to his world than when hunting, since hunting is also a 'taking into possession'. (The expression is the one used by the common law, to describe what happens when a wild animal is hunted and killed by the owner of land.) For this reason, hunting rights and game laws have underpinned the structure of ownership and tenancy in our societies, and have been vivid subjects of political dispute. It is hardly necessary to mention the significance of the royal forests, the eighteenth-century game laws, the decree by the French Revolutionaries that henceforth the people could hunt where they choose, or the monopoly over hunting exerted by the communist Nomenklatura in Eastern Europe. The transcending of the hunter-gatherer economy into the producer economy required that hunting and fishing rights be legally specified and defended. Thereafter you could hunt in a place only if you had the right to do so or were the guest of another whose right it was.

This obvious fact is of some significance. For it has made hunting, shooting and fishing into elaborate forms of hospitality. In all societies, hospitality is a necessary part of ownership, since it is the price paid for the social acceptance of private wealth. Ownership of land is particularly sensitive as it places tangible obstacles in the way of those who do not enjoy it and restricts the supply of every raw material. English law has been lenient and subtle in the distribution of land – granting rights of way and easements, enforcing covenants and prescriptive rights, and producing a unique combination of over-crowding and public access in a landscape which retains its domestic appearance. Nevertheless, even in England, the private ownership of land provokes resentment among those whom it excludes and the Ramblers' Association, for example, has taken an increasingly belligerent line towards farmers who forbid people to cross their property.

The farmer who forbids the rambler is very likely to permit the hunt, regardless of whether he is plagued by foxes and notwithstanding the fact that the hunt does far more damage than a quiet walker in an anorak. The reason is simple. The rambler is an outsider, someone who does not 'belong'. The farmer needs to justify his ownership to his neighbours, to those with whom he lives as one possessor among others. Hospitality extends to them, since they enjoy the same ancestral title to the territory from which his portion has been carved. Hence, when the hunt meets on his land, the farmer will usually offer additional hospitality in order to confirm that the land is open to his guests. In the Vale of White Horse country, where I live, it is normal for a farmer to offer port, sausages and cake to followers on horseback and to make special provision for the huntsman, whose partiality to whisky is well-known. Towards ramblers, however, farmers feel no hospitable urges, regarding them as alien intruders who should stick to public rights of way (not all of which are recognized by the farmers themselves).

Ceremonial hospitality of this kind should be distinguished from ordinary giving. It is an attempt to raise the relations among neighbours to a higher level: to confer legitimacy and permanence on the current patterns of ownership. It is partly in acknowledgement of this that mounted followers wear a uniform and obey a strict dress-code that extends to horse as well as rider. The hunt arrives on the farmer's land not as an ordinary visitor but as a ceremonial presence, endorsing his ownership in the act of exploiting it.

In the hunt, therefore, are revived, in transfigured form, some of the long-buried emotions of our forebears. The reverence for a species, expressed through the pursuit of its 'incarnate' instance; the side-by-sideness of the tribal huntsman; the claim to territory and the animals who live in it; and the therapy for guilt involved in guiltless killing.

But is it guiltless? Hunting, shooting and to a lesser extent angling have been repeatedly condemned as immoral: not immoral *per se*, since they may well be necessary if people are to feed themselves. But immoral in circumstances like ours, when hunting is a recreation rather than a means to food and clothing. The arguments here are involved and various, and there is no short answer to them. Nevertheless, it is not a sufficient justification for recreational hunting that it puts us in touch with needed emotions or that it maintains the boundaries which fence off the 'natural' world. Even if it could be shown that hunting (in one or other of its many forms) is the best that we over-civilized beings can hope for, by way of a homecoming to our natural state and the best proof against the tribal aggressions which otherwise beset us, this would carry little weight in modern times. Many people are also sceptical of the romantic *Heimkehr*. The best hope for our future, they believe, is to live with our alienation, to cease to look for some simulacrum, however sublimated and self-conscious, of the old tribal emotions and to look on the world as a vast suburban garden, an artificial and third-rate paradise, which we must maintain as kindly and responsibly as we can. This means taking the interests of all creatures into account and refraining from pursuits which cause needless suffering, lest the spectacle of suffering should cease to trouble us. The comparative toleration of modern people towards angling stems from the fact that fish are so very different from us, in their appearance, habitat and behaviour, that it is no sign of a hard heart to look on their sufferings unmoved. The hare, the stag and the fox, by contrast, are near to us. Whatever the difference between our thoughts and theirs, we share the circumstances of our pains, our terrors and our death, and to inflict these things on such an animal is to act with a callous disregard.

There is something right in that argument. But it also overlooks the crucial fact from which I began and which is now at the back of all our minds, including the minds of those opposed to hunting. The natural world can no longer look after itself. We are the guardians and keepers of the natural order, which owes its character to us. We could turn our backs on it and cease to interfere. But the result would not be better, either for the animals who live in it or for us, who depend on the natural world for our sense of what we are. If deer were never culled, Exmoor would contain nothing else besides suburban houses, and the highlands of Scotland would be treeless crags. If foxes were never killed, lambs, ducks and chickens would be reared indoors, in conditions that no decent person should tolerate. If angling ceased, our waterways would never be maintained and mink, coote and moorhen would drive all their rivals to extinction. In so far as 'biodiversity' is a wished-for part of our third-rate paradise, culling and pest-control will remain incumbent on us. And it seems to me that the truly callous way of doing these things, is the way that merely attacks the species – as when poisoned bait is laid for rats and foxes, or electric shocks are used to free the waterways of pike. Such practices involve a failure to achieve the 'incarnation' of the species in the individual and so to renew our respect for it. The true graciousness of hunting occurs when the species is controlled through the arduous pursuit of its individual members and so impresses upon us its real and eternal claim to our respect and sympathy. This does not mean that hunting can be pursued in any way we choose. A rifle in the hands of a well-trained stalker may be a permissible way to bring death to a stag; but it does not follow that the very same stag might as well be killed by a grenade, a noose or a handgun. An animal like the fox, which can be cleanly killed only in the open and which is never more quickly dispatched than by a pack of hounds, requires great labour and the cooperation of three species if he is to be hunted in this way. If he is to be hunted at all, however, this is how it should be done. On the other hand, I have tried to show in *Animal Rights and Wrongs* that the concept of animal rights is based on a confusion. It is my view that a true understanding of the nature of moral judgement will find no conclusive argument against properly conducted hunting. Indeed, I incline to Plato's view, defended in *The Laws*, that hunting with hounds is the noblest form of hunting. And this because it is the form in which our kindred nature with the animals is most vividly present to our feelings. The pleasure that we feel in this kind of hunting is borrowed from the animals who are really doing it – the hounds who pursue and the horses who follow them. The residual moral doubts are ours, not theirs, and they must be answered by us – by ensuring that the fox or stag has the best chance of saving himself and the quickest death should he be caught.

Suggestions for Further Reading

CONSERVATISM

Everything that Roger Scruton has written bears the hallmarks of his conservatism. But for those wishing to get at the core of his political conservatism, see *The Meaning of Conservatism* (South Bend: St. Augustine's Press, 2002). One should also read his powerful polemics in *Untimely Tracts* (London: The Macmillan Press, 1987), a collection of his columns written for *The Times* between 1983 and 1986). See also his two collections of essays from *The Salisbury Review* which Scruton edited from 1982–2000, *Conservative Thinkers: Essays from 'The Salisbury Review'* (London: The Claridge Press, 1988), and *Conservative Thoughts: Essays from 'The Salisbury Review'* (London: The Claridge Press, 1988). His fine introduction to *Conservative Texts: An Anthology* (London: Macmillan, 1991) is also a must, as is the chapter entitled 'Xanthippe's Laws' from his hilarious fictional send-up of Plato *Xanthippic Dialogues* (London: Sinclair-Stevenson, 1993, and subsequently reprinted by St. Augustine's Press in 1998). 'How to be a Non-Liberal, Anti-Socialist Conservative' in *The Intercollegiate Review*, spring 1993, is an excellent short summary of Scruton's conservative vision, as are two more recent essays: 'Hayek and Conservatism' in *The Cambridge Companion to Hayek*, Edward Feser (ed.) (Cambridge: Cambridge University Press, 2006), and 'The Limits of Liberty' in *The American Spectator*, December 2008/January 2009. For an overall summary of Scrutonian conservatism, see my *Roger Scruton: The Philosopher on Dover Beach* (London & New York: Continuum International, 2009), Chapter 4: 'The Meaning of Conservatism'.

THE NATION

The reader should certainly look at *The Need for Nations* (London: Civitas, 2004), an edited version of which is included as the first chapter of *A Political Philosophy*, entitled 'Conserving Nations'. *England: An Elegy* (London & New York: Continuum International, 2006) is essential, as is 'The United States, The United Nations, and the Future of the Nation-State' in *The Heritage Foundation: Heritage Lectures*, No. 794 (available at www.heritage.org), and 'The Dangers of Internationalism' in *The Intercollegiate Review*, fall/winter, 2005. For an older analysis, please see 'The Usurpation of Australia' and 'In Defence of the Nation', both of which appear as Chapters 26 and 27 of *The Philosopher on Dover Beach: Essays* (Manchester: Carcanet, 1990 and subsequently reprinted by St. Augustine's Press in 1997). For more on Enoch Powell, see 'Immigration, Multiculturalism and the Need to Defend the Nation State', a speech given to the Vlaams Belang political party in Antwerp on 23 June 2006, and reproduced in *The Brussels Journal* at www.brusselsjournal.com. Lastly, for an overall summary of Scruton's defence of the nation, see my *Roger Scruton*, Chapter 5.

SEX AND THE SACRED

Sexual Desire: A Philosophical Investigation (London: Continuum, 2006, first published in 1986) is, of course, essential, as is his short chapter on 'Sex' in *Philosophy: Principles and Problems* (London & New York: Continuum International, 2005). See also 'Phryne's Symposium' in *Xanthippic Dialogues*; 'Sexual Morality and the Liberal Consensus' in *The Philosopher on Dover Beach*; 'Sex in a Commodity Culture' in *Rewriting the Sexual Contract*, Geoff Dench (ed.) (New Jersey: Transaction Publishers, 1999); 'Bring Back Stigma' in *City Journal*, autumn 2000; 'Very Safe Sex' in *National Review*, 28 July 1997; 'The Moral Birds and Bees: Sex and Marriage Properly Understood', *National Review* online, 15 September 2003; and 'Shameless and Loveless' in *The Spectator* , 16 April 2005. There is also a superb interview with Scruton on the theme of 'Sex and Perversion' on *Ethics Bites, Open2.net*. For the meaning of the 'sacred' in

Scruton's work, see 'The Philosopher on Dover Beach', which appears as Chapter 1 of *The Philosopher on Dover Beach: Essays*; Chapters 7 and 8 on 'God' and 'Freedom', of *Philosophy: Principles and Problems*. More recently see, 'The Sacred and the Human', *Prospect Magazine*, issue 137, August 2007. On the theme of religion in Scruton, see especially Chapter 12 of *Gentle Regrets* (London & New York: Continuum International, 2005), entitled 'Regaining my Religion'; 'Dawkins is Wrong about God' in *The Spectator*, 14 January 2006; 'Religious Freedom in America' in *The American Spectator*, 13 February 2007; 'Islamofascism: Beware of a Religion without Irony' in *The Wall Street Journal*, 20 August 2006; 'Two Virtues of Western Culture: Irony, Sacrifice, and the Transmission of Culture' in *Provocations: A Journal from the Trinity Forum* (www.ttf.org); and Chapter 5 of *England: An Elegy*, entitled 'The English Religion'. Most recently, Scruton has a wonderful critique of 'The New Humanism' in *The American Spectator*, 10 March 2009. Finally, for an overall summary of Scruton's philosophy of sex and the sacred see Chapters 1 and 2 of my *Roger Scruton*.

CULTURE

On art and culture, one should read *Art and Imagination: A Study in the Philosophy of Mind* (South Bend: St. Augustine's Press, 1998, first published in 1974); *The Politics of Culture and Other Essays* (Manchester: Carcanet Press, 1981); *The Aesthetic Understanding: Essays in the Philosophy of Art and Culture* (South Bend: St. Augustine's Press, 1998, first published 1983); *Perictione in Colophon: Reflections on the Aesthetic Way of Life* (South Bend: St. Augustine's Press, 2000); *Beauty* (Oxford: Oxford University Press, 2009); Chapters 8 and 9 of *The Philosopher on Dover Beach: Essays*, entitled 'Modern Philosophy and the Neglect of Aesthetics' and 'Aesthetic Experience and Culture'. On architecture, see *The Aesthetics of Architecture* (Princeton: Princeton University Press, 1979); *The Classical Vernacular: Architectural Principles in an Age of Nihilism* (Manchester: Carcanet, 1994); Chapters 5 and 6 of *Perictione in Colophon*; 'Cities for Living' in *City Journal*, vol. 18, no. 2, spring 2008; and a piece written by Roger and Sophie Scruton, 'The

Future is Classical' on *Opendemocracy.net*, 9 August 2001. On Music, please see *The Aesthetics of Music* (Oxford: Oxford University Press, 1997); *Understanding Music* (London: Continuum, 2009); and Chapters 3–8 of *The Aesthetic Understanding*. Finally, for an overall account of Scrutonian aesthetics, see my *Roger Scruton*, Chapter 3: 'Gazing Aesthetically'.

NATURE, WINE AND HUNTING

On nature and the environment, see 'A Righter Shade of Green' in *The American Conservative*, 16 July 2007; 'Conservatives are Conservationists' in *First Principles: ISI Web Journal*, autumn 2007 (www.firstprinciples.com); and Chapter 21 of *The Philosopher on Dover Beach: Essays*, entitled 'The Red and the Green'. See also Scruton's fascinating account of farm life in *News From Somewhere: On Settling* (London & New York: Continuum International, 2004). On wine, see his regular wine column at www.newstatesman.com; 'The Golden Mean' in *The World of Fine Wine Magazine*, issue 3, 2004; and *I Drink Therefore I Am: A Philosopher's Guide to Wine* (London: Continuum, 2009). For more on hunting, see *On Hunting* (London: Yellow Jersey Press, 1998); 'Fox-Hunting: The Modern Case', A Written Submission to the Committee of Inquiry into Hunting Chaired by Lord Burns (see www.defra.gov.uk); and 'Animal Rights' in *City Journal*, vol. 10, no. 3, summer 2000. A more scholarly piece entitled 'Ethics and Welfare: The Case of Hunting' can be found in *Philosophy*, 77, 2002, pp. 543–564. Finally, for an analysis of Scruton's environmentalism and his philosophy of hunting, see Chapters 2 and 4 of my *Roger Scruton*.

A Bibliography of Roger Scruton's Books 1974–2009

Art and Imagination: A Study in the Philosophy of Mind, South Bend: St. Augustine's Press, 1998 (first published in 1974).

The Aesthetics of Architecture, Princeton: Princeton University Press, 1979.

The Meaning of Conservatism, South Bend: St. Augustine's Press, 2002 (first published in 1980).

The Politics of Culture and Other Essays, Manchester: Carcanet Press, 1981.

Fortnight's Anger, Manchester: Carcanet Press, 1981.

A Short History of Modern Philosophy: From Descartes to Wittgenstein, London & New York: Routledge, 2006 (first published in 1981).

The Palgrave Macmillan Dictionary of Political Thought, London: Palgrave Macmillan, 2007 (first published in 1982).

Kant: A Very Short Introduction, Oxford: Oxford University Press, 2001 (first published in 1982).

The Aesthetic Understanding: Essays in the Philosophy of Art and Culture, South Bend: St. Augustine's Press, 1998 (first published 1983).

Thinkers of the New Left, Harlow: Longman (subsequently London: The Claridge Press) 1985.

Sexual Desire: A Philosophical Investigation, London: Continuum, 2006 (first published in 1986).

Spinoza: A Very Short Introduction, Oxford: Oxford University Press, 2002 (first published in 1986).

A Land Held Hostage: Lebanon and the West, London: The Claridge Press, 1987.

Untimely Tracts, London: The Macmillan Press, 1987.

Conservative Thinkers: Essays from 'The Salisbury Review' (ed.), London: The Claridge Press, 1988.

Conservative Thoughts: Essays from 'The Salisbury Review' (ed.), London: The Claridge Press, 1988.

The Philosopher on Dover Beach: Essays, Manchester: Carcanet, 1990 (subsequently reprinted by St. Augustine's Press in 1997).

Francesca: A Novel, London: Sinclair-Stevenson, 1991.

A Dove Descending and Other Stories, London: Sinclair-Stevenson, 1991.

Conservative Texts: An Anthology (ed.), London: Macmillan, 1991.

Xanthippic Dialogues, London: Sinclair-Stevenson, 1993 (subsequently reprinted by St. Augustine's Press in 1998).

Modern Philosophy: An Introduction and Survey, London: Pimlico, 2004 (first published in 1994).

The Classical Vernacular: Architectural Principles in an Age of Nihilism, Manchester: Carcanet, 1994.

Animal Rights and Wrongs, London: Continuum, 2000 (first published in 1996).

Philosophy: Principles and Problems, London: Continuum, 2005 (first published as *An Intelligent Person's Guide to Philosophy*, 1996).

The Aesthetics of Music, Oxford: Oxford University Press, 1997.

On Hunting, London: Yellow Jersey Press, 1998.

Modern Culture, London: Continuum, 2005 (first published as *An Intelligent Person's Guide to Modern Culture* in 1998).

Perictione in Colophon: Reflections on the Aesthetic Way of Life, South Bend: St. Augustine's Press, 2000.

England; An Elegy, London: Continuum, 2006 (first published in 2000).

The West and the Rest, London: Continuum, 2003 (first published in 2002).

Death-Devoted Heart: Sex and the Sacred in Wagner's Tristan and Isolde, Oxford: Oxford University Press, 2004.

News From Somewhere: On Settling, London: Continuum, 2004.

The Need for Nations, London: Civitas, 2004 (an abridged version of this pamphlet appears as 'Conserving Nations' in *A Political Philosophy*, 2006).

Gentle Regrets: Thoughts from a Life, London: Continuum, 2005.

A Political Philosophy: Arguments for Conservatism, London: Continuum, 2006.

Culture Counts: Faith and Feeling in a World Besieged, New York: Encounter Books, 2007.

Beauty, Oxford: Oxford University Press, 2009.

Understanding Music, London: Continuum, 2009.

I Drink therefore I Am, London: Continuum, 2009.

The Uses of Pessimism, London: Atlantic Books, 2009.

Index